ADVANCE ACCLAIM FOR *SNOW ON THE TULIPS*

"A splendid debut novel! With a tender romance, a gripping plot, and a well-researched setting, *Snow on the Tulips* drew me in to the harrowing uncertainty of life in the Netherlands under Nazi rule. Liz Tolsma's beautiful story kept me up at night—not just wondering what would happen to her endearing characters, but wondering what I would do in similar circumstances. Do not miss this book!"

—SARAH SUNDIN, AWARD-WINNING AUTHOR OF *WITH EVERY LETTER*

"Being widowed at a young age, I once again felt the pain and joy during those days as Cornelia fights her own feelings for Gerrit. The guilt of loving again, the desire to be wanted, set against the backdrop of the Nazi-infested Netherlands brings joy and heartache to the reader. New author Liz Tolsma brings her fresh writing to a tragic time in history. Her use of engaging characters and description should not be missed."

—DIANA LESIRE BRANDMEYER, AUTHOR OF *MIND OF HER OWN* AND *WE'RE NOT BLENDED, WE'RE PUREED: A SURVIVOR'S GUIDE TO BLENDED FAMILIES*

"*Snow on the Tulips* is richly layered with courage, faith, and love. It reminded me of all the things I loved with Bodie Thoene's Zion Covenant series: characters doing more than they thought possible, wrestling with how to live lives of faith in time of war, and history that comes to life on each page. It is a compelling story that will delight readers."

—CARA PUTMAN, AWARD-WINNING AUTHOR OF *STARS IN THE NIGHT* AND *A WEDDING TRANSPIRES ON MACKINAC ISLAND*

D0499551

ALSO BY LIZ TOLSMA

Snow on the Tulips

Novella included in
A Log Cabin Christmas

Daisies Are Forever

LIZ TOLSMA

THOMAS NELSON
Since 1798

NASHVILLE   DALLAS   MEXICO CITY   RIO DE JANEIRO

Published in Nashville, Tennessee, by Thomas Nelson. Thomas Nelson is a registered trademark of HarperCollins Christian Publishing, Inc.

Thomas Nelson, Inc., titles may be purchased in bulk for educational, business, fund-raising, or sales promotional use. For information, please e-mail SpecialMarkets@ThomasNelson.com.

Scripture quotations are taken from the King James Version. Also quoted: Holy Bible: New International Version®. NIV © 1973, 1978, 1984 by International Bible Society. Used by permission of Zondervan Publishing House. All rights reserved.

Publisher's Note: This novel is a work of fiction. Names, characters, places, and incidents are either products of the author's imagination or used fictitiously. All characters are fictional, and any similarity to people living or dead is purely coincidental.

Library of Congress Cataloging-in-Publication Data

Tolsma, Liz.
  Daisies are forever / by Liz Tolsma.
    pages cm.
ISBN 978-1-4016-8912-4 (pbk.)
1. World War, 1939-1945—Underground movements—Germany—Fiction. 2. Germany—History—1940-1945—Fiction. I. Title.
  PS3620.O329D35 2014
  813'.6—dc23   2013047198

Printed in the United States of America

14 15 16 17 18 19 RRD 6 5 4 3 2 1

*To my aunt Lillian Tolsma, thank you for sharing
your story. You are a courageous, godly woman
and an inspiration to all you touch.*

*And to Ruth Lippert. This story is also yours. Your example of
faith in difficult circumstances is an encouragement to many.*

"Without remembrance, there can be no future."

*"Oh merciful Lord . . . crown our effort with victory . . . and
give us faith in the inevitable power of light over darkness,
of justice over evil and brutal force . . . so be it. Amen."*

*"In this world you will have trouble. But take
heart! I have overcome the world."*

*"And he saved them from the hand of him that hated
them, and redeemed them from the hand of the enemy."*

GLOSSARY OF FOREIGN WORDS

GERMAN

ACHTUNG—caution

BAHNHOF—railway station

BITTE—please

DANKE—thank you

DER FÜHRER—the leader

DEUTSCHES ROTES KREUZ (DRK)—German Red Cross

ESSEN KOMMEN—come eat

FLUCHT—escape

FRAU—Mrs.

FRÄULEIN—miss

GUTEN MORGEN—good morning

HALTEN SIE—stop

HERR—mister

JA—yes

KINDER—children

KOMMEN—come

KRISTALLNACHT—series of attacks against the Jews throughout
Nazi Germany

LUFTSCHUTZBUNKER—air-raid shelter

MUTTI—mother

NEIN—no

OMA—grandma

GLOSSARY OF FOREIGN WORDS

ONKEL—uncle

OPA—grandpa

REICHSMARK(S)—German currency

SCHNELL—quickly

STALINORGEL—a rocket launcher nicknamed Stalin's organ

STRASSE—road

TANTE—aunt

TIEFFLIEGER—low-flying German aircraft

VATER—father

VOLKSEMPFÄNGER—people's radio

VOLKSSTURM—German national militia

ZUM ÖFFENTLICHEN LUFTSCHUTZRAUM—To Public Shelter

RUSSIAN

ТИФ КАРАНТИН—Typhus Quarantine

NYET—no

URI—watches

ONE

HEILIGENBEIL, EAST PRUSSIA

February 8, 1945

B right red and orange explosions lit the dark, deep-winter evening. Gisela Cramer hugged herself to ward off the bitter chill. Her warm breath frosted the windowpane and with her fingernail she shaved a peephole. She didn't know what she expected to see. Maybe the Russians surging over the hill.

An icy shudder racked her. She couldn't block out the sights and the sounds of the last time the Russians found her.

Behind her Ella Reinhardt's two small girls giggled as they played on the worn green-and-blue Persian rug that covered the hardwood floors. Gisela's *opa* dozed in his sagging, overstuffed chair, his Bible open on his lap. His skin hung on his thin face. Every now and then he coughed and stirred, then settled back to sleep.

Each day her grandfather grew weaker. His condition worried Gisela, especially since he refused to see a doctor.

A Red Army mortar shell hit its target not far from them in town and rocked the earth beneath her feet. The vibrations almost buckled her legs. Her heart throbbed in her chest. How much longer could the German army hold off the Soviets? What would happen to them when they arrived?

Almost at the same instant, an urgent pounding began at the door, accompanied by Dietrich Holtzmann's deep voice. "*Herr* Eberhart. Herr Eberhart."

Not wanting Opa to have to get up, Gisela spun from the window, tiptoed over and around the children's dolls and blocks, and answered the door.

The breathless older man stepped over the threshold. The wind had colored his cheeks. He pulled his red knit cap over his ears, gray hair sticking out of the bottom. "I had to warn you right away."

Gisela held out her hands to take their neighbor's coat, but he shook his head. "I can't stay."

"Let me get you something hot to drink at least. Some ersatz coffee maybe?"

"Have a game of checkers with me, Dietrich. We can talk as we play." Opa sat straighter in his chair.

"I don't have time. We're leaving, Bettina and Katya and me. Tonight. Whoever is left in town is going west, as far and as fast as possible. By morning the Russians will pour in from the south. You need to come with us. All of you. Take the children and get out of here. It is too dangerous."

Gisela had feared this moment for many days. Though she had pleaded with her family to leave, they delayed. Opa's health was too poor.

Gisela peered at the girls, now clutching their dolls to their chests and staring at Herr Holtzmann with their big gray eyes. Another shudder ripped through her. She knew all too well the peril they would be in if they didn't leave before the Red Army arrived.

Opa's hands shook as he grasped the chair's armrests to stand. "*Ja*, it is time to leave. We knew it would come, though we prayed it wouldn't."

Her cousin Ella stepped into the living room from the tiny kitchen, wiping her cracked hands on a faded blue dish towel, then tucking a strand of blond hair behind her ear.

The cold wrapping itself around Gisela intensified. How would Opa make the trek? They had no car, no horse, only bicycles. "Are you sure they will be here by morning?"

Herr Holtzmann nodded. "If you wait for daylight, it will be too late. Pack whatever you can and get out of here. My sisters and I are leaving within the hour."

Gisela rubbed her arms. "What about Opa?"

Her grandfather shook his head. She recognized the determination in the firm line of his mouth. He couldn't be thinking about staying here. Surely not.

Herr Holtzmann pulled his red knit cap farther over his ears. "Go. Right now. Get out of this place and head west."

Ella ushered their neighbor into the frigid night. "We will be ready in an hour." She took a moment to lean against the door after she closed it, breathing in and out. Gisela followed her lead, willing her galloping heart to settle into a canter. Another nearby blast rocked the house, reverberating in her bones.

Closer. Closer. They were coming closer.

In her memory, she heard those soldiers kick in the door. Heard screams. Gunshots.

She clutched her chest, finding it hard to breathe, and snapped back to the present.

They had to run.

An hour. They would leave in an hour. She drew an unsteady breath and steeled herself. "We can't let them catch us."

Deep sadness and fear clouded Ella's face. "You leave."

Gisela took a step back. "What about you?"

"What about Opa? He will never survive the trip. He needs me. And the Red Cross is depending on me. With so many refugees already in the city, the *DRK* can't do without anyone." She squared her shoulders and straightened her spine.

Gisela glanced at Annelies and Renate playing once more, now pulling a colorful tin train on a string. "What about the girls? They can't stay."

"I want you to take them."

Had Ella lost her mind? Gisela couldn't leave her opa and her cousin here alone to face a horrible, certain fate. Those screams she had once heard rattled in her brain again. "*Nein.* I won't leave without you. Both of you. Let us get packed."

Opa stepped in front of her, his arms crossed. "Ella and I discussed this weeks ago, when the Russian offensive began. You will take the girls and go. She and I will remain here. When the fighting is over, we will join you."

"If all of us don't go, none of us will." Gisela headed toward the kitchen. Ella grabbed her by the shoulder, her fingers digging into Gisela's flesh. "You're not listening to me. I am not going. And Opa can't." Annelies and Renate ran to their mother and clutched her leg.

Ella lowered her voice. "I will help you get ready and give you whatever money I have, but you have to be the one to take my children. I have the nursing skills to take care of Opa. And when the war is over, this is where Frederick will come looking for me. If I'm not here, he won't be able to locate me. *Bitte,* bitte, take my children to safety. Opa and I will join you as soon as possible."

Chilled to the core, Gisela bit her lip. The pleading, crying in Ella's voice pinched her heart. Should she take the girls and leave her cousin and Opa behind? "You know what awaits you if you stay."

"You have to do this. For my sake. Save my girls. Take them from here. It's their only chance."

The fluttering in Gisela's stomach meant she would never see

Ella again. Nor Opa. Her throat constricted, making speech difficult. "Think about this. Your girls need you. Their father is gone and you are all they have left. I'm not their mother. I'm not enough for them. You have a responsibility."

The color in Ella's fair face heightened. "And I have a vow to my husband. This isn't easy for me to send my children west. Believe me, my heart is breaking. And your parents did it for you. I am asking you—begging you—to do this for me."

Thoughts whirled like a snowstorm through Gisela's mind. How could she take care of the girls? Even if she got them to safety, what would happen to them after the war? Their mother would never come and their father would never find them, if he even survived.

And Opa. The Russians would not show mercy to an old, sick man.

Ella drew Gisela's stiff body close and whispered in her ear, her words laced with tears. "I trust you. I have faith in you. Bitte, for my sake, for the girls' sakes, take them."

"I will not separate them from their mother. If you don't come with us, I won't go either."

Ella released her hold and Gisela fled up the steep wood stairs to her second floor bedroom. The pictures of Opa and *Oma* with their children rattled on the wall as another shell hit its mark. They had no time to waste.

The room had a sloped roof and was tiny, with little space not taken by the bed and the pine wardrobe. A small doily-covered bedside table held her Bible, a picture of *Mutti* and *Vater*, and a photograph of her beloved sister, Margot.

Without thinking much, Gisela grabbed all of her underwear, a red-and-green plaid wool skirt, two blouses, and a gray sweater and stuffed them into a well-traveled pea-green suitcase. All of it donated by Ella when Gisela arrived here last fall.

She yanked the drawer pull of the nightstand so hard it shook.

Fighting for breath and to hold back tears, she picked up her Bible, the one she had always kept here, and the photos and stuffed them into her suitcase.

Hurry, hurry, hurry. The words pounded in her head in time to the pounding of her heart. What else must she take? Money.

A rusty coffee tin hidden in the back of her wardrobe held all the cash she had in the world. She withdrew it and removed the small wad of colorful *reichsmarks*, counting them three times to make sure she knew what she had. Or didn't have.

She folded the cash and slipped it into a pocket sewn on the inside of her dress, along with a handful of cigarettes from the tin. They were like gold, barter for whatever they needed. Anyone would sell anything for a cigarette.

She did much the same as she had two years ago when she traveled to East Prussia and to safety, away from her parents, away from the Allied bombs in Berlin. The war had caught up with her when she stayed with *Tante* Sonje and her cousins farther east in the country in Goldap.

And it had caught up again.

Lord, please keep us safe. Let us escape. I can't go through that torment again.

Her hands shook as she picked up her heavy suitcase and headed for the stairs.

Moments later, Ella appeared carrying a small overnight case. Gisela released her breath in a whoosh. At least her cousin had made the only wise decision.

Gisela charged past Ella and down the hallway. "If you help Opa gather his things, I'll pack what food we have, then change into something warmer. After I finish that, I will help you get the children ready." Not waiting for Ella's reply, Gisela made her way to the first level, the suitcase thumping down every step, Ella's footfalls echoing behind her.

The empty kitchen cupboards reminded her of the "Old Mother Hubbard" nursery rhyme her mother had told her ages ago when they lived in California. They contained not much more than those of that fictional character.

Gisela wrapped up what she could—a few loaves of bread, some potatoes and cabbages. She gathered vegetables canned last summer with produce from their garden and sticks of wurst. The sausages would travel well. When they ran out of food, they would have to buy what they needed until they depleted their cash.

She didn't want to think about what would happen then.

Gisela returned to her room. She pulled on two pairs of cotton stockings, three pairs of wool socks, a pair of pants, a serviceable blue wool skirt, a blouse, and a red wool dress. On top, she layered her knee-length black wool coat, thankful that her weight loss enabled her to button it. Like Charlie Chaplin, she waddled to the girls' pink-papered room to help Ella dress the girls. How would they ever walk in all of these clothes?

Her cousin was getting Renate ready but again she didn't speak as she tugged a wool sweater over her daughter's head. As Gisela helped Annelies sit on the bed beside her sister and pull on two pairs of heavy wool socks, the child looked at her with round gray eyes. "Where are we going?"

"On an adventure. Doesn't that sound like fun?" Gisela willed her trembling fingers to tie the little shoe faster. "We will see different places and meet many different people. Perhaps we will get to ride on a train. Would you like that?"

Annelies nodded, her blond curls bouncing. "I want to ride on a train."

Her three-year-old sister refused to be left out of the fun. "I go on the train too."

"Ja, Renate, you may go on the train too."

"Hooray." The girls bounced on their feather mattress.

Ella gave Renate a stern glance. "You must sit still so I can get you dressed. It is going to be cold and you need to keep warm." Cold didn't quite capture the bone-chilling twenty-below Celsius temperature the thermometer recorded.

They carried the girls downstairs because they couldn't move well with the clothes they had on—their two coats each, their toboggan hats, and shoes with boots over them.

Gisela stopped short when she saw Opa, dozing once more in his threadbare chair. He had not begun to prepare for the flight west. She shook him to wake him. "It's time to leave. You must get dressed."

Opa opened his eyes, as blue as the East Prussian sky in summer. He patted her hand. "Gisela, my dear child, I cannot leave. You know that in your heart. Please go. Don't make this more difficult than it is."

She knelt beside Opa and clasped his hands in hers. "How can I leave you?"

"You have a job to do. Get Ella's *kinder* to safety. What happens to us is God's will." He kissed the top of her head, then took his Bible from his lap. The binding was worn, having been opened many times throughout the years. From within the pages, he drew out a paper and handed it to Gisela.

It wasn't a paper, but a daisy pressed in between sheets of waxed paper. The flower looked like it might have been picked yesterday.

"I gave a bouquet of daisies to your oma when we were courting. It was her favorite flower. They reminded her of God's pureness and holiness. She told me that if you put them in water, they last forever. This one she took from the bunch and pressed it in her Bible. When she died, I slipped it in mine, in the same passage where she had it. I want you to take this. Put it in Isaiah chapter 43."

"This is for me?"

"Ja. When the road gets hard, I want you to remember the daisy. And the passage it is in."

Gisela clung to her grandfather, their tears mingling and dripping down their cheeks. A little piece of her heart tore away. How could she do this?

Opa released his hold on her. "It is time to go. Remember. 'When thou passest through the waters, I will be with thee.'"

Gisela nodded and kissed him on the cheek. With trembling fingers, she retrieved her English Bible from her suitcase, the one she had earned for good Sunday school attendance at their church in California. Flipping the pages, she located Isaiah 43. Tears blurred her vision so she couldn't read the words. She placed the daisy between the pages and closed the brown leather cover.

Once outside, the women bundled the girls in the cart, wool blankets and bright quilts covering all but their button noses. Gisela pulled her daisy-studded scarf around her neck.

In the bursts of light cast by the exploding bombs, Gisela became aware of the refugees filing past them, a stream of humanity headed toward safety. She set her attention behind her, to the house they were leaving. Her mother's parents had lived here all their married lives, and she and her parents had come here each summer from the States.

For the last time, she crossed inside and stood in the hall. Closing her eyes, she allowed the memories to wash over her. She smelled Oma's kitchen and the scent of her pink and yellow roses from the garden, felt the cool, smooth wood floors beneath her bare feet and the softness of the feather mattress.

She heard Margot's laugh, her light snoring in the bed beside her, smelled the fragrance of her rose water.

She remembered how her opa's mustache tickled her cheek when he kissed her good night, how he smelled like the pipe tobacco he loved to smoke, how his big hand engulfed her little one as they wandered the streets of the city.

The grandfather clock in the hall, well-oiled with beeswax, chimed the hour.

How many times had she and Margot lain in bed well into the depths of the night, listening to the clock toll each quarter hour? A few tears eeked from the corners of her eyes as she heard Opa's bass, singing German folk songs to her, lulling her to sleep.

Nothing would ever be the same. She would never return to this house. All she would have left would be a handful of memories.

And a daisy tucked in her Bible.

TWO

Mitch Edwards breathed in and out, the cold air stinging his nose, burning his lungs. The winter sun had almost disappeared beneath the western horizon, bathing the East Prussian countryside in red and orange and yellow. A little stone farmhouse stood in silhouette against the sky, a barn a short distance from the residence.

Xavier McDonald, his fellow British soldier and stalag companion, stopped and rubbed his skinny calf, a horde of refugees streaming past them. Muscle cramps again. "Inside or outside tonight?"

Mitch's own legs ached. He shrugged. "What does it matter? This ghastly long line of refugees means we'll either have cold or filth tonight."

"You're a cheery chap."

Mitch scratched at the lice that had established a colony in his matted hair. He had a difficult time with cheer when a hard lump settled in the pit of his stomach. Since slipping away from their German captors a few days ago, he had reason to believe they had been walking in circles.

Just as they had in France in 1940.

Xavier had followed Mitch then. Where would he lead them now? Would they be able to rejoin their mates? His throat constricted. One poor decision years ago with a horrible outcome. Though he tried to deny it, he feared another wretched result.

Xavier should never have put his confidence in him.

Today they had met up with this river of refugees. They had to know where they were headed. If Xavier and he could blend in, they could make it to the Allies.

The trampled snow turned into frozen mud beneath Mitch's worn boots. He blew into his icy hands and rubbed them together. Mitch and Xavier and the line of German refugees—their enemies—trudged on until they approached the neat little farm. The barn rose higher than the squat stucco house, but the windows of the residence gleamed light and smoke spiraled from the chimney.

The farmyard, encircled by the house, the barn, and a couple of outbuildings, was mass chaos. Old people set up camp while children ran in circles, shouting to each other. Women gathered firewood from the row of oak and pine trees along the property line and gleaned root vegetables from the fields.

Xavier and Mitch gathered as much kindling as possible. "My light tonight?" Xavier's hand shook as he grasped the precious match. One of the few they had left from the Red Cross relief packages sent to them in the stalag. Mitch nodded.

Xavier applied the flame to the sticks while Mitch blew a light breath over the brushwood. His Boy Scout skills did not fail him, and within minutes they were melting snow in their dixies, adding a little powdered milk from their almost-exhausted care packages to make a hot drink.

Mitch sipped the beverage, careful not to burn his tongue. "One thing I will miss when the war is over is the powdered milk, eggs, cheese, meat, everything."

Xavier laughed. "It's a sight better than the sauerkraut the German farm woman smothered everything in when the work detail sent me to her."

"Now you're making me hungry. Stay here and man the fire. I'll see what I can find to go with the last of that Spam."

Xavier stared at Mitch with his green eyes. Mitch had seen that look five years ago during the retreat through Belgium and France toward the coast of the English Channel. Mitch pulled his stolen German greatcoat around himself and clapped his hands together, bringing him back to their present reality.

The dark figures of hunched women dotted the open field. Though six inches of snow lay on top of the furrows, he hoped to find a potato or two that hadn't rotted. He pushed away the snow with his boot's toe. Nothing but bare dirt. A shout went up from the far corner of the field. Some lucky bloke would have a feast tonight.

Fifteen futile minutes passed before Mitch struck gold. In his gleaning, he uncovered two small potatoes. If they hadn't been frozen, they would have been mushy, but the hunger gnawing at his insides refused to let him pass over these prizes. He bent and picked them up, then stuffed them into his coat pocket before making his way back to Xavier and their small fire.

He held up the prized potatoes.

"We're blessed tonight." Xavier took them and placed them among the glowing embers.

"Hey, you." A woman's voice came from behind them.

Mitch turned to spot her hurrying toward them. "Ja?"

The slender, beak-nosed woman crouched beside their fire. Her long, jagged fingernails reminded him of eagle's talons. "You and you." She pointed at each of them. "Why are you here and not fighting for the Fatherland?"

They had both learned German during their five years of

captivity, but they had definite British accents. The guards would often laugh at their clumsy attempts to speak the language.

Xavier answered for them. "Separated from our unit."

"Where are your rifles?"

"Lost." Their captors had confiscated them.

She harrumphed before getting up and walking away. How many others questioned why he and Xavier were among this group?

His friend scooted forward, clutching his tin cup with the warm, thin milk. "A close shave, that. What a nosy bird, that woman."

Mitch nodded. "You get us into trouble. I get us out."

"Life wouldn't be fun without a bit a trouble."

Off in the distance, a train whistle blew. Mitch wondered where it might be going. "Like the time we nearly burned down your pop's barn when we threw the chicken on the fire without plucking it?"

"My mum laid into me so hard for that one, I had a tough time sitting in the pew the next morning."

"No surprise that you'd get me to join the army with you on a dare." Mitch shook his head.

"That's what friends do. And you've yet to thank me."

"Father will tar and feather you if he ever sees you again."

Xavier laughed, then sat back and finished his milk. After a while, he rolled the potatoes from the fire with his cup. "Supper's ready, mate. Eat up."

Though the skins burned, the potatoes inside were half raw and half rotten. Xavier nibbled at his. Much too impatient to savor his supper, Mitch scarfed down his meager meal, then took a bite of his Spam.

He had just set his cup on the ground and sat back with a satisfied sigh when they heard the rumbling of a motor. A jeep sped into the farmyard, scattering refugees like a flock of birds.

A pair of Wehrmacht officers jumped from the vehicle, guns

cocked. They appeared nearly identical—tall, muscular, Aryan perfection. "We're looking for two escaped prisoners. Brits."

Mitch clenched his fists. He recognized these soldiers. SS guards watching the men they drove from the stalag ahead of the Russians. Xavier jabbed him in the ribs.

The group melted back. A voice sounded from near the barn. "If we found them, we would have shot them."

A cheer rose from the assembly.

Mitch was surprised the guards had come this far. Surprised they were out searching for them at all, they were in such a hurry to stay ahead of the Soviets. He held his breath.

"They might be impersonating German soldiers."

The woman with the long nose stepped forward. Mitch grabbed Xavier by the upper arm. Crouched low, they inched their way from the fire—and the mob. With everyone's attention focused on the stalag guards, they took the chance to get away. Once they cleared the farmyard, they broke into a full-out run.

Footsteps pounded behind them. *"Halten sie!* Halten sie!" Gunshots punctuated the soldiers' orders for them to stop. In the gathering darkness, their aim was poor. The field was uneven, the furrows impeding the men's progress. Xavier stumbled. Mitch grabbed his mate and dragged him along.

His lungs burned with each frigid breath, though sweat poured down the back of his stolen uniform. His cramped legs cried out for him to stop, but he couldn't. They couldn't. To do so would be to die.

The Germans continued calling for them. At first, their voices came from right behind. Now they sounded a little farther to the side. Could they have lost them?

Mitch didn't stop to think, just kept sprinting. *Lord, don't let me run in circles this time. Help us.*

They reached the edge of the field where pines and oaks grew along the property line and dove for cover in the underbrush.

THREE

The weight of exhaustion bore down on Gisela's shoulders. Her legs burned from the effort of pedaling the bicycle while her toes burned with the cold. Her eyes refused her command to stay open, her eyelids fluttering like flags in the breeze. Annelies and Renate had cried themselves to sleep around dawn. At first Gisela had been glad for the quiet, but now their screaming would help keep her awake and alert.

Herr Holtzmann pedaled behind her, his handcart trailing him. Each time she glanced back, he had fallen a little farther behind. Bettina and Katya trudged alongside. The older of the two sisters, Bettina, drew her blue wool coat around her bony frame. Even with the distance between them, Gisela caught Bettina's remarks.

"Brother, why are we out strolling at this time of night? This is not sensible. I have never heard the likes of such things, have you, Sister?" Her words whistled between the gap in her front teeth.

Herr Holtzmann sighed. He must grow weary of the bizarre questions his senile sisters barraged him with.

All throughout the night, Gisela's thoughts returned to the

little house in Heiligenbeil. What must be happening to Ella? She glanced at the children asleep in the cart. Both of them had inherited their mother's button nose, and both had their mother's freckles spattered across their faces.

With half-frozen fingers, Gisela gripped the bicycle's handle-bars tighter. How would she explain their mother's choices to the children? They had lost so much already.

And what about Opa? Every time she thought about him, her throat ached. He was an old man. Would the Soviets take pity on him?

Nein. She knew the answer. She bit back her tears.

She slowed her pedaling and rode to the side of the congested street to allow Herr Holtzmann to catch up to her. Wagons, carts, and people so clogged the road that he almost drove past. She waved and he pushed his way toward them.

She dismounted. "Your cart is too heavy for you. Let me see what I can take and what we might be able to leave." She rummaged through his belongings, pulling a few cast-iron pots and pans from in between the bedding and setting them alongside the road.

Katya unloaded a box spilling over with picture albums and books and transferred it to Gisela's cart. Bettina joined in, grabbing a load of stuff in her scrawny arms and plopping it on Annelies.

Herr Holtzmann hurried to pull the pile from on top of the giggling girl. "Sisters, that is enough. We can't let Gisela carry all of our belongings."

Still digging in the Holtzmanns' quilts, Gisela pulled out a mantel clock, painted blue with yellow flowers scrolled across the case. She held it high. "Do you need this?"

He swallowed hard and pulled his cap farther over his balding head. "Ursula loved that clock. It has been in her family for a long time."

Gisela tried to ignore the wistfulness in the man's voice. It was impractical. Better they leave his late wife's clock than the pots. You couldn't warm food in a timepiece. His pleading blue eyes begged her not to dispose of this treasure. Then she thought of her Bible and her treasure tucked in its pages. Never would she want to leave it. She placed the clock among the blankets and pillows once more.

Herr Holtzmann kissed her cheek with his chapped lips. "*Danke*. You understand. It is all I have left of her. Sixty years and that is all that remains." His eyes watered with unshed tears. Gisela turned away, not wanting to give way to her own grief.

A moment later, he touched her shoulder. "It is nearly noon. My friend and his wife own a farm along this road. Let's find him and see if he has a place for us to rest and a room for us to spend the night. You look like you need a decent sleep."

Dark circles rimmed his eyes. She imagined she looked much the same. "You too. But are we far enough ahead of the Soviets? What if they catch up to us?" What if they were overtaken while they slept? Gisela's stomach flipped.

In the cart Renate stirred. She scanned her surroundings, her eyes large. Tears gathered and threatened to spill. "Where is Mutti? I want Mutti to come."

Annelies squared her shoulders. Gisela sensed she fought the urge to break into tears herself. Gisela longed for her own mutti as much as Renate wanted hers. Family. Most of these people were going anywhere as long as it was west. She needed to get to Berlin, to take care of her mutti. From there they could travel to Munich.

Renate continued to cry for her mother. How could Ella have abandoned them? At least when Gisela's parents sent her east, she was an adult.

She pulled the girls from the cart and gathered them close. "Your mutti will be along very, very soon. She had to finish some work and take care of Opa, and then she is going to join us. Remember, we are having a great adventure. We will make new friends and see new things. You have to be big girls." They didn't understand their loss.

Annelies blinked away her tears. "I can be a big girl."

"Me too. I be a big girl." Renate refused to let her sister get the last word.

"Very good. I'm proud of you."

"Tante Gisela, would you sing the wagon song for us again?"

"Ja, wagon song."

"You walk and follow Herr Holtzmann, and we can sing the song."

Herr Holtzmann mounted his bicycle and the group rolled down the streets of the sleepy village, the girls in all their clothing waddling along like two penguins.

> High on the yellow coach
> I sit in front with the coachman.
> The white horses start trotting,
> Merrily peals the horn.
> Meadows, pastures, and marshes,
> Ripening grain shimmering gold.
> How I would like to stay,
> But the coach rolls on.

The group sang the refrain several times—the Holtzmann sisters the loudest—before they arrived at a squat stone farmhouse, brightly lit windows staring at them. A huge barn overshadowed the cheery, inviting home, the once-vivid green exterior in need of a new coat of paint.

An older woman met them at the entrance when they knocked. Her mouth dropped into an *O*. "Oy, Dietrich, is it good to see you and your sisters. And this." She scanned the bedraggled band and a smile curved her lips. "Who is this you have brought us?"

"Let me introduce Gisela Cramer and her cousin's children, Renate and Annelies Reinhardt. Ladies, this is *Frau* Becker."

Annelies went to shake the woman's hand, polite as her mother had taught her. Instead, the woman, a heavy crown of braids ringing her head, pulled the child into a grandmotherly hug. "Little girls. So long it has been since we had little girls."

Renate flung herself into the old woman's embrace. "Me too."

Frau Becker laughed. "Of course. We should not forget you."

For the millionth time that day, Gisela's heart tugged with thoughts of her grandfather. He loved the girls so much. They should have had more years together.

God, please take care of him.

Frau Becker ushered the group into the house, already overflowing with refugees. Bedding covered the parlor floor and the couches and chairs. Farther into the home, women jostled for position at the stove. Frau Becker patted her hand. "You see, we don't have much room. What we have, though, you are welcome to."

The noise and heat and confusion started a pounding behind Gisela's left eye. "That is very kind of you." If they stayed here, they would have to sleep standing up.

Herr Holtzmann cleared his throat. "Your husband, is he around?"

All at once, the joy left the older woman's eyes. "Heinz had a stroke this fall. He cannot move his left side, and his speech isn't so good anymore. That is why we stay. We cannot leave with him like this."

Herr Holtzmann nodded and rubbed the spot between his nose and lips. "I would like to see him."

Their hostess pushed her way through the crowd and down the hall to the last of two doors on the left. "You visit with him for a while. We have some room in the attic. There is no heat, but you are welcome to stay there. Or the barn, but I fear those conditions are worse. That is all I have. Come, girls, let me help you settle." Herr Holtzmann slipped inside and shut the door.

Frau Becker never stayed still, her hands moving even when the rest of her body didn't, and she reached the top attic step before Gisela had willed herself to reach the third. When Gisela was a child, Mutti had always wished for a tenth of Gisela's energy. She now understood the feeling. She had to drag her feet up the flight of stairs.

The sloped roof, its rafters exposed, covered the large space. Even here, though, there would be no privacy. Groups had spread blankets and duvets over almost every square inch of the room. Gisela stared at one woman, her round face unlined though gray streaked her dark hair. The strands hung loose and dirty around her face. She held a screaming infant and patted the child's bottom.

The stench of unwashed bodies pressed in on Gisela. She squeezed the girls' hands. She had imagined conditions to be poor, but not like this.

Frau Becker shook her head. "These people keep coming and coming, and they don't stop. More and more every day. You don't want to sleep in the barn. I wonder, where will this crowd go? Is there food for so many in the west?"

After they had hidden in the underbrush for a while, Mitch and Xavier continued to run across snow-covered fields, tripping and stumbling along until the world spun in front of Mitch's eyes. When his legs cramped so he couldn't take another step, they sought shelter on the dark side of a barn. This farm stood off the main road.

Over their panting, Mitch listened for any sound of approaching German soldiers. He strained his ears for the slightest giveaway—a footstep, a cough, a whisper. The night remained still. He put his hands on his knees and took several deep breaths.

Xavier slapped him on the back. "Away by the skin of our teeth, mate. That was grand fun."

Mitch raised his eyebrows. "Grand fun? You've gone crackers. Let's not do that ever again. We have to be more careful from here on out. Follow the crowds but at more of a distance."

"Trouble is, we've left our dixies and pans and Spam at that farmhouse. Not to mention our last couple of matches."

It was an awful blow, but what could they do? There was no way Mitch was stepping foot back on that property. "We'll have to improvise."

"I improvise that we go back and retrieve our supplies."

"Now I know you're crackers, Xavier. That woman would turn us in without blinking an eye."

"Listen, I have a brilliant idea. We'll slink in and grab our supplies and out we go. In an hour or two, everyone will be sleeping and no one will know we've been there."

"And that's your brilliant idea?" Over the years, Mitch had to talk Xavier out of more brilliant ideas than he could dare count. And there were plenty he hadn't talked him out of. His dad disapproved of Mitch palling around with Xavier, afraid he would get a criminal record and ruin his chances at becoming a solicitor.

"And yours is what?"

"Getting some sleep." Mitch pushed open the big barn door just enough to slip inside. Xavier, thankfully, followed.

"You can get all the sleep you want. I'm going back. Without those supplies, we're sunk lower than a U-boat." Xavier stomped out.

After all these years, he knew how to get under Mitch's skin. "Xavier, listen to reason. Is a nearly empty can of Spam and two old tin cups worth a shot through the heart? Not to me. Not by a long sight. We can eat snow and raw potatoes."

But Xavier didn't listen. In the glow of the snow, Mitch watched him march off. Did he dare shout after him and risk waking the farmer's family? Mitch stomped after his friend. You'd think so many years in a POW camp would have taught Xavier some common sense.

Mitch caught up and marched alongside Xavier, not saying a word. At least this time they wouldn't end up walking around in circles, their footprints from earlier their guidepost.

The cold night air bit through his coat and his worn gloves. Mitch had no feeling left in his toes and doubted he ever would again. Each step brought excruciating pain to his legs. "Is this worth a can of that rubbish they call meat? You do realize that one refugee or another will have gobbled it up by now. If not handed it over to the Germans as proof we were there."

"We're this far. Let's keep going. There's no harm in looking, is there?"

They walked and walked, never getting to that farm. Where could it have gone? It was impossible for them to go wrong this time. They had run far and long and fast, but even so, they should have come upon it by now.

Lost in the whiteness that was East Prussia.

Survived five years to die like this.

Xavier was right. He was a cheery chap tonight.

He wanted to lie down in the snow and go to sleep.

Xavier marched alongside him. "Keep awake, mate. Don't let hypothermia get the best of you. We're almost there. I have the feeling we've been here before."

"Am I supposed to laugh at that?"

"I mean it. Is that it?" Xavier pointed at a light on the horizon. "Fires in the farmyard, perhaps?"

Mitch couldn't be sure. "Let's head in that direction. The worst it could be is our friends from the stalag."

Xavier clapped him on the back. "That's the spirit. I like your optimism."

Just when Mitch believed he couldn't put one foot in front of the other yet again, they made out the small house and the large barn. A farmyard. The layout matched with the one in his memory. As the first rays of sunlight pinked the sky, they arrived full circle at the place they had fled.

They slunk into the still-quiet yard. A few unlucky ones slept out of doors, wrapped in layers of blankets near their fires. Together they searched the area without success. Mitch shot Xavier an I-told-you-so glance. He had the gall to shrug.

Motioning that it was time to get out of here, Mitch turned to leave. As he did so, he bumped into someone. Not just anyone.

The scrawny, greasy-haired woman from the night before.

She stared at him. He peered at the point where her gaze bore into him. His lapel. The Nazi SS uniform that he and Xavier had stolen before their escape. Why was she so intent on what he wore? He crossed his arms to keep them from shaking.

The woman stood, jiggling her wailing infant on her hip. He turned away from her, pretending he was looking for something.

He was.

A way out.

He nudged Xavier and tipped his head in the woman's direction.

The woman stepped in front of him. *"Guten morgen."* Her breath stank of rotting teeth.

His mouth went dry. "Guten morgen." Why didn't she leave him alone?

"What unit did you serve with?"

Mitch pointed to the stylized SS on the lapel of his dark coat, hoping his shaking fingers wouldn't give him away. "Stalag guard."

She tucked one dirty strand of hair behind her ear and leaned over him. "Then why aren't you with the prisoners?"

"Separated from our unit. I told you so last night." Xavier stood tall.

She tilted her head and squinted her lifeless blue eyes. Then she spat at their feet. "You are no SS guards."

"We are."

"Nein. Listen to you talk. You are either American or British."

"German," Mitch growled at her. If she found out the truth . . .

"You killed him."

"I killed no one." The unfortunate truth.

She lunged at him. "My husband was in France, you dog, on the beach. The British killed him."

War slapped him in the face. His legs quivered. She would turn him in to the authorities who, busy driving westward, had little time to deal with escaped prisoners. They shot the escapees before they could defend themselves.

"Go away." He ground his teeth to keep them from chattering.

"You killed him."

FOUR

February 10

Gisela woke, stiff and cold in the early morning hours, surprised she had slept at all, what with the crying babies and the old man who talked in his sleep. Most of her companions continued to slumber in this dark, freezing attic. Even Renate and Annelies still dreamed. Beside them, the Holtzmann sisters snored. Off in the distance, mortar fire broke the stillness.

Gisela had left her hairbrush in the cart. The girls needed to have their hair rebraided, and she wanted to work out her own tangles. Compared to all that was happening around them, it was a minor thing, but it would make her feel better. More civilized.

She rose and Herr Holtzmann stirred beside her. "Where are you going?"

She bent over him and tucked the blanket around his shoulders. "I need something from my cart. Stay here and stay warm as long as possible. I'll be back soon."

She picked her way over and around the prone, sleeping forms of her fellow refugees. Playing on her tire swing as a child in her yard in California, free and happy, her sister Margot at her side, Gisela never dreamed she would find herself in this kind of situation. Not even when Vater moved them to Germany nine years ago.

Downstairs, a few women used the small stove. She predicted that within an hour, the kitchen would be packed, humming with women cooking breakfast for their families. Not too many people had roused themselves in the yard yet. Horses munched on a little patch of grass they had uncovered. While a horse and wagon would make their burden much lighter, the animals required food and care. Their bicycles did the job just fine.

She stopped to think a moment, trying to remember where they had left their belongings the night before. On the far side of the yard, she located their carts.

But no bicycles.

Where were they? Gisela pivoted around, sure they would appear.

Her search yielded nothing.

This couldn't be happening. Did they unhitch them and park them somewhere else? No, she would remember doing that. Then again, she had been exhausted.

She turned and stared at her cart. And at Herr Holtzmann's. How would they pull them, loaded as they were, without the bicycles? And how would she tell him? Her head spun. She stood with her hands on her hips and closed her eyes, trying to wish this all away. Yes, when she opened her eyes, she would see those bicycles.

Or better yet, find herself snug and warm and safe in her bed at home.

One, two, three.

Nothing.

She scurried from cart to cart, examining each bicycle. Someone must have mistaken Ella's for theirs. Many were similar. One looked like it but didn't have a scratch on the frame. She had fallen one day when the road was muddy and a rock nicked it.

Only looking at the bikes and not at where she was going, Gisela slammed into an older man, almost knocking him over. She took hold of his arm just in time. "I'm so sorry. I wasn't watching where I was going."

The man's mustache twitched. "No harm done. What are you looking for?"

Gisela swallowed back the tears. Crying would accomplish nothing. "Our bicycles. Someone stole them during the night. We left them hitched to our carts, but they're gone. Herr Holtzmann needs that bike."

He patted her shoulder with his gnarled hand. "Slow down, *fräulein*, let me help you."

"Have you seen them? Can you help me?"

But they were nowhere around. They had vanished. She rubbed her throbbing temple.

Shouting drew her attention. The woman with the bedraggled hair and the screaming baby towered over two soldiers. "You dirty Brit, you killed my husband in Normandy. You are those men the SS was looking for last night."

"Nein, nein. We are German officers." The one man's hand shook as he drew it through his dark, wavy hair.

The woman, however, was right. She could tell it in his speech. He was British.

A friend.

An ally to an American such as herself.

She scanned the crowd. The woman's outburst had awoken and captured the attention of many. They knew the truth. Such a mob would be all over him in a matter of minutes. And they would do away with him.

Her legs moved forward of their own volition and her mouth formed the words she hadn't bothered to check. "Leave them alone. This one"—she pointed to the dark-haired one—"he is my husband. He fought bravely for the Fatherland." She stepped beside him.

He gave her a tepid smile, doubt and confusion in his fabulous brown eyes.

The woman shifted her weight and jutted out her right hip. "If so, then who is he?" She motioned toward the fair-skinned man with a shock of bright red hair sticking out from under his hat.

Her heart pounded, the full impact of what she was doing dawning on her. "My brother-in-law."

"Why are they here?"

Very good question. Very, very good question. She hugged herself to still her trembling. If she had thought through her actions, she would have a ready answer. She turned to her supposed husband who lifted his shoulders in an almost-imperceptible shrug.

Her mind refused to conjure up a reason.

The woman tapped her foot.

"They were shot."

"Sure. Millions of our boys have been shot. If they don't die like my husband did, they keep fighting."

The man beside her tapped her arm, then his chest.

"My husband was shot near the heart. Ja, the bullet just missed his heart. They were unable to remove it."

"I thought he was a POW guard."

The man could have told her that. Or he could have answered the question. "Ja, after he was shot, he went to be a guard. He can no longer handle the rigors of marching and fighting. It could kill him. He served our homeland."

"And your brother-in-law?"

"He is carrying a special message for the Führer."

"The Führer?"

Both men gazed at her, as did the woman shaking her head. With her stomach dancing in her abdomen, Gisela nodded.

The woman gave them all a look as hard as stone, then turned away.

Gisela released a breath she didn't know she had been holding.

"Brunhilda." The man touched her hand.

Warmth spread through her despite the frigid temperatures. "Pardon me?"

His eyes widened when he heard her speak in English. He replied in that tongue. "That's what I'm calling that old bird. Rather appropriate, don't you think?"

"I think you're lucky she didn't turn you in."

"Thank you."

"You're welcome."

"American?"

She nodded.

"Now I understand why you helped us. You're a swell gal."

"It would be best if you didn't speak at all. Your German is poor and your English is dangerous. I'm Gisela Cramer."

"Mitch Edwards."

"Xavier McDonald."

Gisela pointed at the tall, thin man, Xavier. "You are Siegfried Munchen." She pointed at his friend who stood three or four inches shorter. "And you are Josep Cramer. You are supposed to be German and I am supposed to be your wife. Too many people heard that little exchange, so we will have to continue the charade for a while longer. Where did you come from?"

"Stalag XX-A." Xavier cracked his knuckles.

"A POW camp."

He nodded.

Great. Not only were they English, but they were escaped prisoners of war. Her headache got worse. "Are you going to wait here for the Soviets?"

Mitch leaned forward, his eyes darkening, intensifying. "Too much of a risk. We've heard that oftentimes the Russians treat other Allied soldiers no better than their German prisoners. They're brutal. That's the rumor in camp. Not the allies we want to meet up with. So we'll be moving on."

Gisela rubbed her hands together. This posed a problem. "You need to stay with me then, since we're supposed to be together and all. I'm traveling with three old people and my cousin's two young daughters. I have to tend to them, but be ready to leave as soon as possible."

One positive to the situation was that Mitch and Xavier could pull carts. Though they were skinny, they had to be stronger than Herr Holtzmann. They could prove useful.

She spun to return to the house to awaken the rest of her group.

Whether Herr Holtzmann liked it or not, their party had grown by two.

"Gisela, what took you so long?" Herr Holtzmann stood in the middle of the clan waiting for her in the front hall, the sisters carrying beat-up suitcases. The girls grinned and ran to hug her legs. She could manage nothing more than a slight smile.

"You look like the world is going to end." His words, as soothing as her opa's, almost did her in.

She studied the cracked leather of her brown shoes. So much had happened in the little while she had been gone. "That sounds very good right now."

"It is better if you spit out poison."

He had a point. "A thief stole our bicycles last night."

Herr Holtzmann sucked in his breath and let it out little by little. "Then we have to pull the carts by hand." He said it in such a matter-of-fact way.

"It will slow us. And we have two other members of our party."

Bettina shoved her bony elbow into her sister's equally bony ribs. "A party. What a splendid idea. Do you think my pink dress will do? Perhaps it needs to be altered."

Herr Holtzmann ignored his sisters as they planned the shindig of the century. "Anyone is welcome."

She dropped her voice to a whisper. "They are escaped English POWs masquerading as German SS officers. My concern is for the girls. Is it too dangerous?"

"Danger is what life is about these days. We never know when our time will come. Do you want to help these men?"

Crazy as it was, she did. The Lord had pricked her heart. She nodded. "They would be assets, helping pull the carts or carry the girls."

"That's fine with me. Bigger problems are in front of us. Frau Becker told me, and I overheard it from some of the other men, that the road to Elbing has been cut off."

"Cut off?"

"Ja. The Russians are to the south of us and to the east and west."

The Frische Haff, a large lagoon on the Baltic Sea, lay to the north. "We're trapped."

"I would say so."

Much as she tried to control herself, her voice rose in pitch. "Then what do we do? Where do we go? Back to Heiligenbeil to face the inevitable?" Screams echoed in her head. Pleas for help. She took a deep breath. They couldn't go back. They couldn't. The girls stared at her, their mouths open.

The Holtzmann sisters took a break from their party planning. "Swimming in the Frische Haff in this weather?" Bettina tapped her forehead. "Brother, you have become addle brained in your old age. Wouldn't you agree, Sister?"

Katya nodded, her speckled gray hair peeking out from underneath her brown hood. "I don't much care for swimming myself."

Annelies tugged on Gisela's arm. "Are we going swimming?"

"Nein." Though if the Soviets continued their three-way assault, they may have no other choice. Her stomach clenched. She leaned closer to Herr Holtzmann. "How will we escape? Is there a way?"

"Don't worry. We will go over the Frische Haff."

"Your sister is right. You have lost your mind."

He chuckled. "My mind is right here. The lagoon is frozen. We will walk over it."

"Just like that?"

"Just like that."

An hour later, the vast whiteness of the Frische Haff stretched in front of the little band. Gisela stood unbelieving as a sea of humanity flowed forward, plodding across the ice of the lagoon, dark against the frozen brightness. She thought of her own black coat and how it made her vulnerable.

A road of sorts had been sketched out across the ice. The German army had placed small trees along the way to mark the path the refugees needed to take. Out in the blinding, unending whiteness, it would be very easy to get lost.

Mitch caught up to her and stood at her shoulder. "A far cry from the green hills of England."

"So you're not from London?"

"Not quite. The little town of Kendal. My mum and pop have lived there all their lives. My sister too, until she moved to Dorchester."

"You miss it. And them."

"My mum, anyway. It's been a long five years."

"That's how long you've been a POW?"

"Yes."

"Has your father passed away?"

"No. Why do you ask?"

"You said you miss your mother, but you said nothing about him."

"We have a complicated relationship. Shall we?" He led the way down the beach and onto the ice.

Gisela took the hint and dropped the subject.

After a while, the trees became redundant. The side of the "road" was littered with dead horses, discarded goods, and broken-down carts. Gisela tried to take it in at the same time she tried to close her mind to what played out in front of her.

They plodded farther in silence, needing every bit of every breath to continue trudging forward. In places, small holes littered the ice. Herr Holtzmann had gathered a stick from the bank and walked in front of them, testing the depth of the water on the surface at those points. In some places, it was more than ankle deep. Their shoes and stockings and pants legs were wet.

And cold. Gisela shivered.

"How are you doing?" Mitch pulled the heavy cart without complaint.

"Swell." Ella and Opa had been right. He would never have survived this trip. Would any of them?

"You've taken my title as the cheeriest chap on the planet."

She had to give him a little smile for his effort. "I'd like to feel my toes again someday."

"You will. And when you do, they'll hurt like the dickens."

"Ah, now I see how you earned that title in the first place." But Mitch was correct. She tried not to think of the pain that awaited her when they finally left the ice. Whenever that would be.

They continued the trek, the line of refugees stretching as far in front of them as they could see and as far in back of them. The scene was surreal, like it should be in a motion picture and she should be Greta Garbo.

"I want to get out." Annelies leaned over the side of the cart as she whined. Poor kid. She had to be restless. Mitch lifted her and set her on a stretch of ice not pockmarked by bullets and missiles. She gave him the biggest grin and began gliding across the slick surface.

A little bit ahead, Gisela spied a dark bundle on the right side of the road. Probably left there by someone who could no longer carry the heavy burden. The goods were wrapped in a gray army-style blanket. She broke off from the group. "I'm going to see what's in that package."

Herr Holtzmann on her left nodded. "Do you need the extra weight?"

"Nein, but there might be valuables in there we could use. We have two strong men now." She removed her heavy wool mittens and unwrapped the blanket.

Her breath caught in her throat. A baby. Eyes closed, lips blue. She cradled the infant in her arms.

Cold.

Stiff.

Dead.

Her eyes stung.

Who would leave their baby like this? How could they walk away from their child? The thought sickened her.

A Soviet plane droned overhead.

A *tiefflieger*.

The single plane broke through the clouds, its shiny silver fuselage catching the light. The pilot wheeled around and gunfire rained down on them.

Rat-a-tat-tat.

Gisela spun to the left and to the right. Bright-white ice surrounded them. No trees. No ditches. No homes.

Rat-a-tat-tat.

Annelies broke off her gliding, her gray eyes huge in her face, her mouth hanging open. Mitch tackled the child to the ground like an American football player.

Rat-a-tat-tat.

Renate shrieked in the cart. Gisela flung herself on top of the toddler.

All around, women and children screamed. They melded with the screams of her aunt and cousins. Screams of the present, screams of the past.

Gisela clutched her chest, finding it hard to breathe. The Russian pilot continued to shoot in the midst of the stream of refugees.

Nothing but innocent ladies and babies.

A bullet screeched past Gisela's ear.

She trembled and Renate shook under her.

Only the dead infant laid still and quiet.

FIVE

The whistle of bullets and the screech of bombs scrambled Gisela's thoughts. The sound of shooting, yelling, dying filled her ears and reverberated in her head. She quivered like a poplar tree in the wind.

Renate whimpered underneath her.

"Hush, little one, hush. God will take care of us." But did she believe that? Had God truly watched out for her that one awful night last fall?

The pilot wheeled around and the gunfire continued. With her face buried in the duvets, breathing was difficult.

She didn't dare raise her head to look for the other members of their party. Was Annelies safe? And the Holtzmanns? What about Mitch and Xavier?

Time lost all meaning. They may have lain there for five minutes or five hours. The plane flew back and forth along the column of refugees. Would the shooting ever stop? Or did the Russian intend to kill every last one of them?

The plane's whine grew higher in pitch, coming closer. The incessant firing fractured the ice. It moaned as it split.

Another bullet whizzed next to Gisela's right ear. Renate screamed. Gisela held her breath. *Dear God, dear God, dear God.* She couldn't control her shaking. How much longer until she awoke in glory?

"*'When thou passest through the waters, I will be with thee.'*" Among Opa's last words to her.

"Are You here, Lord?"

Rat-a-tat-tat.

Shouts and prayers and curses. So much crying. Some of it was Gisela's. But it surrounded her on every side.

And then the Russian decided he'd had enough fun. He rose above the clouds.

All sat silent, except for the cracking of the ice. No one dared to breathe. Was the tiefflieger gone for good?

Time slipped away. A voice spoke here and there, joined by a few more. The plane had indeed left.

Gisela gathered her courage and lifted her head. Blood soaked the ice, horses lay fallen, wagons split in two. She rose from on top of Renate and lifted her from the pile of blankets. She checked her over and saw no blood, though the toddler screamed at the top of her lungs.

Gisela's heart banged against her ribs, with a beat like a Duke Ellington song. Her knees were so weak she had a difficult time holding herself up.

And right beside the indentation Renate's head had made, the hole from a bullet burned through the quilts.

So close. They had come so close. She held on to the cart to avoid slumping to the ice.

Mitch lifted his body off of Annelies. She hurried to Gisela's side and wiggled her way into Gisela's embrace.

"Are you okay? Did you get hurt?" With quaking hands, she examined the child. No blood. But the girl didn't blink.

Gisela kissed her cheek. "You're fine now. The plane is gone and can't hurt us anymore." Annelies began to cry and Gisela cradled both children.

She turned to the Englishman. "Thank you."

Mitch nodded, his brown eyes darker than she had noticed before. "Are you hurt?"

She shook her head, then turned to see to the welfare of her other charges. The old ladies knelt on the ice beside a prone form. Gisela set Annelies on the ice.

The chill permeated to the depth of her being.

Mitch turned his attention to the place where Gisela's gaze was directed. The old people huddled together. And Xavier . . .

Where was he?

Mitch's gut clenched and his world narrowed until he saw nothing but the Holtzmanns.

God, no. Please, not him.

He hurried in their direction, slipping and sliding. "Xavier. Xavier." God couldn't do this to him.

"Hush, dearie, he's sleeping." One of the elderly women patted his shoulder.

He dropped to his knees by his chum's side, his face ashen, lips blue, a crimson puddle spreading across the ice. "No. No!"

Mitch's throat constricted. He couldn't breathe. His child-hood pal. Always able to get him into scrapes. Always able to get him out.

Gisela was there then, beside him. She placed her fingers on Xavier's neck, searching for a pulse, he presumed.

"One last crazy adventure, chap. I should have talked you out of it. Why didn't I?" He wiped the moisture from his eyes.

Perhaps it would've been better had they stayed with their

fellow prisoners, marched westward by the SS guards, instead of slipping away that day, burrowing into a snowbank and hiding there until the Germans cleared the area.

"He's gone." Gisela touched his shoulder. Mitch pulled away. What had he done? He shook his fists at the heavens. An ally. An ally took Xavier's life.

A fire burned in his gut. If he ever got his hands on a Russian . . .

"You saved Annelies's life." Gisela's words were little more than a buzz.

He scanned the scene around them. The family in the wagon ahead of them lay unmoving, their bodies riddled with bullet holes. The women behind them stroked their dead horse's mane. A wail of grief rose from this frozen grave.

He added his to theirs. He sat shivering on the ice, wet through to the skin with water and blood.

Annelies came and touched his wet cheek. "What's wrong?"

"Xavier died."

Katya, her brown hood askance on her head, kneeled on the ice beside Xavier but did not say a word. Perhaps, even in her senility, she understood.

But they couldn't understand. No one could. God should have taken him instead.

Gisela put her arm around him and helped him stand. "We have to keep moving and get off this ice before more planes come."

Herr Holtzmann nodded. "She's right, son. We can't linger."

Mitch stared at the other bodies strewn over the white bareness of this place. Just leave Xavier here? To sink to the bottom of the Haff when it thawed?

A physical pain clawed at his chest. Xavier deserved better. "Give me a minute." Herr Holtzmann and Gisela led the two pairs of sisters away.

This wasn't right. None of this was right. If only he could undo what he had done five years ago.

Tears blurred his vision as he bent and retrieved Xavier's dog tags, then slipped them over his neck. His parents would want them.

The stream of refugees swung a wide berth around the little group, but continued unabated.

Mitch covered Xavier with a green blanket Gisela brought him from her cart. She placed the baby beside his lifelong chum.

Then they turned away, leaving the bundles on the frozen Haff.

Like Lot's wife, Mitch turned back, the sight of Xavier's body seared into his memory.

Time blurred for Gisela. How many minutes and hours passed as they struggled across the ice, she had no idea. Night came and they slept in the carts, huddled together under the duvets for warmth. The morning sun did nothing to change their circumstances.

All she wanted was to get to the Frische Nehrung, the narrow spit of land separating the lagoon from the Baltic Sea and their road to Danzig. And safety. Out here, they were too vulnerable, too exposed.

Every little bird that flew across the sky caused her shoulders to tense. They fooled her into believing they were tieffliegers.

The Frische Haff was only twenty kilometers or so wide, yet they continued across the endless stretch of white. Unable to see either shore, it felt like they would never reach land.

Mitch pulled the Holtzmanns' cart with his head down, his back rounded, not saying a word. She wanted to comfort him, but the words stuck in her throat. In this situation, they sounded false and hollow. There was no comfort here. Even the Holtzmann sisters were subdued. They walked on without a word.

The bullet-riddled ice creaked and cracked as the wheels of the cart rolled over it. She had lost feeling in her feet many kilometers ago. Her coat and dress and pants never had a chance to dry. Her ears burned.

Renate whimpered at each little noise and insisted that Gisela carry her. Gisela's arms ached after five steps, but Renate refused to be happy anywhere else. When Gisela tried to settle her in the Holtzmanns' cart, she protested that idea in no uncertain terms. Gisela held Renate in one hand and pushed her cart with the other. She had a difficult time putting one foot in front of the other. Even plodding was too much work.

The blisters and calluses on her hands hurt. By tonight, they would be cracked and bleeding. Her shoulders begged for mercy. The load became too much and she had to drop the handles and rest for a bit. She set Renate on the ice.

The entire party took its cue from her and paused. She rummaged through her cart, filing through the items they had taken from her grandparents' home. Oma's silver, picture albums, quilts she had stitched by hand, and duvets filled with goose down. And Gisela's Bible.

What should she keep? The silver could buy them food, lodging, and train tickets. Parting with her Bible, Opa's daisy pressed between the pages in Isaiah, was out of the question. Some of her clothes? No, she needed those.

In the end, she discarded her coffeepot, the partial set of china, and all but a few pictures from her album. She repacked the cart and settled Annelies inside once again.

Mitch came to her. "What can I take for you?"

"Nothing. You have a heavy enough load."

"Every now and again we were sent to work on farms while we were prisoners. Manual labor was new to me, but I managed."

Yes, he looked strong despite his captivity. Still, she didn't want to burden him. "This will be enough for now. Later, we will have to see."

Situated for the time being, they continued their slow trek north, each turn of the cart's wheels taking them that much farther away from the Russians. Even so, Gisela could almost feel them breathing down the back of her neck. Maybe they would be waiting for them on the other side of the Haff.

A loud, sudden snap sounded.

Her heart roared to life.

The ice under their feet cracked.

She flicked her gaze to Mitch. He stared at the frozen Haff.

With another great creak, the chunk of ice under Herr Holtzmann's cart broke. The handles slithered from Mitch's grasp.

His eyes widened as the cart sunk into the water.

He slipped and slid.

The ice snapped.

SIX

Mitch was helpless against the frigid water as it pulled him down. So cold it took his breath away.

As he sank, he grasped for something, anything, to hold on to. He raked his glove-encased fingers across the frozen surface. He couldn't get a grip.

Voices, people shouting, sounded like he was already underwater.

Strange, really it was, that he wasn't afraid.

The German greatcoat served as an anchor, dragging him down.

The last thing he saw was a pretty pair of brown eyes. He waved as the Frische Haff claimed him.

Then fingers clamped around his wrist, like a vise crushing his bones.

In that moment, the panic rushed over him. His heart revved into high gear. *Dear God, help me.*

He kicked his legs, though they were weighted down by his heavy boots. Dizziness threatened, blackness at the corners of his mind.

Harder, harder he fought. Kicking. Reaching.

Lord, get me out of here.

Would he end up at the bottom of the Haff, dead like Xavier? His throat constricted. All thanks to the Russians.

Whoever tugged on him had incredible strength. He rose toward the surface.

His face broke the plane. He gulped in air. It stung his lungs. Bright sunshine assaulted his eyes.

Another couple of pulls and he lay panting on the ice.

He was alive. *Thank You, thank You, thank You.*

Gisela pounded him on the back.

"What on earth are you doing?"

She fell over on the ice beside him. "Getting the water out of your lungs."

"What kind of way is that to go about it?"

"I don't know. I saw a lifeguard do it once to a woman he pulled from the water, so I gave it a try."

"Rest assured, I haven't any water in my lungs." Then he thought about what she said. "You rescued me? A tiny girl like you?" A beautiful, tiny woman like her with a heart-shaped face.

She crawled to her cart, sat up, and rubbed her arms. "Don't act so surprised." He followed her lead. She stood and offered him a hand.

He declined it and got to his feet on his own, flashing her a smile, his teeth chattering. "My chums are going to razz me about this one."

"Instead of telling them Gisela rescued you, maybe you'd better tell them Herr Holtzmann did." No amusement in her voice. Was she teasing him or not?

"They'd tease me about that too. No, I like a good story. I'll tell them I rescued Gisela, my wife." Even that didn't elicit the laugh he hoped for. He rubbed his arms in a desperate bid to get warm.

Herr Holtzmann brought them towels from Gisela's cart. "You are going to freeze to death."

The magnitude of what happened hit him then. The Holtzmanns had just lost all of their possessions. They owned nothing more than the clothes on their backs. Even when trying to do good, he failed to succeed. "Herr Holtzmann, I don't know what to say. I apologize for losing your cart."

The old man clapped him on the back. "More important than possessions is that you are safe."

"If I had been more careful, had watched the color of the ice, I'd not have lost it."

"Blame the Russians for that. It is their bombs and bullets that weakened the ice."

He would. No worries about that. He shivered and shivered.

"Don't take the guilt on yourself."

Mitch appreciated Herr Holtzmann's words. His own father would have berated him for his carelessness and rebuked him for not being able to complete such a simple task. "I am sorry."

"We know that. No apologies are necessary."

"I will make it up to you."

"You don't need to. They are just things." Herr Holtzmann tapped his chest. "In here is where your memories are. In your heart. Those, no one can take away. I tried to hang on to Ursula's clock, but now it is gone. Yet she is with me. I hear her laughter and feel the touch of her skin against mine. Those things do not fade."

Mitch didn't miss the implication that replacing the items would be impossible. He heard his father's voice. *"How could you be so careless? You lost all this poor man had left in life. He's destitute because of you."*

And Xavier wasn't around to tease him. His chest ached.

Gisela held out a red wool sweater and a pair of pants. "Will these help you?" She bit her lip.

"Help with what?"

"You have no clothes to change into and you're soaked to the skin."

The corners of his mouth curved as he towered over her by a head at least. "I believe they would be a wee bit too small."

She peered at the offering in her hand.

"Thank you, anyway."

Away she bustled, slipping the sweater over her own damp blouse before buttoning up her long black coat.

"How much farther?" Mitch rubbed his hair and handed the towel back to Herr Holtzmann.

"Can't be too long." The older man sounded out of breath. "Perhaps another couple of hours."

All this occurred while the line of refugees snaked around them, careful to avoid the thin ice. No one came to their aid. With faces pointed north, they marched ahead. Like the wind-up toys he'd played with as a child.

Katya stepped to her brother's side and shook her index finger at Mitch. "Sister and I told you that swimming in this weather was lunacy. You should always listen to us."

Reprimanded like a tot, Mitch nodded and shivered.

As dry as they could be, they set off once more. Mitch was now able to pull what was left of Gisela's belongings while she carried Renate and kept an eye on Annelies. At least the work warmed him.

Herr Holtzmann plodded along, holding his sisters' hands. He limped and breathed heavily. Mitch stopped. Worry knotted his stomach. "Come on, Herr Holtzmann. It is your turn to ride in the wagon." The old man needed to rest.

"Nein, danke. See up there?" He let go of Bettina's hand and pointed to the gray streak on the horizon. "Land. Tonight we will sleep with a roof over our heads."

Gisela watched as the old man lowered his arm and rested it over his chest.

Herr Holtzmann's footsteps slowed the closer they came to shore. His sisters dragged him along with them. Every few minutes he stopped to catch his breath, his face devoid of color. His state of health concerned Gisela. She set Renate in the cart, went to him, and rubbed his back.

He bowed his head. "You need to go ahead. My sisters and I are slowing you. Don't worry about old people like us."

"Nein." She and Mitch spoke at the same time.

"No one gets left behind." She glanced at the girls, their gray eyes large in their peaked faces. She had made a vow. "No one."

He shut his eyes. "I pray that you and this soldier and the girls will be safe. For myself, God has other plans."

"I have plans of my own. And they include getting us out of harm's way. No matter what, I will do it."

He touched her hand. "You are sweet."

"Ja, sweet and right. We stay together." Mitch nodded at her and she appreciated his support.

"I beg you to leave me here. Take my sisters, but go on without me." Herr Holtzmann gripped his heart. A physical pain cramped her chest as well.

"Are you ill?"

"Nein, just old. And slow."

"We can see land now." And they could. A few trees and scattered houses. Hope lay ahead of them.

Mitch cleared a spot in the cart, making a nest of sorts. "We all get a chance for a ride. Now it is your turn." He led the old man by the elbow to their makeshift form of transportation and got him settled.

Gisela pulled a blanket over his thin frame, worrying the satin edge of it as she kissed his wrinkled forehead.

A smile crossed Herr Holtzmann's face. "If Ursula could see me now, like a king riding in his chariot, she would tell me to stop being so lazy and put a hoe in my hand."

His little joke eased Gisela's concern just a bit.

Not too long afterward, the travelers stepped from the Frische Haff to the Frische Nehrung, their feet soaked. The last few meters, the ice had been almost nonexistent. But they were once again on solid land, wet feet a small price to pay.

They had fallen far behind those they had started this journey with. No matter how far they fell back, though, they never reached the end of the line. Gisela hadn't known this many people existed on the face of the entire earth. As far as she could see in front of her there were people, and as far as she could see behind her there were people.

They had come to a populated area—as much as this narrow strip of land was populated. The tiny fishing village was full to over-flowing with people. Scattered homes rose over what would be a sandy shore in summer. A single chimney jutted from each steeply sloped roof.

Not trusting Mitch's German, she left the girls and the old people in his care and went to search for a warm place where they might be able to rest. Herr Holtzmann needed a good place to sleep.

Gisela pushed through the crowd, jostled by women and old men.

She knocked on the door of the first house she came upon. A haggard middle-aged woman answered the door. "No room." She slammed it in Gisela's face before she even asked the question.

At each of the half dozen or so homes, she got the same response. She deflated. No one would take pity on the elderly and the children. Because they weren't any different from the norm. The Frische Nehrung was laden with the very old and the very young.

But what would she do? She feared for Herr Holtzmann's

health. Everyone's health. They had all gotten wet. No matter which way she looked, no answer presented itself. There were no barns, just fishing shanties and summer homes.

A rumble sounded in the distance. She gazed at the sky, expecting more fighter planes, wanting to shake her fist at them. They couldn't leave civilians alone. But then again, they didn't sound like aircraft. She cocked her head. More like trucks. From the sound of them, a convoy of trucks.

Lord, is this the answer to my prayer?

A short time later, a dozen or more green canvas-covered trucks rolled into the village. The throng surrounded them so they were forced to stop before rolling over the clamoring crowd. Gisela shoved aside those in her way. A German officer sat inside the first truck she came to, his billed hat embellished with a brass eagle.

"Where are you headed?"

"To Danzig."

"Don't leave." As if he could. She twisted her way through the crush of bodies to where she had left the rest of her band. "Come on, we have to hurry. Leave the carts. Stuff the rucksacks with everything we can carry and go. There's a truck headed west."

Herr Holtzmann rubbed his eyes and stretched his limbs. "God does provide."

"He did this time." Gisela nodded.

Everyone pitched in to pack what few possessions they had left. The old women stuffed sweaters and wool pants and the girls' underwear into the bags. Gisela added jars of pickled beets and the remaining sausages wherever she found room. In her search, her fingers touched her leather Bible.

Opa, what is happening to you? Are you still alive?

She pressed the book to her chest, feeling her opa's work-roughened hand on her cheek. Not much room remained, but she packed it among their clothes.

More refugees joined the crowd. Mitch slung a rucksack over his shoulder, then picked up the girls—one in each arm. Herr Holtzmann hung on to Katya. Gisela grabbed three bags and Bettina's hand. "Come on. We don't have a minute to lose."

Already a few men clung to the running boards of the idling trucks. Gisela hauled her band to the first vehicle where she had told the driver to wait. She had never seen even sardines packed as tightly as the people in the back. "I'll see what the driver can do."

She dashed to the cab. "Can you fit in a few more? I have little children and old people."

"Fräulein, if there is not room back there, there is not room up here."

Now she noticed the four other soldiers who filled the seats. "What am I going to do?"

"Whatever it is, do it fast. Frauenberg fell yesterday, the eleventh of February."

First Elbing and now Frauenberg.

"The Soviets will be in Danzig very soon."

"Are the trains still running out of there?"

"If you find one, get on it."

The noose around the refugees tightened. When they were all pressed against the Baltic Sea, then what would happen? They had to get to Danzig and onto a westbound train without delay. With their slow progress, they would never be able to walk to Berlin and keep ahead of the Russians.

She scooped up Renate and grabbed Annelies. "Let's go." She pushed and pulled the group down the line of trucks.

All of them were filled to overflowing.

They came to the final truck, revving its engine. No matter how full it was, she would get them on board. She felt the Red Army's breath hot on her neck, and it made her shiver.

This time, she wouldn't fail.

Mitch climbed up. "Hand me the girls." He had to shout above the noise of the crowd and the vehicles.

Diesel fumes choked her and she coughed. She lifted first Renate and then Annelies into Mitch's arms. The trucks ahead of them in line pulled away, one at a time.

Bettina and Katya proved to be nimble and, though not very ladylike, climbed aboard without assistance, then tumbled over the closed tailgate.

The truck's lights went off as she turned to help Herr Holtzmann. The tires rolled, splattering mud. The crowd parted and the driver picked up speed. She screamed for them to stop.

Gisela's stomach dropped to her feet, her heart taking its place, her entire body thrumming with each beat.

"Halt! Bitte halt!"

SEVEN

Gisela held on to Herr Holtzmann's hand, squeezing it, pulling him along. Her legs burned and she gasped for breath. "Halt, bitte halt."

She ran behind the transport truck like a lion runs for its prey. With its heavy load of passengers and baggage, it moved forward at a crawl. The old man's hand slipped from her grasp.

"God, help us!" If she shouted at the heavens, would He hear?

The truck lurched forward. It would leave and she and Herr Holtzmann would be stuck here, at the mercy of the Russian soldiers.

Her memory echoed with her aunt's voice. *"Run, girls, run."*

But she couldn't run. To do so would leave the old man to face his fate. And she had promised she would leave no one behind. She grew light-headed and her ears buzzed. Every muscle in her body quivered.

"Halt! Halt!" The shrieks tore the inside of her throat raw.

With a sudden squeal of brakes, the truck stopped. From the corner of her eye, a dog darted from in front of the truck.

She clutched her neighbor's hand once more and dragged him behind her.

"Leave me, Gisela, leave me."

"Nein. Nein. Don't talk like that." *God, get us all on this truck.*

"I cannot continue. Take care of my sisters."

"Ja, you can. You must."

But two steps from the truck, he wrenched his hand free. She stumbled forward. Fingertips brushed hers and a strong hand gripped her wrist, pulling her into the truck. The bone in her shoulder joint shifted and her legs lifted off the ground. She swung her feet until she kicked the truck's bumper.

Feeling a solid surface beneath her, she climbed over the tailgate. As she turned to help Herr Holtzmann, the truck jolted forward. "Nein. Nein. We can't leave him."

He made no attempt to catch the transport.

In the distance, explosions rocked the ground.

She leaned forward and banged against the gate.

Hands held her inside. She fought and wriggled but couldn't free herself.

Herr Holtzmann waved with his right hand, his left over his heart.

A Russian plane zoomed from the heavens, spraying the ground around the truck with bullets. The rocks they kicked up clanged against the truck's metal body. Without warning, the driver sped up.

Gisela bounced against a solid chest.

"Let me go. I have to help him. I have to get him."

"You can't. It is too late." The deep voice in her ear was pure German. No British accent.

"Then let me off." She kicked at the stranger's shins.

Her blows proved futile. Herr Holtzmann grew smaller and smaller.

"Good-bye, Brother. Catch the next bus and meet us in Venice." Bettina stood next to Gisela, now waving to Herr Holtzmann and blowing him a kiss.

Gisela fell backward.

The stranger wrapped his arm around her and steadied her.

She peered at her rescuer. A man in a German soldier's uniform met her gaze, the picture of Aryan perfection with blond hair and eyes as blue as the Baltic itself.

The Russian pilot shot a few more rounds at the convoy of trucks. Screams erupted from those in the vehicles in front of them. Her stomach vaulted into her throat.

The tide of tears spilled over, down her cheeks. "Nein, not him. Not him. Dear Lord, not him too." She clung to the stranger who still held her.

He let her cry for a good long time, until her tears turned into hiccups.

"Are you going to be all right, fräulein?" His voice was deep, lilting, almost hypnotizing.

"Gisela." Mitch's voice came from beside her, though the stranger continued to hold her.

"Oh." She stopped short, almost calling him Mitch. "Josep, Herr Holtzmann didn't make it on. He stopped running. I couldn't . . ."

"I know."

"Then this man pulled me inside."

"Kurt Abt." The man's right sleeve hung empty. He must have a very strong left arm to have lifted her into the truck the way he did.

"I should have stayed with Herr Holtzmann, held on to him tighter. If only you could have rescued him."

Kurt's blue eyes frosted. "He was an old man, not long for this world."

"He was my opa's best friend. Neither of them will make it." The empty space in her heart pained her. She swallowed around the lump in her throat.

At last Kurt released his hold on her. "He could get on the next truck."

"How many more will there be? If Elbing and Frauenberg have fallen, how much longer until Heiligenbeil and Königsberg do too? The Russians could already be in Danzig. We don't know."

Mitch touched her back. "These soldiers wouldn't be on their way there if it was in Soviet hands."

But they all understood that it wouldn't be long.

"Tante Gisela." Renate cried for her and she became aware of the little girl beside her and the gorgeous platinum blond woman holding her.

Gisela took Renate and snuggled her.

Mitch spoke in her ear. "If you hadn't made it onto the truck, the girls would have been without you."

She squeezed Renate. "Then what was I supposed to do?"

"Just what you did."

"Was it the right choice?"

"The only one."

Yet she heard the huskiness in his voice. He had to miss his friend as much as she missed Opa. And now Herr Holtzmann. There had to have been a way to save them.

"You did the right thing." The woman beside her with the Hollywood looks nodded. "When the Russians entered my village last year, they ran over the fleeing civilians with their tanks."

"I know. I know." Gisela would never forget the sickening sound of bones being crushed. All night long that horrible last fall in Goldap, she listened to the Russian tanks roll over those fleeing them. She shuddered. How many more lives would the Soviets demand?

Gisela studied the young woman, her wavy hair escaping her rolls. She had seen her before. But where?

A moment's consideration gave her the answer. "You are Audra Bauer, a seamstress at the shop where my cousin buys her dresses, aren't you?"

The woman tipped her head. "Ja. I always remember these sweet girls. Frau Steinmetz gives them candy."

Gisela introduced herself and Mitch.

Audra wrinkled her forehead. "That soldier is your husband? I don't remember you or Ella mentioning him when you came to the shop."

When would she learn to think before opening her mouth? Or at least have an excuse at the ready. Gisela paused for a long moment before an answer came to her. "We are newlyweds. You know how wartime romances go. You meet one day and are married the next."

Audra giggled like a schoolgirl. "He is very nice."

Gisela had to admit she was right. His dimples got her every time, making her want to smile. And the way he raked his hand through his thick, dark hair . . .

Person upon person had crowded onto this truck tighter than pickled eggs in a jar. The truck flew over a bump and she and Renate jostled against Mitch. As if touched by fire, heat suffused her body. She managed a cautious peek at him. His prominent Adam's apple bounced as he swallowed.

He smiled a sort of sad smile, biting his lower lip.

Her head spun.

The world buzzed.

Then there was blackness.

Gisela, standing in front of Mitch, slumped into him. He grabbed her under her arms. If there had been a spare centimeter to move, she would have fallen to the ground. The hair on his arms bristled.

They bumped along the road, jostled and shaken until every muscle in his body hurt. The smells of human waste, the taste of fear, the packing of one body against another reminded him of that horrific trip in the cattle car from France into Germany five years before. Their captors had been less than kind. The POWs had been packed tighter than in this truck. Men prayed. Men cried. Men died.

Renate, wedged between Gisela and Audra, cried a pitiful howl until Audra held her.

Mitch shook Gisela. "Wake up." She had to come to. "Come on now."

He slapped her cheeks, though not hard.

She didn't stir.

With quivering fingers, he felt for a pulse. Good and strong.

"Gisela, let's look lively now. Come on now. Come on."

Her eyes didn't open, her long lashes brushing against her pale cheek. He peered at the crowd pressing on every side. "Give her air. Back up."

But where could they go? The truck hit a pothole, jolting them. Gisela continued to sleep.

"She needs fresh air."

Kurt whistled, quieting the throng, Mitch's ears ringing with the shrill sound. "This woman has fainted. Now, everyone, step back so she can catch her breath."

They did their best to obey their wounded war hero. Not a lot of extra air circulated around Gisela, but enough that her eyes flickered open. Confusion clouded them.

"Mitch? Mitch."

He covered her mouth, hoping to cover her slip of the tongue. "Ja, Gisela, it's your husband, Josep. Are you feeling better?"

She righted herself. "What happened?"

"Have you had much to eat?"

She shook her head. "With Herr Holtzmann's food lost, I was trying to ration what we have left."

"You fainted." He dug in her rucksack, found a loaf of bread, and tore off a chunk. "Eat this."

"I'm not hungry." She turned her head away.

He clenched his teeth. Stubborn woman. "Suit yourself. When you faint again, I won't try to revive you."

She grabbed the bread and stuffed it into her mouth. After she swallowed, she grinned, a most insincere smile adorning her heart-shaped face. He returned the gesture.

Renate, Audra still holding her, patted Gisela's arm and made an announcement. "I go potty."

Did she mean she had to or she already had? If she went right here, both she and Audra would smell awful within minutes. And would keep smelling that way for days to come. Judging by the eye-watering odor in the truck, many had.

Mitch took a two-second survey of their surroundings. Nowhere at all for the little one to use the loo. There was only one choice.

He lifted Renate from Audra's arms. "Take off her pants."

Gisela leaned back and stared at him. "You want me to do what?"

"Take them off. You don't want her going potty with them on."

"What are you going to do?"

"Help her go."

"Right here?"

"Not exactly." He lifted Renate over the tailgate and held her out.

Gisela grabbed his arm and screeched. "Stop it! Stop it. Don't throw her."

A bubble of laughter rose in his chest. It was the kind of prank Xavier would have pulled. He'd be disappointed if Mitch didn't play along. "How far do you want me to pitch her? I toss a mean game of cricket."

Gisela tugged on him and he had to tighten his grip.

"I won't drop her. I promise. Renate, go potty."

And the child did so, while hurtling through the East Prussian countryside.

When she finished, Mitch pulled her inside and held her while Gisela dressed her. Renate laid her head on his shoulder.

He gave a short chortle. "Now wasn't that fun, Renate? When you grow up, you will tell your children all about this."

"My turn, my turn." Annelies wriggled out of her own clothing and he repeated the process.

He lifted Annelies inside the truck and she pulled up her pants. Then he faced Gisela. "Is it your turn now?"

She sniffed. "I don't think you could lift me like that."

"I could try."

Bettina began unbuttoning her knee-length wool coat. "I want to try. That looks like fun."

"Nein, nein." Gisela grabbed her hand. "That is a game only for the children. You will have to wait until we stop."

"I want to soar. One day Sebastian took me in his plane, so high above the clouds I never wanted to come down. That is the one and only time in my life I have ever been in an aeroplane. He can lift me out of the truck so I can fly."

"You are crazy, Sister." Katya played with a gray curl that had escaped her hood. "You can't fly in a truck. Wherever did you get that idea?"

Mitch remembered wheeling over the English countryside in his uncle's biplane. Uncle Roger taught him how to operate the controls. Mitch loved every minute of it. He also recalled his father's stern look, the hard set of his mouth and the jut of his chin, not understanding. After all, a solicitor didn't need to know how to fly.

Mitch shook his head. "Bettina, I don't believe I'm up for that challenge. But perhaps someday we can arrange for you to fly again."

"A plane would get us there faster. It would take us farther away from this awful place." Gisela bounced against him.

The German army's truck engine ground to a halt, emitting a terrible squealing sound. Not one a vehicle should make.

Mitch peered around the edge of the canvas. Nothing but snow-swept farmland.

This couldn't be their destination.

EIGHT

The soldier's footsteps crunched in the snow as he approached the back of his truck. Mitch inhaled and held it in.

"Where are we?" Gisela's breath tickled the back of his neck.

"I've no idea. I got a D in geography." Much to his father's consternation. A solicitor would need to do better than that in school. Perhaps if Mitch had paid better attention in class, he wouldn't have never ended up in a POW camp to begin with. "Don't look to me for directions." *Please, don't look at me.* The muscles across his shoulders tightened. "If you don't know, we're in trouble."

One thing he did know was that he wanted to stay out of the soldier's sight. He didn't want to have to speak to him in German. He didn't want to have to come up with another excuse. So Mitch leaned back and behind the German with one arm. Kurt.

The driver lowered the tailgate and banged his hand on it twice. "I don't know what is wrong with the truck. I can't get it going again. The others have gone ahead. There was no room for you."

So they were to sit out here, target practice for Soviet planes? Would he ever rejoin his mates?

"We may not even be able to fix the truck. Danzig is just a few kilometers that way." He pointed in the direction the truck had been headed.

"Danzig?" Mitch whispered to Gisela.

"Where the Frische Nehrung meets the mainland. You should have paid better attention in class." She sighed. "Danzig has a train station. That's why we have to get there. If the trains are still running, we can make our way to Berlin."

"Can you walk into town? What about the girls and the old women?"

Dark half circles rimmed the bottom of Gisela's eyes. "We're not invalids."

If he could, he would have raised his hands. "Don't go crackers. They are young and old. That's all I meant."

The driver busied himself under the bonnet. Most of the truck's occupants filed out and wandered away over the frozen landscape.

When he helped Gisela and the children down from the truck, Mitch was surprised to see Kurt and Audra waiting for them. Bettina and Katya stood between them.

"Sister." Bettina grasped Katya's age-spotted hand. "It's Barcelona. I would recognize it anywhere. I can smell the paella. What a cosmopolitan city it is."

Katya shook her head. "I don't smell anything. You are addle brained to think this is Barcelona. More likely, it's Madrid."

They continued arguing about which Spanish city they were in, appearing not to understand their brother was no longer with them. Was that a good thing or not?

He found himself often turning to speak to Xavier, only to catch himself at the last minute. Xavier wasn't with them.

Gisela asked the driver for directions to the train station and relayed them to Mitch. "He says we only have to follow this road and we will find it. We can't miss it."

He closed his eyes for a moment.

She didn't know his history.

Kurt watched as Gisela limped behind her husband. Her foot was bothering her, but she said nothing. And Josep was so busy playing the hero, he didn't notice.

She should remember he pulled her into the truck. He saved her from the Russians.

And what was an SS officer doing marching westward with this crazy band of misfits?

Kurt slogged on, his eye always on the beautiful woman in front of him. Her long amber hair had escaped its pins and flowed free and loose around her shoulders.

Beautiful. A Mozart concerto began to play in his head. His missing fingers ached. He longed to run them up and down a piano keyboard.

He hadn't heard the music or desired to play his instrument in months. She made it happen.

Ja, he was smitten with Gisela for sure. And God—if there was one—had dropped her into his lap. Literally.

Too bad she was married. Gisela caught up to Josep and spoke into his ear. He smiled at her but . . .

But what? While the man gazed at his wife with longing, it was the look of longing unfulfilled. Of holding back. Of guarding his heart.

Kurt rubbed his forehead.

"Have you been to Danzig before?" Audra's voice at his side startled him. The music ended.

She had linked arms with each of the old sisters and the three walked together. Her pale cheeks had pinked in the wind.

"Never. I never had the intention to visit the city either. London, New York, Paris. Those were the places I wanted to see."

Her green eyes grew large. "Ja, those are grand places. I want to go to Hollywood, like Marlene Dietrich. Be a famous actress. Imagine, your name on a theater poster."

"Or on the top of a concert program." The war began and there went his dreams. Shattered. Like his arm.

"Perhaps you will see those cities someday. If you get to America, you can visit me in Hollywood. I will be a movie star by then. I could drive you around the city in my car. Or better yet, my chauffeur can drive us."

Kurt leaned back. "How will you get to Hollywood?"

"I don't know yet. But I will. You can count on that."

Out of the corner of his eye, he watched Gisela pull one of the girls' hats farther over her ears. Such tenderness in her touch. For a moment, he forgot the woman beside him. Again she startled him when she spoke. "I'm from Schirwindt. On the border with Lithuania. I doubt you ever heard of it."

"Nein, I never did."

Gisela stroked the golden curls of the oldest child.

"Is something wrong?"

He forced his attention back to Audra. She did have a beautiful puckered mouth. "Why would you say that?"

"Because you get this faraway look in your eyes. Like you are having a pleasant dream."

He cleared his throat and attempted to make his expression as blank as possible. It would do no good to let people see how struck he was by a married woman. A woman he could never have. "Pleasant dreams are difficult to come by these days."

"Ja. I don't know anything about my family—if they are alive or dead. Nine brothers and sisters."

"I'm sorry. Those Russians are brutal. Heartless. They all deserve to be dropped in the cold, hard ground forever."

Josep spoke to Gisela again and she stopped and turned to face them. Fine lines radiated from her brown eyes. This war took too much from them too soon.

"Do either of you know Danzig?"

Both Audra and Kurt shook their heads at Gisela.

She shifted a sleeping Renate on her hip. "We will have to find accommodations for all of us. Tonight I would like to sleep in a house. No cart. No barns."

Audra patted Bettina's hand. "A roof and a floor. No hay."

Gisela's smile broke like a crescendo. "Ja, no hay. No horses or cows or pigs."

Josep nodded. "Perhaps smaller groups. It will be easier to find a place."

"Nein." Gisela spat out the word. "We will stay together. If need be, we can sleep on the floor of the same room. Just to be warm and dry, I would do anything. And together we can work on catching a train west."

Kurt was glad she voiced her opinion about splitting up the group. He didn't want to be separated from her. With these crowds, he might never see her again. "I agree. And you will be safer with a soldier with you."

Josep pointed to his chest. "She will have a soldier."

Kurt watched his sleeve flop in the breeze.

Empty. Like his soul without the music.

Gisela trailed Mitch into the city, the blister on her heel burning with each step. It had started even before the truck picked them up. When they had been able to get a ride, she hoped she wouldn't have to walk much anymore. With each step, the pain increased. Her stocking was sticky with blood.

Renate had fallen asleep on Mitch's shoulder and Annelies's feet dragged more the farther they walked. Bettina clung to Audra and Katya grasped Kurt. Gisela didn't think she had ever been so tired in her life.

She had failed Herr Holtzmann, like so many others. He should have rested more. She pushed him too hard.

They passed a shop with a few boxes of powdered milk in the window. A sign hung on the glass.

Soldaten meldet euch bei der nächsten heeresdienststelle. Wer mit ziviltrecks zieht oder sich in privatquartieren herumdrückt, gilt als fahnenflüchtig.

Mitch stood beside her. "What does it say?"

"Soldiers, get in contact with the nearest army base. Anyone who attaches themselves to civilian convoys or hangs around in private homes is considered a deserter." She shivered. Mitch grasped her hand and squeezed it.

The others caught up to them. Mitch turned down a side street in a residential area. Where it was dangerous for him. Though it was dangerous for him everywhere. Kurt would not have to report to the army base. Not as a wounded hero.

She turned her attention to the neighborhood. Neat houses lined the road. They slumbered, all quiet, unaware of who waited on the doorstep to their city.

Mitch went no farther than the second or third home before he climbed the steps and knocked on the door.

A stooped, elderly woman answered. Her hands and head and even lips shook. Mitch waved Gisela forward. "We are looking for a place to stay. Do you have room or know of someone who might take us in?"

The woman shook her head, her long gray braid bouncing. "Nein. We aren't well enough to have boarders, especially ones with little children."

"Bitte, I'm begging you. The old women and small girls are exhausted. We need a warm place to rest for the night."

"There is no way I can take you." She began to close the door.

Gisela stuck her foot on the threshold and prevented the woman from shutting them out. "We will be quiet, I promise. We are so tired, we will sleep. No fuss."

The home owner grasped the brass knob. "Nein. They are taking people at the school. That is where you can stay."

"Bitte, how do we get there?" While Gisela desperately wanted a little peace and quiet, time away from the crowds, the school had to be better than the outdoors.

Gisela bobbed her head when the old woman finished giving them directions. "Danke, danke."

They stepped back into the deserted street. Mitch adjusted the sleeping child on his shoulder. "Were you paying attention to those directions?"

"I was."

"Good. I had trouble following her German."

Gisela led them up and down a few blocks before they came to the unassuming red brick building.

The gymnasium was packed with people. Wall to wall. Where would they even go? She looked at her crew. The old women had ceased their chatter some kilometers before Danzig. They had hardly been able to put one foot in front of the other between the house and the school.

She turned her attention to Mitch. He shrugged.

Then Kurt stepped forward. She had felt his gaze on her back the entire way from the truck to this spot. She wanted to squirm under his scrutiny. "They will make room for a hero of the Reich."

He proceeded to pick his way through the throng, which parted for him like the Red Sea parted for Moses. He chose a spot close to the door. With one sweeping motion of his hand, those huddled there made room for their party.

Kurt flashed her a crooked grin, a triumphant light in his cold blue eyes.

She shivered. Together with the rest of their bunch, she made her way to the place Kurt had cleared.

"I told you I would be able to make room. For a hero, these people will do anything." He cast a glance at Mitch. Mitch glared back at him.

She settled on the hard floor and Mitch handed Renate to her. The child stirred, then nestled her warm body into Gisela's. How blissful to be so innocent, to have someone looking out for you so you never had to worry.

Kurt positioned himself on Gisela's right, a little too close for her liking. Trying not to appear obvious, she slid over a few centimeters. Mitch lowered himself to the floor on her left. A man sandwich. Stellar.

Mitch leaned over. "How about that foot?"

"What about it?"

"You have been limping since we got off of the truck. Those boots are much too small for you. My guess would be that you have a nasty blister."

"I'm fine."

"Let me see."

"That's not necessary."

"Let me determine whether it is necessary or not."

More to make him stop pestering her, she handed Renate to Audra, who sat across from her.

When she tried to pull off her shoe, Gisela sucked in her breath with the fierce pain.

Mitch ripped off her boot and her blood-soaked sock.

NINE

Mitch tightened his grip on Gisela's ankle when he saw her heel. Her small, thin foot was caked in blood. He examined the blister. White puss oozed from the raw wound. She tried to pull it back, but he held her fast.

"We need to get some medication for that."

"I'll wash it out with soap and water and it will be fine. Now please, hand me my sock."

He clung to it. "I'll rinse this when I get ointment."

"You have some in your pack?"

"No, but I'll get some."

"How?"

"You ask too many questions." Best not to let her know he planned to rifle through the sack of a woman he saw applying ointment to her own blisters earlier.

Gisela lowered her voice. "You're not going to steal it, are you?"

Kurt leaned over, attempting to catch their conversation, Mitch assumed. He kept his mouth shut.

She reached out and grabbed the filthy sock from him. "You can't do that."

"Why not?"

"You'll get caught and be in a world of trouble."

"What is wrong with your foot?" Kurt couldn't keep his nose out of their business.

"Nothing."

"I will take care of her." Mitch swiped the sock back. His burst of possessiveness surprised him.

With an abruptness that startled Mitch, Kurt rose and walked away, fisting his hand. More than likely, he was off in search of medicine for Gisela's foot. Watching the German clear a spot for them in the crowded school gave Mitch confidence. He pointed to the stylized SS on the tab of his shirt collar. "They'll hand the medicine over to a soldier."

"And you'll explain what you need in your terrible German?"

He flashed her a rakish smile. "Nein. I won't have to explain. Kurt cleared this area with one gesture. That is all it takes." At least he hoped it was.

"I won't let you put it on my foot."

"Unless you want to limp all the way to Berlin and risk gangrene, I suggest you let me treat you."

He'd had enough of arguing. Mitch turned and stomped over the mass of refugees, much as Kurt had moments before.

A pleasant surprise awaited him in the washroom. Running water. Not hot, but a trickle of water from a faucet all the same. He rinsed out Gisela's sock. He'd love to rinse the lice from his hair.

His reflection in the mirror startled him. Two weeks' worth of beard covered his face and lines rimmed his eyes. Over the years in the camp, he had lost a good deal of weight. And some muscle. His mum would never recognize him when he got home. His dad might not accept him, a failure several times over. A stabbing pain sliced through his chest.

Mitch stepped into the crowded room once again. The owner

of the sack had walked away for the moment. Mitch didn't see her as he scanned the mob. Not saying a word, he crouched and loosened the drawstring.

He avoided eye contact with those surrounding him and picked through the bag. *Lord, let me find this liniment soon.*

A pair of black boots and legs encased in long black socks appeared in his line of sight. Ignoring them, he continued his search. *Don't let this be in vain.*

"What are you doing?" The husky voice of this rather large woman gave him shivers.

He pointed to the SS on his collar, just as he had with Gisela. "I need this." At that moment, his fingers closed around a bottle. With a flourish, he pulled it from the rucksack.

He held a brown bottle of beer in his hand.

"You are stealing."

"Nein. My wife must have this." Again he pointed to his chest. Why wasn't this working as well for him as it had for Kurt? And why did she carry a bottle of the liquor when most other refugees had dumped their unneeded supplies?

The woman stood tall and puffed out her chest. "This man is stealing." She called with enough volume for the entire room to hear her.

Only a few took notice of the announcement. Stealing to survive had become commonplace.

"What do you need it for?"

"My wife's foot." Even to his own ears, his German sounded broken.

The woman stood with both hand on her hips, her legs parted. "Why would you need beer for a foot?"

He didn't know the German word for *blister.* His brain sparked to life and he fumbled to find the correct words to answer the woman. "It is bleeding." At least that's what he thought he said.

Yet again, he prayed the officer's uniform would be enough to keep him out of trouble.

Gisela watched Mitch walk across the gymnasium and heard the rotund woman's accusation that he was stealing.

He stood at such a distance that she couldn't see what he held in his hand. He gestured at his chest. He had been foolish to think his uniform would do him any good.

The sack's owner hesitated for a moment before nodding. Mitch straightened his shoulders and tipped his head to the woman. Then he marched in Gisela's direction.

No sign of Kurt. Just as well.

As he sat beside her, he produced a beer bottle. She took it from him. "What do you intend to do with this?"

"Treat your blister. What else did you think I might do with it? The alcohol will kill any infection." He smiled his rakish grin.

"So I'll get to smell like beer all the way to Berlin?"

"There is running water here."

That was the best news she had heard in a long time. She hadn't washed any part of her body since they left Frau Becker's house.

Herr Holtzmann had been with them then. They didn't know what lay ahead of them. She drew in a deep breath to keep the tears at bay. If only they could go back to the way things used to be. Peaceful. Quiet. Loved ones around them. Like Opa. Gisela pinched the bridge of her nose.

Mitch lifted her foot and turned it so he could see her heel. His touch was tender, careful. Though she hated how he had come by the remedy, she relaxed under his ministrations. For a little while, it was good to have someone take care of her. Good to know someone watched out for her.

Like Mutti always had.

A terrible wave of homesickness crashed over her. She so wanted to be home with Mutti, for them to be a family, for all of this to end. Surely it was a nightmare. Surely she would wake up soon.

Just as Gisela relaxed a bit, the girls happily brushing Audra's almost-white hair, Kurt returned, strips of cloth in his hands. "Move over, Cramer. I will bandage Gisela's foot."

She stiffened at the casual way Kurt addressed her. Mitch did it and it didn't grate on her nerves. Why, then, did it bother her so when Kurt spoke the same way?

He grabbed her ankle and Mitch was forced to release his grasp. He rubbed his stubbly chin. "I believe it would be more proper for her husband to do this."

Kurt, his touch rough, growled. "I will do it. I have dressed many wounds on the field of battle. You babysat for a group of aristocratic Brits."

Mitch clenched his jaw as he eyed the roll of bandages in Kurt's hand. "Bitte, I will take care of her." The more he spoke, the more his accent became apparent.

Not wanting Mitch to be exposed and a brawl to break out, Gisela pulled her foot from Kurt's possessive grasp. She hugged her knees to her chin. "I don't need any bandages. You two are making such a fuss over nothing. Just leave me alone."

Audra held out her hand to Kurt. "Let me bandage Gisela's foot."

It was crazy the way the men fought over that woman. She was nice enough but nothing special. Not pretty enough for Hollywood.

Kurt looked every inch the perfect Aryan—blond hair, blue eyes, features that could have been carved from stone. He held himself tall and proud.

She had never seen a man like Josep. He was the definition of Kurt's opposite—dark hair, olive skin, and a boyish and impish grin.

"Ow. Don't tug it so tightly." Gisela pulled her foot away.

"I'm sorry. Please hold still now so I can finish."

Katya bent down to inspect Audra's work. "Dearie, is she going to lose her foot? How dreadful. I was a nurse in the Great War, you know. I saw too many men lose their feet, even their entire legs. But never a woman before. Just awful."

Audra concentrated on her task, noticing that Josep watched. "She will not lose her foot. It is nothing more than a blister."

Gisela pulled away again and finished tucking in the ends of the bandage. "Exactly. Nothing like this fuss should be made about it. I believe I will survive." She pulled on her sock and squeezed her foot back into her too-small boot.

Audra reclaimed her brush from the girls and drew it through her tresses one last time, hoping to restore them to order. Her task completed, she set Renate on her lap and maneuvered closer to Josep.

"Isn't she such a sweetheart?" She kissed the child's forehead.

Josep nodded.

"I have nine brothers and sisters, all younger than me, so I am good at handling children."

Josep smiled at Audra, a grin that made her stomach flip like a trapeze artist. "Good."

"Do you have any siblings?"

"A sister."

Did he ever answer in anything other than monosyllables? He spoke to Gisela freely enough. Then again, she was his wife. Just a minor detail. "It's nice to have brothers and sisters around to keep you company, to play with you when you are small. Family means so much to me."

Again he smiled and nodded.

From the corner of her eye, she spied Kurt watching her. A

light danced in the depths of his steel blue eyes. Did he think it funny?

She sat back against the hard wall, gaze cast to the ceiling.

She thought Kurt to be very handsome. When she made it big, she would need an escort on her arm. She imagined him dressed in evening wear. Josep had a boyish charm that was appealing. He would be a good man to have too. So what if he was married?

Actresses broke up marriages all the time.

Annelies slept in Mitch's arms. He stared at her freckled face, her nose upturned just enough to be cute. He cuddled her as Gisela pushed the child's golden hair from her face. His breath caught in his throat at the intimate, maternal gesture.

She was beautiful.

She kissed the girl's cheek and spread a blanket from the pack over her. She pulled out an old quilt for Renate. A long stretch of silence passed, a hush falling over the crowd in the gymnasium as one by one, people fell asleep. Only he and Gisela from their group remained awake.

He should be exhausted, but he wasn't. He should be able to sleep, but he couldn't. His thoughts tumbled one over the other. Xavier. This flight from the hated and feared Russians. Their safety. His home.

Father. He had never written to Mitch in the camp. Not a single line. The only letters he received were from his mother and sister. He disapproved of Mitch's joining the army in the first place, even though he was in the 5th Queen's Regiment. Especially not the way he joined. According to Father, Mitch should have stayed at home and followed the family tradition of studying law.

He had to prove to his father that he made the right choice. He had to rejoin the British troops so he could fight for his country.

Then, perhaps, his father would understand.

Gisela leaned over to whisper in his ear. Her breath brushed his neck and every muscle in his body came alive.

"I can't sleep. Do you want to come outside with me for fresh air?"

"Good idea." He set Annelies on the floor and pulled the blanket around her thin shoulders. She turned on her side and resumed her light snoring.

They exited the stuffy building, a heavy blanket of stillness over all. The cold wind bit him through his greatcoat, refreshing after the close, stifling quarters. A military truck rumbled past, and out of instinct, he flattened himself against the rough brick facade.

She laughed, then took his hand. Her slight form swayed in a pleasing way as she led him to the opposite side of the building. He gulped the clean air.

She stood next to him, her shoulder brushing his. "I don't think Kurt likes you very much."

Mitch shrugged. "That's fine. I've had enough of German officers to last me a lifetime. In the camp, you got to know the men. Some were decent chaps, others not. You always tried to have one of them on your side, never knowing when you might need a favor from them."

She gasped. "Did you ever try to escape before this?"

He rubbed the muscle ache at the base of his neck. "No. Most who tried weren't successful."

"That's a long time to be in prison."

"Some of the time I worked on a farm. The hausfrau was kind, but it wasn't home."

"Did you steal from her?"

Her question caught him off guard. There was no teasing in her tone. "What is that supposed to mean?"

"You don't seem to have a compulsion to steal. I wondered if this was your first time."

"Desperate times call for desperate measures. You should know. You're a brilliant liar."

"A blister is not a desperate measure, Mitch. Saving your hide is." He didn't miss how she didn't comment on his remark.

"Not unless you want an infection. Do you want Katya to be right about you losing a foot?"

She blew out her breath, and he figured he won that battle.

"You have to be careful with using English. Don't let anyone other than me hear you. And don't speak in German."

"Not unless it's necessary."

"Don't let it be."

"Are you always this bossy?"

Even in the semi-dark, her amber eyes sparked. "With the girls and the old women, I have enough people to keep safe. If you get into trouble or draw attention to yourself, you put me at risk. And when you put me at risk, you put the others at risk. I've watched you with the children. I know you don't want to do that." She pulled the ever-present daisy scarf around her neck. "Are we in agreement?"

"About what?"

"You don't speak German or English."

"May I speak French? How about Spanish?"

She huffed, then began to turn away, her brown hair bouncing on her shoulders.

His heart pounded at her beauty and his instincts took over. In three long strides he reached her, spun her around to face him, and kissed her full on the lips.

Hard.

Until he couldn't breathe.

TEN

S tunned and shocked, Gisela allowed Mitch to kiss her for what seemed like endless minutes. His kiss was firm and sure, though not demanding. She enjoyed it.

Then reason returned and she pushed herself away and landed a smack on his cheek, her hand stinging.

He put his hand to his face. "What did you do that for?"

"What did you kiss me for?" She backed up a step.

"Because I wanted to."

The whir of a plane's engines broke the stillness of the night. This one remained high in the sky and faded away. Her shoulders relaxed, then tightened again. "Do you always do whatever you want?"

He tapped her chin with his finger. "You're a beautiful woman. And the only ones I've seen for five long years have been large, old East Prussian farm women. Not very attractive."

"That doesn't give you the right to kiss me whenever you want."

"You're supposed to be my wife."

"But you aren't my husband."

"I apologize."

"As do I. And it won't happen again."

"You are controlling."

"I am not. Don't ever call me that. Ever." She balled her fists and dug her nails into her palms.

"Again, I apologize."

"Are you laughing at me?"

"You intrigue me, Gisela."

"And you infuriate me, Mitch."

"Let me ask you a question. And I'm not making sport of you. You're American and German. Or are you German and American?"

"I thought you weren't making fun of me."

"I'm not. Where do your loyalties lie?"

"Then I'll tell you. Yes, I belonged to the Hitler Youth when I was younger. Does that shock you?"

"So, you are pro-Hitler?"

"I didn't say that."

"I can't figure you out, Miss Cramer."

"That's good."

"These German soldiers are boors. You've spoken about California. I don't think you'll remain in Germany after the war."

She sighed and leaned back against the wall. "For the right man, I might."

He lifted one dark, bushy eyebrow.

Why had she said that?

The low din in the gym roused Gisela from her light slumber. Every muscle in her body ached. She sat slumped over, her head on Mitch's shoulder. She bolted upright, not wanting him to know she had leaned against him in her sleep. A great desire to stroke his stubbly cheek came over her. She combed her fingers through her hair instead.

They had to get out of here. A train would be the fastest way to

Berlin, if they still ran. The last one had pulled out of the Heiligenbeil station weeks ago, in January. She needed to get to Mutti.

Mitch still slept, his black hair mussed and in need of a cut. She touched his upper arm and he opened his eyes.

"Guten morgen."

"Good morning to you too." He smiled a rakish grin, his dimples deepening.

"I thought your friend said you weren't very cheery."

His expression dropped and his dimples disappeared.

"I'm sorry. I . . ."

"Don't be. I only wish Xavier could have seen the end of this dreadful war."

She understood.

"Are you going to slap me again?"

"Are you going to kiss me again?"

"Touché."

Kurt yawned and stretched. "What is this talk?"

"We need to find out if we can catch a train. As soon as possible."

He straightened, his piercing gaze boring into her. "You and I will go. We don't know if there will be one today—or if the trains are even running from here anymore. They would have to let a wounded soldier on board."

Annelies's eyes flew open. "Tante Gisela, can't I come with you?" Her fair eyebrows scrunched.

Gisela squeezed her eyes shut, trying to block out the remembrance of another time she had left someone behind. She had vowed to Heide's and Lotta's memories that she would never desert another person under her care.

She stroked Annelies's hair, her heart breaking for the little girl. "Of course you can. I will never leave you, I promise." She stood and swiped her hands over the rough wool of her skirt. Why would

Kurt want to separate her from the girls? And the rest of the group? His frosty eyes gave away nothing.

Though she would prefer to leave Kurt behind, they had to stay together. "Nein. We will all go. If there is no train today, we can come back. Before one of us could return from the *bahnhof* and retrieve the rest, the train could be gone."

Mitch nodded. "Ja. Good plan."

Hadn't she told him not to speak German? She caught the way Kurt raised one blond eyebrow. They incited too much suspicion.

Bettina grabbed Katya's hand. "Sister, we are going exploring in Barcelona. What an exciting day this shall be—all the wonderful architecture."

Katya struck her forehead with the palm of her hand. "That would be lovely, Sister, but we are in Madrid. You are so addle brained."

Bettina humphed. "*You* are addle brained. This is Barcelona."

All Gisela needed was for the two of them to argue today. It was bad enough she had to referee Ella's children. "We are neither in Barcelona nor Madrid. This is Danzig."

Bettina shook her head, her words eeking out from between the few teeth she had left. "Danzig? I've never heard of that river."

Kurt shook his head. "It's foolish for all to go. We will have to fight the crowds and might become separated." Gisela squirmed under his heavy gaze.

Renate climbed into her lap and began sucking her thumb. Gisela kissed the girl's golden curls and her heart expanded. "Nein. I refuse to leave either set of sisters."

Mitch jabbed her in the side. "Or your husband."

Heat rose from her neck to her cheeks. "Of course not." She fiddled with securing the straps on the rucksack to cover her discomfiture.

They ate a little of their ever-dwindling rations, packed up their few possessions, and were ready to leave in short order.

Gisela shouldn't have been surprised at the large number of women already up and about, heading out the door. None of them wanted to stay here.

Daylight revealed what had been hidden by shadows in the night. In the center of the schoolyard, a bomb crater yawned wide. Gisela shivered and clutched Annelies's hand a good bit tighter. They needed to get out of this place. Now. Next time the bombardier might be more accurate.

Mitch clutched Gisela's hand in his right, Renate's in his left. Kurt and Audra brought up the rear with Bettina and Katya. He paused a moment to stare at a church steeple. The base was a large ball with consecutively smaller balls—maybe four or five of them—reaching toward the gray sky.

The city's main thoroughfare was clogged with wagons, most pulled by two horses, some covered with canvas. Here and there he spied box wagons. No matter which direction he turned, person upon person moved forward. Away from the Soviets.

He leaned over to Gisela. "This is worse than London traffic."

"I thought you lived in a small town."

"I've been to London several times."

"Which do you like better?"

He shrugged. "My pop would move to London if he could. Katie is happy in Dorchester. But Mum and I like it where we are. There is open space and sky. Flying above it is a thrill."

"Is that what you want to do? Be a pilot?"

A woman scurried past them with her three small children. A horse whinnied.

"Yes, it's what I want. Crackers, isn't it, since I'm in the army?

But you should come with me once. In an open biplane. Feel the wind on your face."

"You said you couldn't figure me out. Well, I can't figure you out either."

Mitch grinned. "I like it that way."

The crowd pushed them forward. Whether based on rumors or facts, these people were terrified of the Red Army. He, too, had heard the tales of raping and plundering. If true, they had good reason to be afraid.

They became caught in the ceaseless flow of refugees. What they needed was the train station. Gisela was right. The faster they could head west, the better.

Gisela stopped a woman on the street, a white scarf on her head, her black coat buttoned to her chin.

"Bitte, where is the bahnhof? We are trying to get to Berlin."

The woman—he couldn't tell her age—peered at their group and then at Annelies who clasped Gisela's hand and moved to hide behind her. "I am going there now. Come with me and I will show you the way."

"Danke, danke." Gisela's head bobbed and they followed the woman who set a brisk pace. Fine with him.

"Why do you want to go to Berlin?"

"My mutti lives there. We will get her and continue to safety."

The woman nodded. "What I hear, the Allies are bombing every day there—all day and all night. You do not want to stay."

Mitch intended to go farther than Berlin—however far he had to go in order to meet up with either the British or the Americans. He'd miss Gisela's banter, but he'd not stay in Berlin.

But how far would that be until he met up with his mates? And how would he cross enemy lines? He swallowed hard. Sooner or later, the war would catch up with him.

Their guide pumped her short legs and in short order brought them to a building that resembled a church more than a train station. A square pink-brick tower with multiple spires rose over another building highlighted by a huge arched window.

The woman swept her hand across her body. "Every day I look for my daughter and grandchildren, hoping they will come from Königsberg. I pray they will be on the next train."

Gisela shook her head and patted the woman's hand. "No more trains are running from Königsberg. They haven't been for a while."

"I pray and I pray."

The woman had nothing more to hang on to but the hope that she would be reunited with her family. Gisela's insistence that they go to her mum in Berlin was much the same. He understood that need. The need to smell his mum's bread baking in the oven. The need to make his father proud of him. It propelled them forward, through this madness.

They entered the main terminal that was crowded with people, some scurrying to and fro, others milling about. The train tracks sat empty.

What if they didn't get out of here?

Holding to Gisela and Renate and motioning Kurt and Audra to follow, Mitch meandered to a group of about five or six women, all with packs on their backs. "Any trains west today? Perhaps to Berlin?"

Gisela stepped on his foot. He hid his grimace. Yes, he would hear about his transgression later. He almost wanted to laugh.

A young woman, perhaps still a teenager, her hair rolled in two sausages on the top of her head, answered. "Nein, they are being stingy with the information they give. They said they never know when a train will roll in or where it might end up going."

Another adjusted the little blue hat on her head. "They haven't had regular train service in weeks. Sometimes one can get through. Other times the Russian planes will shoot at it and it might be delayed for days. Many days they have no trains, and every once in a while, they have two or three."

Gisela stepped in before he could violate their agreement again. "How long have you been here?"

"Three days." The slightly older girl shook her red hair. "Still no train."

Mitch willed away the panic crushing his chest. What if no more trains ran? The children and the old women would never be able to survive the grueling trip west on foot.

The information they gleaned from other groups they asked was much the same.

Though he wasn't physically traveling in circles as he had in France and again in East Prussia, the result was similar. He never got any farther ahead than when he started.

He huffed in and out.

Kurt tapped him on the shoulder. "This is crazy. Why don't you take the others to the school and Gisela and I will find a train. We will come for you."

Gisela spun around. "Nein. We stay together."

He wouldn't be surprised if she spit fire from her mouth. She sure was insistent that they not be separated. Not that he could blame her.

Getting split from your group brought tragic consequences.

ELEVEN

K urt sat on the cold, hard floor of the train platform and watched Josep, Annelies on one knee and Renate on the other. Gisela sat next to her husband, her knees drawn to her chin, hugging her legs. She had limped along this morning in their vain search for information about a train.

While the old ladies snored away, one leaning on each of Audra's shoulders, Annelies and Renate fussed, antsy, not finding much to like about the way Josep bounced them on his knees.

Kurt dug through his rucksack to the bottom. While in the hospital in Braunsberg after his injury, the nurses had given him some paper and pencil so he could write home. He never did. How could he tell his parents they were right? They had said he would never make it as a musician. And now he would never become a concert pianist.

He pulled the crumpled sheets from his bag and withdrew the pencil. The girls ceased their squirming and watched his every move. He handed the paper to Annelies and the pencil to Renate. "You have to take turns drawing." The older one nodded, face somber but a light in her gray eyes.

Gisela smiled at Kurt. "Danke."

His fingers, the ones that were no longer there, could almost feel the cool ivory piano keys. A warm satisfaction spread through him. "They need to be entertained." He aimed an expressionless stare in Josep's direction.

Annelies stuck her tongue out and concentrated on the scribbles on the page. "I need to eat."

Josep rumpled her hair. "Are you hungry?"

Annelies nodded. "Ja, *Onkel* Josep. I want candy."

Kurt's rival smiled that ridiculous smile. "Nein, no candy."

"I will get you some soup from the Deutsches Rotes Kreuz. The Red Cross has a table on the other side of the bahnhof. How will that be?" Kurt stood and brushed off his pants before grabbing Gisela by the wrist. "Tante Gisela and I will go."

She tugged her arm from his grasp. "Nein. Where I go, the children go."

Josep also rose. "Me too."

Kurt sighed. Would he never be able to get Gisela by herself?

Annelies dropped the pencil and it rolled away. "I want to go."

"We all will. Audra, you stay here with Bettina and Katya."

Audra's green eyes turned cold, but she nodded her consent. "Don't be long."

What a hassle it was to do such a simple task as getting a bowl of soup.

Josep swung Renate on his shoulders and the little girl shrieked in delight. Kurt stared down at Annelies, expectation written across her face.

Curse his empty sleeve.

Unwashed bodies pressed in on every side of Gisela. The crowd in the bahnhof had swelled throughout the morning. She wandered in the general direction of the soup kitchen the DRK had set up.

She wished they still had their cart, loaded with food, packed with love from home. But wishing wouldn't bring it back. Envy rose in her chest when she spied two middle-aged women munching on a large stick of knockwurst. Her stomach growled. There were two of them with plenty to spare. It had never been her favorite food, but it would be more filling than a bowl of thin soup. She had to ask.

"Excuse me." They kept on chewing, the heavier woman wiping her mouth with the back of her hand.

The thin woman fluffed her gray-speckled hair. "What can I help you with?"

"These are two soldiers who fought gloriously for their fatherland." Never mind that they fought for opposite countries. "Could you spare a little of that sausage?"

They stared at Gisela, then at each other. The thinner one scooted closer to her traveling companion and motioned for Gisela to sit. "What sweet little girls. How old, do you say?"

Play on a woman's nurturing instinct to get her what she wanted. "Just three and five. They have been through so much."

The bigger one stopped chomping on her food. "Oh, look at their freckles. My granddaughter has freckles. I love them. What is your name? Where are you coming from?"

"I'm Gisela Cramer from Heiligenbeil. We've run low on food because one cart fell through the ice on the Frische Haff and the other we had to abandon to catch a truck. The walk was too hard on the girls."

"I can imagine. My granddaughter would never be able to walk all the way from Heiligenbeil to here. And she's ten." She turned to her friend. "What do you say?"

The smaller one nodded. "I think so." She produced a knife and proceeded to slice a generous hunk from the sausage and wrap it in a cloth napkin. "What about these soldiers? Where were you injured?"

Kurt jumped in with an answer. Just as well. Mitch wouldn't have to open his mouth. "Russia. Both of us."

"Ach, surely we have a few slices of bread and some cheese for these poor men."

Her friend got busy searching through their backpack. Before too long, she produced the requested items.

Gisela dug out a few cigarettes, the day's currency, from her pocket. "Danke, danke. I wish I had more for you in return."

The skinny one waved away the offering. "You keep those. You never know when you will need them."

"But I insist. Vater always told me to never be a borrower or a beggar. I've done the begging, but I'd like to pay for what we have taken from you."

Again the woman declined the offer. "Are you headed west on that ammunition train due today?"

She spoke so low, Gisela was sure she had heard wrong. "There is a train coming? Is it going to Berlin?" Mitch stepped beside her and touched the small of her back. Was the thrill she felt from his contact or from the news about the possible train?

"The rumor is that one is due. Be on the lookout. I don't know where it is headed, but anywhere west is fine with me."

"I have to get to Berlin."

The chubby woman smacked her lips. "I wouldn't worry about the destination right now. Just get on that train and get west as fast as possible."

"But . . ."

"You don't know when the next one will come. Or if it will."

Mitch broke their agreement for the umpteenth time. "Ja, she's right, Gisela. Whatever train comes, we take."

But west without Mutti? "Danke. For everything. We will think about it."

Their newfound friend locked gazes with her. "Nothing to think about. Whatever you have to do, get on that train."

Kurt chatted beside her as they turned back toward Audra. Gisela tuned out his senseless babble. They did need to hurry west. What if they were too choosy and missed their opportunity entirely? They could get caught by the Soviets and be in worse shape than they were now.

But more than anything, she longed to be with Mutti. It had been two years since they had seen each other. And she had to make sure with her own eyes that Mutti was safe. Especially when she heard about the bombing of the capital city.

They located Audra and their two elderly companions with little trouble. Gisela sat beside her. "I have a surprise for you." She opened the off-white napkin and revealed the treasure.

Three sets of eyes lit up like candles in a dark room.

Audra leaned forward. "Where did you get this?"

"We found two women a little way from here. They were eating knockwurst and I couldn't resist the temptation to ask them for some."

Kurt drew a pocketknife from his coat, divided the meat, and gave it to the girls. Noticing that her part of the share was much larger than the others, Gisela switched portions with Mitch. She avoided looking at Kurt.

Gisela bit the once-despised, now-loved meat. "That's not the best part." She whispered and Audra leaned closer. "They told us an ammunition train is due here today, headed west. I just don't know if it's for Berlin or not. I have to get home."

Mitch broke off a piece of the sausage for Renate. "We have to get on the train."

"What if it is headed more south than west? It could be going to Frankfurt or Bavaria for all we know."

Mitch pulled her to the side and spoke in English. "Do you want the Russians to catch you?"

She shook her head.

"With trains no longer running on a regular basis, who knows when one will show up." His cheeks bore no signs of his dimples.

"I have to protect the children."

"Then get on the next train, so long as it's headed west. No matter where."

She choked down the meat. If she ended up in Frankfurt or Dresden or any city other than Berlin, how would Mutti ever find her? Would they ever be reunited?

Annelies pulled on her coat. "I want to go on the train. I don't want those bad men to come here."

Gisela peered at the little girl, her pert nose turned up a bit. Pleading, excitement, and fear all shone in her pretty eyes. The same emotions churned in her own stomach. How long would it be before the Soviets entered Danzig? She couldn't risk letting the Russians catch them. Not again.

"If the train comes today, we'll go on it. How is that?"

Annelies nodded and so did Mitch.

The day wore on with no sign of a locomotive. They dozed the afternoon away until the sun stopped streaming in the windows and darkness fell.

Gisela rubbed her eyes and ran her fingers through her greasy hair. "The train isn't coming today, is it?"

"Train, train." Renate bounced up and down.

Mitch caught the child when she tottered over, then shrugged. "Hope and pray God will send one."

As if he were a prophet, in the distance a train's whistle sounded. "Train, train," repeated Renate.

Gisela laughed. "That sounds like one, doesn't it?"

Mitch shot to his feet and pulled Gisela to hers. "Let's go. We have to be in front if we ever expect to get on."

They grabbed their sacks and Gisela clung to each girl's hand, desperate not to lose them in the crush of people headed toward the tracks. As a group, the three of them twisted and pushed and maneuvered to position themselves as close to the arriving train as possible. Kurt and Audra came behind them, each dragging a Holtzmann sister. Several meters from the tracks, they could go no farther. People were packed in shoulder to shoulder and hip to hip. They couldn't have moved even if they wanted to let the little party to the front.

The train chugged into the bahnhof, like Santa Claus dragging his feet on the way to a child's house. No sooner had it slowed to a near stop and belched a puff of steam and coal ash did the crowd surge forward.

They were carried onward by the wave. Women with sweet, round faces pushed old men to the side without apology. The old men swore. The girls cried as they were pressed against Gisela's legs.

She turned her head to see if Mitch was still behind them. Nowhere in the crowd did she see his dark head. Where did he go? They needed to stay together. "Josep! Josep!"

The shouts of the horde drowned out her screams. No one answered.

She glanced to her left, hoping to see him. Instead, Kurt headed in her direction. He beamed a crooked smile. Another heave by the crowd and he joined her. "Keep moving forward."

She squeezed each girl's hand to make sure she still gripped them. The throng squashed her so she couldn't move her arms from her sides. She propelled herself forward, no matter how small the steps. Her goal, their salvation, lay mere meters in front of them.

The black iron horse grew larger and larger, and after several more minutes riding the ebb and flow of the mass, they reached the tracks.

They stood in front of the passenger car, the steps several meters on either side of them. The windows were either cracked or missing altogether. Women handed their children to strangers through the openings. If moving forward had proved difficult, moving sideways toward the stairs was impossible. They were unreachable. She didn't know what to do.

Two graying heads popped out of the window directly in front of them. The thin woman with the knockwurst leaned out as far as she could. "Hello there, Gisela."

She would have waved but couldn't.

Kurt pulled Annelies from her grip.

Gisela's throat threatened to close. "What are you doing?"

"Getting the girls on the train."

"Nein, nein." Even her shouts were ineffectual against the racket of the crowd.

"Do you want them on here?"

"Not without me. They have to stay with me. I made a promise. If you put them on this train, I will never find them again. I won't leave them with strangers."

Kurt took no heed of her pleas. With his one strong arm, he lifted Annelies to the window. "Grab her and take her in," he shouted to the woman.

"Ach, of course. We'll take the kinder."

One plump hand and one bony hand each reached from the window and grabbed Annelies by the wrists.

"Don't take her from me." *Oh God, don't take her from me.* Before she could reach to pull Annelies back, the worn soles of the child's shoes disappeared from sight.

Gisela picked up Renate and pressed her against her chest. "Don't take this one. She stays with me."

But despite the fact that she clung to Renate with all of her might, Kurt tugged the child from her grasp and handed her up in the same manner. She beat his single arm, but he didn't let go.

Renate disappeared from her sight.

Annelies appeared at the window. "Aren't you coming with us, Tante Gisela? I don't want to go with these ladies."

"I'll come, I promise. They will watch you for a little while until I get onto the train." She turned to Kurt. "Lift me up. Now."

"I can't. There is no way I can lift your weight with my one arm. The kinder are smaller."

"Then bend down and let me stand on your back. Or shoulders."

The engine hissed and blew another puff of steam, then another. The couplings creaked as the wheels began to turn.

"Now. Lift me up now." Gisela couldn't catch her breath. She had to get on the train.

It chugged and chugged some more, picking up speed and momentum.

The carriage containing the girls moved away from her.

The train was leaving.

With the girls.

Without her.

TWELVE

Mitch scanned the crowd in the train station, first to his left, then to his right. The engine belched steam. Where were they? They had to be here. Right beside him. How could he have lost Gisela and the girls? Not to mention the rest of their little band. He beat his arms against the people mashed against him. If they would just move. At last, he managed to get his arm above his head to wave it. "Gisela! Gisela!"

No return wave. No answer to his call. Sweat trickled down the side of his face.

For a moment, just a small moment, he had leaned to the side to try to gauge how far they were from the train and what the chances were they would be able to get aboard. In that split second, someone had pushed between him and Gisela and then more and more people until she was lost to him.

By the time he turned back to them, they were out of sight. Gone. All of them. In this vast train station, he couldn't locate anyone he knew.

Separated.

Again.

He couldn't swallow.

The crowd pressed in on every side, cutting off his breathing and his circulation. "Bitte, bitte." He dared to use his German.

The wiry, pimple-dotted teenage girl next to him took up his cry. "This man is a soldier. Let him through. Get him on the train."

"Nein, nein." What if they didn't get on? They needed his help. He needed theirs. Like Gisela would insist, they had to stay together. "The women and children go." He pushed a pretty young blond woman with four children ahead of him and up the steps to the compartment.

The girl was insistent. "You gave yourself to the Fatherland. You deserve to get on. You soldiers are all heroes."

Not him. He was far from heroic.

If the teen only knew. Instead, with trembling hands, he pushed her forward, onto the carriage.

Then it began to huff and puff, steam streaming from the engine. Without warning, it inched its way forward like a caterpillar. "Gisela! Gisela!" The noise of the crowd intensified, swallowing his words.

How would he ever find them? But he had to. No matter how much she infuriated him.

Had she and the girls managed to get on? Should he try to board? His heart drummed against his ribs. He couldn't leave them here alone. He couldn't let them go ahead alone.

The train chugged and moved faster. If he didn't act now, he would lose his chance. But if they weren't aboard . . .

He jogged along the train, as much as he could in this mass of people. He had to commit. Now.

"Annelies! Renate! Girls, girls, girls!"

Gisela screamed for the children, her words lost in the clicking of the train wheels against the track. Kurt had gotten lost in the crowd. How would she ever get aboard? She should have never let Kurt push them through those windows. Never.

When the train left the station, they would be lost to her forever. Two little girls, alone in the world.

And she, nothing but a failure.

She could no longer keep pace with their car. Her breathing became labored. Soon the train would pass her by.

"Nein, Lord, nein."

Then two long arms reached from the broken window of a car several removed from the girls. If she could get on the train—anywhere on board—she would have a chance at finding them.

Lord, may this man be strong. Don't let him drop me. If he did, the train would run over her. Her palms perspired.

She grasped his hands and held on for dear life.

Audra telescoped her vision and focused on the train in front of her. Her heart pounded in her throat. If she didn't think about the number of people pressing in on her, she would be fine. She had to just focus on breathing.

This was nothing like her brothers locking her in the outhouse for hours. Nothing like the dream she kept having, the one where her bedroom walls pushed in on her, strangling her.

She had to fight for air.

She pulled Bettina and Katya along with her. They hampered her forward progress. How had she gotten stuck with them, of all people? The iron giant loomed in front of her, large and menacing, yet welcoming her with open arms. She surged forward with the crowd.

Another few pushes and she stood on the edge of the platform, the steps to the compartment immediately in front of her. Here was her chance.

"Sister, we will get to ride the train. What a thrill." Bettina was always up for adventure.

"There are so many people here, Sister. Will there even be seats for us? Is this our train? It looks rather old." Katya was more lucid today.

Audra wondered herself whether there would be room on the train for them. Or would it pull away and leave her here with the Holtzmann sisters?

All Audra knew was she couldn't miss this train. It might be the last one out of Danzig. Forever. If she didn't, she would never make it big. She would be doomed to a life of poverty, like the rest of her family.

The women and children pressed hard around her. She pushed Bettina ahead of her and shoved her up the steps, then repeated the process with Katya before Audra raised her foot and set it on the metal step.

The force of the crowd squeezed them farther and farther into the car. The world began to spin and blackness closed in. She swayed and grabbed the edge of the once-plush seat, crushing the velvet with her fingers.

Her knees buckled. In moments she found herself landing on a lap.

Kurt's lap, to be specific.

"Fräulein Bauer, what a pleasant surprise." Very little light graced his eyes.

She studied his face, the angles of his cheekbones, the rise of his eyebrows. The world stilled even as the train lurched forward. "What are you doing here?" She slid from his lap, stood, and brushed off her coat.

"Some would call this a providential meeting."

"Would you?"

"Providential or not, we will be riding this train together for a while."

"I would say you're following me." Still dizzy, she had to catch her breath.

"Are you feeling any better?"

"Some, danke. There are so many people in this car."

He moved over on the seat already overflowing with three amputees. "There is no reason you should stand."

"The Holtzmanns should be the ones to sit."

Pink suffused his face. "Of course, of course. If you feel fit enough."

If she could forget the mass of humanity around her. "I will be fine."

He rose from his seat and offered it to the women. Bettina cackled. "What a gentleman you are. God bless you, sir, for taking pity on a couple of old biddies."

Katya glared at her sister. "I most certainly am not a biddy."

"I am. And I'm not ashamed of it."

Audra chuckled until the train jerked ahead, along with her stomach. They moved forward, picking up speed. Outside the window, people screamed, frantic to get onto the train.

Light streamed into the window and she knew they had passed from the bahnhof into the countryside. The wheels clacked against the track in a steady rhythm, one she wished her heart would copy.

Kurt had to shout above the noise of the crowd and the train even though she stood shoulder to shoulder with him. "Where are the others?"

"You don't know? They aren't in this car?"

"Nein. I shoved the girls on the train, but before I could get to Gisela, the crowd had separated us and I lost her."

"At least we know the kinder are aboard."

The train clacked along and Bettina's and Katya's excitement waned until they dozed in their seats, heads back, snoring like men.

Kurt leaned into her. He must not have been incapacitated for very long. His body was still lean and muscled. Nice.

"Josep is a good man, nein?"

Kurt's question startled her. "I don't know him well enough to say." She noticed his intense blue eyes. He was screenworthy.

"You should talk to him some. Find out what he's like."

Why would he suggest such a thing? "I could."

"You are very pretty."

"What does that have to do with Josep?"

"He has a strange accent, when he speaks at all. You should ask him where he's from. He's dark. Perhaps he's Jewish."

Audra couldn't care less about the Jews. "Why are you so interested? Are you going to turn him in?"

Kurt cleared his throat and stared out the window. "I am not. Not at all. But you should talk to him anyway."

He fell silent. What a strange man.

She swayed on her feet, in rhythm with the train.

The Holtzmann sisters stirred. "Sister, look at that." Katya pointed out the window.

Bettina squinted. "Cannes. You can smell the sea salt in the air. There is no other place I love more than the French Riviera."

In a way, Audra envied the Holtzmanns, unaware of the trouble around them. She allowed her mind to wander. Bright flashbulbs would blind her as she stepped out of her car onto the red carpet. People would shout her name and ask for her autograph. Her house would be the biggest, grandest of them all.

She would make it. She would.

No matter what it took.

The strong arms lifted Gisela from the wooden platform and through the carriage window. She heard her coat tear on a shard of glass. Grateful to be wearing pants, she planted one foot on the sill and pushed her body inside. She fell across several laps and wondered if she would ride all the way to Berlin with her feet hanging out of the window.

The man who brought her inside pulled her the rest of the way through. She managed to get to her feet—though she still stood between the seats—and examined the rip in her coat. The jagged tear extended from her elbow to her knee. Even if she had needle and thread, she might not be able to repair it. She tried to be thankful to have a coat at all.

"Danke, danke." As she lifted her eyes to look at her hero, she noticed that his pants leg was empty, pinned up with a safety pin. The other men in the seat were also missing either legs or arms. The women with the knockwurst called this an ammunition train, but this car, at least, carried war wounded.

The soldiers sat in the faded and worn red-velvet seats. The women and children who managed to get aboard took up every available inch of aisle space. A little boy pressed against the side of the seat and clung to her leg, the three middle fingers of his right hand stuck in his mouth. No mother claimed him.

She turned to her rescuer. "I'm sorry to have caused you trouble."

"I couldn't leave behind a beautiful woman like you." He tipped his curly head.

She had landed in the lap of a flirt. Like she needed another one of those. "I'm looking for my husband and my nieces."

"Oh." The single word carried his apology. "What do they look like?"

She didn't know what help he would be. "Two little girls, three and five, blond hair, gray eyes, freckles. My husband is an SS officer. He has dark hair."

The soldier put two fingers in his mouth and whistled. The

sharp noise halted the many conversations. "Looking for two girls and a man." He rattled off the information Gisela gave him. "Has anyone seen them?"

"I know they aren't in this car."

"You are sure they got on?" he shouted over the already resumed din.

"Ja, the kinder did. My husband, I don't know about." The thought of leaving Mitch behind, of never seeing him again, was almost too much to bear. If they parted, they would never be reunited. A hard lump pressed against her windpipe.

The soldier shook his head. "I hope you will be reunited with them despite this chaos. They will pass the word to other cars and maybe you will get good news."

"But I have to take care of them." She should have never allowed Kurt to rip them from her arms. She had tried to stop him, but she should have tried harder. *I can't fail them.*

Another woman shouted above the noise. "My boys. I don't know where my boys are. Ten and six. Blond, blue-eyed."

Yet another woman's voice rose to an anxious pitch. "My little one is missing. Just a year old. Wrapped in a blue blanket."

"Bitte, help me find my babies."

Oh Lord, help me find the girls.

Mitch didn't know how much longer he would be able to keep pace with the train. The cars passed him one by one until there were only a few left. His legs cramped, his ears buzzed. The faces in the windows blurred.

What chance did he have of reuniting with his chums if he got stuck in Danzig? What if the rumors about the Russians were true?

And Gisela, all alone. He could hear his father's words. "A

gentleman always takes care of a lady." Mitch had no true obligation to her, but something drew him to her.

Then there was the fact that she had been part of the Hitler Youth. Might have supported this madman who had caused this trouble for all of them.

The whistle blew. His feet hurt with each step.

Out of the corner of his eye, he caught sight of a man who leaped for the train. He missed. The train's wheels took his life.

Five cars left. Now four. Now three.

Should he? Shouldn't he?

The second to the last carriage.

With all he had in him, he leaped for the handrail. In the split second he flew through the air, he prayed as he had never prayed before. *Lord, let me catch this train.*

His fingers grasped the metal and he managed to get all ten of his toes on the bottom step. That is as far as he could go. The stairs were jammed. All of them like a flock of birds, flying away in front of a predator.

Men, mostly older, clung to the ladders ascending the box-cars. The train picked up speed and the bitter cold wind bit his face. The countryside whipped by—farms and villages and burned-out towns—destroyed in the initial German attack in 1939. Not too many kilometers into the trip, his hands froze to the railing. His shoulders ached, then went numb.

The train made steady progress westward, away from tyranny and death, toward freedom and home.

Home. He imagined himself sitting in front of the fire, his mother's red-and-gold Oriental rug at his feet, his springer spaniel Charlie by his side. Wonderful smells emanated from the kitchen and a pot of Earl Grey tea sat on the small, round table beside him.

The simple joy. One he used to take for granted. To be in that spot again.

Warmth rushed through him, even as he lost feeling in his toes.

And to tell his father he was sorry. No, not that he'd joined the 5th Queen's Regiment with Xavier. He just wished he would have had his father's blessing first.

Not that he would have given it.

Mitch's arms quivered. His muscles screamed in pain and his eyelashes were almost frozen shut.

An old man fell from the car in front of him. The chap's screams penetrated over the train's clattering and chugging.

That man may have been the first, but he wasn't the last. As the train puffed its way along, more of the men clinging to the outside of the train let go. Certain death. Those who weren't run over by the steel wheels would freeze in the fields and forests.

Would he ever see the rolling green hills of his boyhood home again? Would he fish in the cold streams, race his car up and down the hills, fly over the countryside?

Not only his arms, but now his entire body shook. His grip slipped. He would never make it like this.

His hold on the railing slid a little more.

And more.

Then he heard the unmistakable drone of a Russian plane.

THIRTEEN

The train screeched to a halt. Mitch tried to grasp tighter, his hands frozen to the railing. He clutched to his tenuous position on the outside of the car, his boot-encased toes clinging to the edge of the step. In the quiet, fighter engines roared.

Like on the ice.

Like the day he lost Xavier.

These were Allies. He should celebrate the sound.

But these pilots shot at innocent men and women. Little children like Renate and Annelies.

War no longer held appeal. The luster had worn off.

And it ripped a hole in his heart. The tear he shed froze on his cheek.

Heads poked out of the windows, peering toward the sky. The crowd pushed outward now and Mitch lost his grip and his footing. He fell to the hard ground, the breath knocked out of him. He rolled out of the way to avoid being trampled by the women and children rushing from the train. They sprinted, fanning over the countryside.

He scrambled to his feet, but instead of running away from the train, he jogged the length of it. His stiff, cold muscles protested the movement. He urged himself forward. Had Gisela and the girls managed to climb aboard?

"Gisela, Annelies, Renate." Over and over he screamed their names. No one answered.

"Please, God, please, help me."

His continued shouts met with no response. His voice grew hoarse.

He tripped over his own tired, aching, frozen feet, stumbling along the uneven ground. He slid on the icy gravel and fell, rocks stabbing his frozen fingers.

The plane made a wide arc and flew directly over the train. In one brilliant, deafening explosion of ammunition, the engine took a direct hit. Mitch caught the sinister grin of the Soviet pilot in the plane's cockpit.

If he could, Mitch would shoot that pilot out of the air.

Once again the Russian turned and this time strafed the passengers lying on the ground.

Mitch dove to the earth, dirt and bullets spraying around him.

The jerking halt of the train slammed Gisela out of her light doze. Why were they stopping? Had they arrived at their destination? With all the bodies between her and the window, she couldn't tell if they had entered a city.

"A tiefflieger! A Russian plane is firing on us!"

The cry and the accompanying screams cleared her head. A single plane after them. She had to get off now. Had to find the girls. If the plane struck the engine, they would be consumed by the fireball. If they were in the middle of the countryside, surrounded by farm fields, they were ripe for the picking.

The boy at her side whimpered even as he sucked his fingers. She reached down and took him in her arms. Then she grabbed the soldier's crutches from under the seat and threw them at him.

Minutes and more minutes ticked by as they inched their way toward the exit. The *rat-a-tat-tat* of the airplane's guns punctuated the air. Women screamed and children cried. The little boy in her arms buried his head in her shoulder. The wounded veteran tromped after her, his single footfall heavy.

At last they reached daylight and fresh air. As soon as her sole hit the ground, she began to limp-run, her heel burning in pain, looking back for the soldier.

He hobbled along. "Go on without me. Stay safe."

"But . . ."

"Go, go."

She didn't want to leave him. She had to help him.

A blinding flash was followed by a thunderous boom. The engine had been bombed. Like Lot's wife, she couldn't help but turn around. The iron horse had been destroyed.

The child in her arms screamed as the whine of the plane's engines faded, then roared back to life.

"Annelies! Renate!"

Her words died on the air as the Russian pilot turned his plane and began to fire on the crowd. Bloodcurdling cries raced across the fields. Bodies thumped to the ground.

"Get down! Get down!"

In an instant, not caring who issued the command, Gisela obeyed. She belly flopped to the frozen ground on top of the boy, his arms squeezing her neck. She lifted as much of her weight from him as she could while continuing to shield him.

The past blended with the present. The screams of the women could have been those of Tante Sonje. The cries of the children could have been those of Heide and Lotta.

Not again, Lord, not again. Wasn't once enough? Why can't we shake these Soviets?

Bullets zinged from the metal monster less than a hundred meters from them. Feet rushed past her, most of the shoes worn, some rags replacing proper footwear. One set of heavy boots entered her line of vision, then stopped.

The body of the wearer fell on top of her.

Her stomach rose to her chest and threatened to empty its meager contents. Gisela's elbows collapsed and she pressed her weight on the boy. With all of her might, she straightened her arms and managed to roll the woman off of her.

The strafing continued for several more minutes, though it could have been a lifetime. Even after the plane departed and the air grew still, Gisela held her breath. If she moved, the plane might return and mow her down. For all she knew, she was the lone survivor.

Then the child stirred under her. Like Renate had on the ice. Other children cried and women screamed. At least she wasn't alone in the world.

Alone. Annelies and Renate. Were they even alive?

She sat and brushed the snow from her torn black coat. The living around her rose as well. She picked up the child and brushed him off. His right cheek was scraped and he cried all the harder when she swept her hand across it. She had hurt him when she'd lain on top of him. He tore away a tiny part of her heart.

Balancing the boy on her hip, she rose to her feet and scanned the crowd. Dazed women walked in circles, crying for their children. The bodies of little ones, old ones, women littered the ground, the snow tinged red.

This field that had once nurtured wheat or oats or maybe even daisies—the flower of innocence—had become a place of carnage.

She directed her attention to the deceased woman lying prostrate beside her. Her dark brown coat was old but in good repair. The heavy boots that encased her feet showed no scuffs or scrapes or wear on the soles.

Gisela glanced to her right and to her left. She winced at her next thought. Would anyone notice if she took the coat and the shoes and anything else of value the woman had on her person? And she, who had reprimanded Mitch for stealing, was stealing herself.

Mitch lifted his head from the ground as silence roared in his ears. He searched the sky but found no trace of the plane. As he sat, so did a multitude of people. But not all of them.

Panicked women clutched wee ones to their breasts. Was Gisela one of them? Had she even been on this train? Even if they didn't continue on together, he wanted to know whether she lived or died.

He had to find out. This was his chance. And if they weren't to be found? He didn't know. Hiking back to Danzig would be suicide. As if he would even run into them there.

Not to mention he would be going in the opposite direction he wanted to.

He walked a few steps one way, then spun and marched a few steps in the other. Where should he begin to look?

The long train wound like an injured snake against the snowy-white background. The hulking engine flamed and smoked and a few other cars burned. He blew his warm breath across his hands and rubbed his fingers together. They didn't tingle, didn't hurt.

He slapped both thighs, hoping for feeling to return to them.

Moving would help. He decided to make a complete circuit of the train. Gisela's green scarf should be easy to spot. *Please, Lord, don't let them be dead. Help me in my search . . .*

He set off at a slow jog, screaming their names at the top of his lungs. Still no one answered his cries. Some began to file back into the train and the relative warmth of the cars. A few dark figures crossed toward what looked like a church steeple. Perhaps a town was there.

What if they now headed in that direction? His chances of locating them among these seemingly thousands of passengers were small.

His heart rate ratcheted up two notches. He ran faster, called louder. "Gisela! Annelies! Renate!"

He scanned the crowd as thoroughly and as quickly as possible. No woman with amber hair and eyes to match. No little blond girls with freckles.

Upon reaching the caboose without spotting any of the three, he stopped to catch his breath, his hands on his knees. If they were even on the train, he had to keep moving. He rounded the back and started down the other side, his eyes flicking right and left and right again.

His throat burned, but he continued to yell their names. A few cars from the end, not far from the train, he saw it. A green scarf. Perhaps he was hallucinating. It seemed too good to be true. But this woman wore a brown coat, not black, and carried a child that, though she sported bright white hair, was too small to be either of the girls.

And there was but one child.

But it looked like Gisela.

He took a deep breath, fighting to stay calm.

Not trusting his eyes, he tramped toward the woman who now stood. She picked up the child and placed a kiss on his forehead.

The way Gisela kissed Renate. His heart hitched. He hurried in her direction. "Gisela?"

The woman focused her attention on him. "Mitch? Oh, Mitch."

She lumbered toward him through the snow, the child on her hip. He rushed to meet her in the middle.

She fell into his arms, her chest heaving. He patted her back until her breathing returned to normal. His breathing grew more erratic.

She stepped back. "The girls. Have you found them? Do you know where they are?"

"I haven't any idea. Did they make the train? I didn't know for sure if you did."

"We did. Kurt handed them through a window, but the train started moving before the women who pulled them in could grab me. I managed to get on a few cars later. I haven't seen them since. Not Kurt nor Audra nor the Holtzmann sisters either."

"Whose lad is this?" Mitch rubbed the small boy's back.

"He stood next to me. No one claimed him, so when the plane came, I grabbed him. But I hurt him when I fell on top of him."

Mitch stroked the toddler's cheek. "A little scrape is nothing. You may well have saved his life."

Filled with unshed tears, her eyes glistened bronze.

A man on crutches, one pant leg pinned up, hobbled toward them. "Gisela."

"Ja, Rolf."

"You found your husband, then?"

A blush crept up her neck. "Ja. This is Mit . . . um, Josep."

"Not the little girls?"

She shook her head.

"That is too bad." The soldier leaned on his crutches and stuck out his right hand, examining Mitch. "SS, is that so?"

Mitch nodded. "Ja." He shook the man's hand, though the soldier's perusal made him uncomfortable. "Any needs? We have to find the kinder."

"Go, look for them. I will keep my eyes open."

Gisela stomped her feet and hugged the child to her. Her forehead furrowed and indecision crossed her face. When she was little, she must have brought home all kinds of lost animals. Mitch didn't want this German soldier joining their group. One was more than enough. The time had come to move on.

Mitch nudged Gisela with his shoulder. "Then let's go." Not waiting for an answer, he trudged off. In a moment, he heard light footsteps squeaking in the snow behind him.

Both of them raised their voices, hoping for the girls to answer them. He checked around them for a little red hat and a little blue one.

The boy began to cry, his wail building with each passing minute. If the girls did answer them, they would never hear. Mitch stopped, took the baby and slung him over his shoulder. His arms ached from hanging on to the side of the train, but he galloped in a semi-horse-like fashion and the child quieted.

They had almost reached the end of the passenger cars. "You said Kurt handed the girls through a window?"

"Ja. I don't remember which one."

"So they wouldn't have been in a boxcar?"

"Nein, he would never do that." Her words were sharp.

"I'm only trying to glean any information that will help us find them."

Her shoulders slumped.

They marched along. She was young and fit but fell behind him, even though he carried the boy. The boy who smelled like his nappy needed to be changed. She looked more deliberately, more carefully than he did. He scanned the crowds faster.

"Annelies! Renate!"

Their cries met nothing but silence.

Gisela and Mitch had almost reached the end of the crowd. They dared go no farther, no closer to the train. There might be more ammunition that would explode. Her heart beat with a wild rhythm for a moment, then stopped altogether for a few more before resuming its untamed ride.

Where could the girls be? Were they even alive? *Please, God, let them have had a kind soul to help them. May they be safe. May they be alive.*

Mitch marched on, not looking hard enough. A quick scan of the area satisfied him. But not her. They needed to make a thorough search of each and every person that had been on that train. Two girls didn't disappear into thin air, no matter how small they were.

She left Mitch's side, the boy crying again, and picked her way over and around people, refusing to let herself think of them as the dead bodies they were. "Annelies! Renate! Where are you?"

A hand tugged at the coat she wore—the dead woman's much warmer coat.

She spun to find an older man. "Can I help you?" She had nothing to offer him.

"Fritz? Oh, that is my Fritz. My grandson."

The little one wiggled and held his hands out to the older man. "Opa. Opa."

"God bless you, fräulein. I don't know where his mother, my daughter-in-law, is, but I found him." The man buried his head in the little boy's neck.

Gisela couldn't wipe the smile from her face if she wanted to. "He was alone on the train."

"Danke, danke. My sweet boy. How can I ever repay you?"

"Only if you help me find my nieces." Since they called her tante, she might as well claim them as such, not just as cousins.

"Ja?"

She gave him a description of the girls.

"One you say is Renate?"

"Ja. Do you know where they are?"

"I remember Renate because that is my daughter-in-law's name." He swallowed a few times.

She crossed her arms and hugged herself. Was he preparing her for what he had to say? She squeezed herself hard.

Mitch drew her close. "Where are they? What happened to them?"

FOURTEEN

The crackle of the fire burning the train and the crunch of footsteps in the snow whooshed in Gisela's ears. Even if the news
from this old man was bad, she needed to hear it. Now.

"Bitte, if you know where they are, tell me." She scanned
around them, but no sign of Annelies and Renate. The bile she had
tamped down earlier rose in her throat.

The little boy, Fritz, squirmed in his opa's arms, still sucking
the three middle fingers of his small hand. The man, shivering,
smacked his tongue against the roof of his mouth a few times.
"Saw two pretty ladies with them heading in that direction." He
pointed to the farm in the distance and the river of people streaming that way. "They were afraid to go back on the train, but the
girls needed to be somewhere warm. Told me that if I saw a young
woman with a green daisy scarf I was to tell you where they went."

The description fit. Did she dare to hope?

All proper social convention long since abandoned, she hugged
the old man, almost knocking him and Fritz to the ground. She
steadied him, then kissed him on the cheek. "Danke, danke."

"I am glad I could repay the favor."

With her throat burning and aching, she kissed Fritz good-bye. Before her heart broke, she spun on her heel and set out across the white expanse.

Mitch tramped in the snow behind her. "Is this a good idea?"

She kept her focus on the farm. The frosty vastness of fields and small groves of trees stretched out before them, leading to a tiny village, the white houses all red roofed. "What choice do we have?"

"If the Russians return, we are exposed out here."

"Those girls are my responsibility. If you don't want to come, don't. Whether or not you join me, I'm going to that barn. I'm the one who left them alone on the train. I'm the one who has to retrieve them. Before the train leaves."

"Calm down. It's not going anywhere for a while. Maybe never."

"I heard talk they are sending another engine from Stettin. An engine alone should travel quickly and be here in a matter of hours. If you want to stay here, that's fine. I'm going to find the girls before it arrives."

"Even knowing what might happen."

She stopped and spun around. Mitch had been following in her shadow and ran into her when she halted. He reached his hand out and wrapped it around her to stop her from falling. How could he smell so manly when there was probably no cologne left in the entire country?

"Even knowing what might happen. Especially knowing what might happen."

Mitch released his grasp and stepped forward. "Then let's find the others and get back to the train."

"You're coming with me?"

"Why not?"

She shrugged. "I don't know. I didn't think you would. You have to get back to the Allies. A woman with two missing children and two AWOL senile ladies is holding you back."

He motioned to the train behind them. "That doesn't matter. I'm not going west anytime soon. Besides, for little girls, Annelies and Renate are pretty swell."

She leaned away from him and took a good look. His face remained serious. But weren't soldiers trained not to give away their emotions?

"I want to."

"Fine. Then let's go." She picked up her pace.

Right alongside of her, he laughed. "You're a tough bird."

She didn't feel tough. The few contents of her stomach agitated like butter in a churn.

What would she do if they didn't find the girls? The man might have confused them with someone else. He might have pointed them in the wrong direction.

How would she ever tell Ella that she had lost her children?

Audra sat shivering in the snow, Bettina and Katya standing nearby. The feeling of Kurt's body on top of hers while the tief-flieger fired on them hadn't faded. A wonderful dream combining with a bad nightmare.

"Are you hurt?" He touched her shoulder, a charge like electricity zinging up her arm, nearly stopping her heart, and she jumped.

He kept his distance this time. "I'm sorry to have frightened you. I only meant to protect you from the shooting. That Russian aimed for whatever moved."

"It's what they do. What they always do. They want to kill and maim as many as possible." She clutched her hands to her chest.

"You are trembling. Come on. It's warmer on the train."

She gave her head a vigorous shake. "I'm not going back on there." She never wanted to be in such close quarters again.

"Why not?"

Bettina bent over, hands on her thighs. "She doesn't like crowds or small spaces."

"Is that true?" Kurt towered over her.

Katya had to insert herself into the conversation. "Every bit of it. Dietrich is afraid just the same way. He always said it made his heart flutter. Where did that brother of ours go, anyway?"

The old woman spun in a circle. Gisela had told Audra about the Holtzmanns' brother. Katya searched for the sibling she would never find. Audra studied the tamped-down snow. "You will see him later."

"He always did like to go exploring on his own. He must have gone off to the Louvre."

Kurt blew out what sounded like an exasperated breath. "What about that farm? We have to get inside and get warm."

True. Darkness would soon descend and Bettina and Katya would die if they had to spend the night outside. Kurt stood and offered his hand to her. She declined the invitation, not wanting his touch to upset her balance, and rose to her feet on her own. The horde of people who had packed every available inch on the inside and outside of the train strung out across the ground.

She looked to the skies. All quiet. For now.

Kurt kept pace with her. "What about your family?"

Did he ever stop prying? "Why do you want to know?"

"I'm making idle conversation to pass the time."

"I don't like idle conversation."

"So I've gathered. I'm trying to change that."

"If I tell you about my family, will you stop asking questions?"

"Maybe. You told me you had nine siblings, but not how many of each." A hint of a grin softened his sharp features.

"I had six brothers and three sisters. Two of my brothers have died and one of my sisters." If she didn't think too much about what she said, it didn't hurt. "Does that satisfy your curiosity?"

"Older or younger?"

"All younger. I left home because there was nothing for me there. My parents were always busy with the other children. There was never enough to go around. I want more. So much more."

The cold wind whipped up, biting her face. What a wonder it would be to be warm. "Now you must tell me about your family."

A muscle jumped in his jaw. "A much quieter household. I am the only child."

"What did you do before the war?"

"You thought I was inquisitive."

"If I have to answer questions, so do you."

"I asked them. I never said you had to answer."

"Don't change the rules now."

He clamped his jaw shut, then released the pressure. "I was a pianist. Set to travel to New York to play in Carnegie Hall."

She stared at his empty sleeve. To go to New York, he must have been very talented. And now . . . He would never get to play there. Or anywhere. "New York. Broadway wouldn't be quite like Hollywood, but it would be good. I would like to go there one day too."

She almost missed the ladies' chatter when they fell silent. The cold made it too difficult to talk. They passed old people and little children struggling in the snow. She wished she could help. It would be pointless.

Up ahead, against the pallid ground, she spotted a little blue pointed hat and a little red one, both familiar to her.

No adult held their hands. No one offered them assistance. Where was Gisela? What happened to them?

She pointed her mittened hand in their direction. "Look at those hats. Just like Annelies's and Renate's. I think they are alone."

Kurt shook his head. "That cannot be them."

"What happened to Gisela?"

"She wasn't in the same carriage. The two women who gave us the knockwurst pulled them inside the train."

Audra's stomach churned. She chewed on her bottom lip as she picked up her pace, Kurt following, dragging the old women with him. With each step, she grew more frustrated at their lack of progress. As they neared the farmhouse, she ran, heedless of the three behind her.

"Annelies." Audra tapped her shoulder.

The older child tugged on her sister's hand and pulled her in close, her gray eyes wide. Audra pulled her hood from her face.

A grin spread across Annelies's features like light at sunrise. "Tante Audra."

"Tante Audra." Renate mimicked her sister.

Kurt came puffing beside her with the old ladies. "Where are the women who took you on the train?"

Annelies's smile drooped and the sunshine fled. "They fell down in the snow and wouldn't get up."

Like so many others. The bitter cold killed them.

Audra turned to Kurt. He scrubbed his whiskers with his hand.

Annelies pulled on Audra's heavy blue skirt. "Where is Tante Gisela?"

Audra knelt so she was at eye level with the girl. "We know she was on the train but not in your carriage. She will catch up to you soon. Would you like to go with us to the farm to warm up?"

Her lip trembling, Annelies stared at Audra.

"Don't worry. Tante Gisela will find you in the barn, maybe even before we get there. I will hold your hand and watch out for you."

Annelies reached out her hand, encased in a blue mitten, hesitated a moment, then slipped it into Audra's. She clutched the child's fingers and picked up Renate.

The six of them tramped across the fields, tripping from time to time on the furrows hidden below the white blanket. Annelies lifted her short legs as high as she could, but their pace slowed as she tired. Renate fell asleep on Audra's shoulder.

She had attempted to sound cheery and optimistic for Annelies's sake, but Audra worried about the tiny odds they would find Gisela in the mob. And what about Josep? The train left a swarm of people on the platform as it pulled from the Danzig bahnhof.

What would she do with the kinder if they didn't find Gisela? Or if Gisela wasn't alive? Audra had no idea where to take them. Gisela had mentioned she was headed to Berlin, but beyond that, Audra didn't know.

Despite the exercise, the brisk air bit through Audra's thin coat. Her fingers, ears, and toes were all frozen. Here, too, just as on the Frische Haff, the old and the young succumbed to the elements. She stopped and rubbed Annelies's arms and hands to keep the blood flowing. The child's nose was bright red.

Renate stirred on her shoulder. Good, she hadn't frozen to death. What would they do if the girls got frostbite or hypothermia?

They said no more until they approached the farmyard. A low stone wall surrounded the house and barn. A stork's nest, a couple of meters in diameter, rose on a pole high above the scarlet roof. The house's white stucco exterior blended into the snowy background.

Of course, they should have known there wouldn't be enough room in the home or the adjoining barn for all of them. A lucky few crammed into the dwelling, their faces peering from a bevy of windows, while others spilled out from the arched doorway.

Someone had built a fire in the middle of the farmyard, in the corner created by the L-shaped barn and house, protected from the wind. The crowd stood many, many deep. Those on the outskirts must not even be able to feel the fire's heat. Audra imagined the barn would be equally as crowded.

She patted Renate's back as she spoke to Kurt. "Now what?"

He shook his head. "I don't know. We will search for Gisela and Josep here. Then we should return to the train. We can get on one of the cars, stay warm, and not miss it when it leaves."

"Nein." She couldn't make herself get back in that sardine can. It had blown up once.

It might again.

FIFTEEN

Kurt stood in the farmyard, wanting to stomp his feet. So he did. Audra would think he stamped them from the cold, not from her stubborn declaration that she wouldn't return to the train.

He had taken Renate from her. Now his arm had gone to sleep, the weight of the child on his shoulder cutting off his circulation. If he possessed two good hands like God intended, he could have traded positions. Instead, he had to rouse the girl and slide her to the ground. "We'll argue the train part when the time comes. If I can get up each day and face life without an arm, you can get on a train. Right now I'm going to look for Gisela. Stay here and let everyone get warm."

Worry gnawed in the pit of his stomach. They had to find her. Without her, he would never hear the music again. His life would never have beauty or wonder. Or meaning.

Her daisy scarf should help her to stand out in the throng. But what a throng it was. Even with such a bright article of clothing, it would be difficult to impossible to locate her.

Kurt pushed his way into the crowd of women gathered around the fire. Some of them chatted like this was a Sunday social. Some stood with sullen faces, beaten and dejected. "Excuse me, have you seen a woman with a bright green scarf?"

One of the ladies pointed to the other side of the fire. "I think I saw a woman with one over there."

Could it really be this easy? He had heard that with God, nothing was impossible—except maybe growing a new arm—so he pushed and shoved his way around the huddled group. He spotted the scarf almost immediately. The woman, her face leathery and tanned, was most definitely not Gisela.

Just as he had suspected, it was too good to be true. Still, it wouldn't hurt to ask. "I'm sorry to bother you. Have you seen a woman with a green scarf?"

"Other than myself?"

"Ja. It has daisies on it."

"There are women with scarves every color of the rainbow on this train. What makes her so special?"

Kurt, unwilling to answer that question, moved away and found Audra and the girls where he left them. "Do you know how many women have green scarves?"

Audra fingered her gray one. "I have counted seven so far. None of them Gisela. No one I have asked knows of a woman who fits her description."

"Stay here and keep watching. I will search the barn and the house." He would go faster alone and they would find each other easier.

Though he conducted a frantic yet thorough search, he didn't locate Gisela. His muse. His empty sleeve slung around as he stood in the farmyard and pirouetted, holding his breath.

No Gisela. No woman with a green scarf who resembled her. It was as if she had fallen off the edge of the world.

Kurt returned to the women. "Our best bet would be to return to the train. If Gisela is among us, we should have an easier time finding her there. She might be searching right now for the children."

Audra licked her cracked, red lips. "I can't get on that train."

"You have to."

She shook her head so hard she must have given herself a headache.

"I will be with you."

She peered into his eyes, her pupils small. Fear radiated from her.

An intense desire to protect her took over. "For the kinder's sake, at least walk in that direction. No one says we have to get on." He would drag her aboard when the time came. For now, let her think she didn't have to climb into the carriage.

"You won't make me?"

He turned into a liar. "Nein."

She gave a brief nod, then turned and walked in the direction they had just come.

Gisela set a brisk pace across the snow, now trampled by many feet, making it icy.

Mitch reached out to her. "Take my hand so you don't fall."

She shook her head. "There is no need for both of us to break our necks."

"Are you always this stubborn?" The dimple in his right cheek deepened.

"Always."

"Suit yourself. If you fall and break an arm, I'm not going to help you."

"Fine."

"Fine."

They walked what felt like miles, the exertion warming her from the inside. Only the tips of her fingers and the tip of her nose were cold now. "They have to be up here. They have to be. With such little legs, they can't walk fast. We should catch them soon." She gulped frigid air through her mouth but pushed on.

Mitch's long strides matched hers. She glanced at him and his smile reassured her. They continued forward, passing slower parties on the left and the right. Each time they asked if anyone had seen the two little girls. No one had.

Dear Lord, help us find them. Please, keep them safe.

They walked in silence, saving their breath so they could maintain their rapid pace. Her new, larger boots didn't chafe like her old ones. She could walk with greater ease.

Darkness had fallen, but the snow glowed in the moonlight. Enough, Gisela hoped, so they would be able to see the girls. They couldn't stay out here in the open with the temperatures dropping.

Mitch soon outpaced her with his long strides. He turned and looked at her over his shoulder. "Come on."

"You go. I'll catch up. Just bring them back to me." Despite her best attempts to sound optimistic and cheerful, she couldn't keep the worry and panic from her voice. Her airway constricted and threatened to close altogether.

"Are you sure?"

"Go. Please, go."

"I don't want to leave you."

"You'll get to them faster."

And he did, leaving her on her own in this wasteland. Why had she told him to move on without her? Loneliness enveloped her. No Mutti. No Vater. No one who loved her.

Would she even make it to Berlin?

The wind gusted. Her eyes watered, the tears freezing on her cheeks. Her nose ran and she wiped away the moisture with the back of her mitten.

Perhaps she might be as fortunate as Dorothy in *The Wizard of Oz.* Her cousin from the United States wrote to her about the movie that was not released in Germany. Hitler hated the fact that many movie producers were Jewish.

But her cousin had relayed the story, and Gisela liked it. If she clicked her heels together, she might wake up in Kansas. Close enough to California. To freedom and happiness. When Margot was still with them. Before that awful disease claimed her life. And snuffed the life out of her family.

She didn't even try what Dorothy did. She was too cold, too tired, too hungry for this to be a dream.

For the longest time, she trudged onward. The farm never appeared to get larger. Was she even moving?

She imagined warm sea breezes, hot sand between her toes, sunshine pinking her cheeks. She remembered Mutti humming as she washed dishes at the kitchen sink and hung the laundry on the line in the sun. Vater wasn't home very often because he traveled for his business. She and Margo spent many happy hours playing in the grass. Wherever Margot went, Gisela went.

The fantasy helped a little. Her fingers didn't ache so much. Then the gust picked up and tugged at her coat and her warm imaginations fled.

More steps and more steps and more steps.

Just ahead, someone jumped up and down, waving his arms. "Gisela! Gisela!"

Kurt? "Kurt!"

Two little voices chorused. "Tante Gisela! We found you."

Like a bullet from a rifle, she shot forward, stumbling across the field. Her lungs expanded and contracted as fast as she ran. She passed Mitch. "Annelies. Renate."

A squeal came from Annelies. She let go of Kurt's hand and raced toward Gisela. "Tante. Tante."

Nothing had ever felt as wonderful as having this little girl's arms around her neck. Never mind that she couldn't breathe. She had found the children. "Oh, my girls."

She tore her gaze away from the pale face to assure herself it was Renate in Kurt's arms. The tiny girl wriggled free, ran to her, and joined in the hug.

The other members of their party arrived. The Lord had orchestrated events to bring them together for a second time. *Danke, Lord, danke.*

Mitch arrived, kneeling beside them, alternating between kissing Gisela's cheek and the girls'. His grin was as wide as the Atlantic. "What did I tell you? We found them. God brought them to us."

She pulled the little ones close to her. "I will never, never leave you again."

Annelies patted Gisela's face. "Do you promise?"

"I promise. A hundred million times, I promise."

"That's a lot."

Gisela laughed. A moment ago she believed all laughter had ceased forever. Joy truly was a balm to the soul.

"Audra? You found the girls?"

Kurt didn't give the poor woman a second to answer. "I noticed two little girls with hats the same color as theirs wandering ahead of us. They didn't look like they belonged to anyone. Just alone. I sent Audra to investigate, not wanting to frighten the girls with my big, deep voice."

Gisela took note of the quizzical expression that crossed Audra's face.

"Ja. I saw their hats and knew it was them. They were alone and I couldn't leave them."

Gisela stood and embraced Kurt, then kissed him on both cheeks. "Danke, danke. I will be forever grateful to you."

He clung to her a moment too long. She had to pull herself from his hold.

Audra took Katya's hand in her own and rubbed it. "We were going back to the train to search for you. Unless you want to continue to the farm. They have built a fire in the yard."

Kurt nodded. "Ja, that is true, but we would have to sleep outside. The barn and the house are too full. In the train, we can huddle together and stay warm." He smiled at Gisela as he spoke the last sentence.

Mitch slipped his arm around her waist. "The train, then."

Would he never stop speaking his horrific German? "If that is what you feel is best."

"Nein. No train for me." Audra stepped back. "Go on without me. I will be fine."

Without much tenderness, Kurt grabbed Audra's wrist. "We will all go to the train." He turned to Mitch and Gisela. "She is afraid of the crowd and the small space."

Gisela directed her attention to Audra. "I understand. If we had to climb a mountain to get west, I wouldn't be able to go. I get nervous looking out of a second-story window. Right now it sounds as if most of the passengers have gone to the farm. The carriage won't be crowded. You will see."

Without further comment, Gisela grabbed Annelies's hand and began the trek toward the tracks.

Kurt glared at Mitch and Mitch wanted to squirm under his gaze. The same kind of look his mum had given him multiple times throughout his childhood. Like the time he had knocked over the cookie jar and broken it. Or the time he had ripped his knickers playing in her rose garden.

She had an uncanny way of sensing he was lying. And of drawing the truth from him.

He glanced at Kurt, who turned away, caught in the act of staring.

A few minutes later, though, Kurt decided to start a conversation. Or rather, an interrogation. "Which company did you serve with?"

Thankfully, Mitch's captors allowed the prisoners to listen to the radio once a week, so he had an answer for the man. "Fourth Panzer Division. Left me for dead during the battle of Kursk." He spoke slowly, measuring each word and attempting to recreate every syllable of the guards' pronunciation.

"I had a buddy in the Fourth Panzer. Heinrich Hoffman. Did you know him?"

Now what should he say? He scrunched his face. "Heinrich. Hoffman, you say?"

"Ja."

"I remember the name. Never met him."

"Too bad. I'll introduce you to him once the war is over. You will have many stories to share."

With any luck, Kurt would disappear from their lives long before the cease-fire.

"But your uniform is SS."

"After I was hurt, I wanted to serve the Fatherland. I could be an SS guard." He could only hope his explanation was plausible.

The low whine of yet another Russian plane filled the air.

Not taking a moment to think, Mitch pushed Gisela and both girls to the ground.

"Hit the deck. Hit the deck." Mitch screamed in English, his heart matching the *rat-a-tat-tat* of the guns. He flung himself on top of the pile but didn't lean down hard on them, mindful of the little bodies underneath his own. Kurt pulled the old ladies and Audra to the ground, lying next to her instead of on top of her.

"I want to see the fireworks. Stop blocking my view." One of the Holtzmann sisters raised her head. Mitch pushed it down.

Underneath him, Renate began to cry. "Hush, little one, hush," Gisela crooned.

"I'm scared, Tante Gisela." Annelies's body trembled.

Mitch whispered to her. "You are safe. Soon it will be over and we can get back on the train."

"I want Mutti."

"Let me tell you about where I was born." As Gisela described California, her soft words stopped Annelies's trembling. She made it sound so idyllic, so inviting. He wanted to visit there one day. Especially if that meant seeing her.

The *rat-a-tat-tat* of machine gun fire interrupted her story.

It was close. So close. Too close.

He would never get home.

Icy pellets stung his face as the bullets pierced the ice-crusted snow in front of them. Pain exploded in his hand. He bit back the scream that rose in his chest.

Lord, make it stop. Please, make it stop.

Each breath sawed in and out faster than the last.

Moments passed, perhaps only a few minutes, before the plane rose in the sky. *Father, keep him from returning.*

As before, they lay still for several minutes after the shooting ceased. Mitch rolled off of Gisela and she picked up the children and hugged them with all of her might. They continued to sniffle.

Mitch examined them and found no visible damage. "It's okay. You're fine. Everyone is fine. That bad man is gone now and you're safe."

Mitch swiped his fingers across Gisela's cheek. "You're bleeding."

"Snow sprayed in my face." She shivered.

Before he could draw away, she grasped his hand. "You're hurt."

Blood covered his fingers.

SIXTEEN

Mitch stared at his bloodied, throbbing hand. Was it his? "A bullet grazed me. Imagine that. I survived the entire war only to get injured by an ally at the end of it."

"Let me look at it." Gisela held his hand, her touch gentle, soothing.

They had drawn attention. Audra, Kurt, and the two old ladies gathered around.

"My boy, you must be more careful when you use a saw." Bettina leaned in close for a better look. "See that, Sister? Just see that."

Katya nodded, her salt-and-pepper hair sticking out from underneath her brown hood. "Will he lose his arm?"

A flash of hurt crossed Kurt's face.

Gisela continued to hold Mitch's hand. "Let me try to fix you up."

He didn't want her to let go. "Are you a nurse?"

"Even if I wasn't, you wouldn't have any choice but to trust me, would you?"

"You are a nurse, then."

"I never said that."

"Should I be worried?"

"Since I don't have to remove your appendix, probably not." One corner of her mouth hooked upward. A bit of the pain subsided.

Audra came to his side. "Can I help? Growing up, I had to care for many injured animals on the farm. And my little brothers and sisters."

"A bullet grazed his hand."

Audra set her pack on the ground and rummaged through it. She pulled out her white nightgown and ripped a length of it. Then she wound it around Mitch's hand. "When we get to the train, I'll get my needle and thread. It's going to need stitches."

He backed away from her. "Nein. No stitches. Bandages are good enough."

Kurt tried to stare at Josep without being obvious. When the tief-flieger had swooped down, he had shouted. But his words didn't sound German. Kurt didn't understand them.

He now felt certain that Josep hid a secret. He was no SS officer. A thousand scenarios streamed through his mind. Was he a spy? And Gisela his partner? But spies wouldn't be on a train in the middle of Poland. There was no military information to be gleaned here.

Perhaps he truly was Gisela's husband. She had married this foreigner and brought him to Germany. But then he would be—should be—off fighting. In this case, he would be a coward.

Kurt narrowed his eyes and studied Josep. His dark hair and just-as-dark eyes told the tale. Kurt was positive Josep was no Aryan. There was a chance he had been a prisoner of war. Now escaped. On the run from his captors.

As they made their way to the train, Audra sidled up to him, Bettina and Katya trudging ahead of them. "What are you thinking about so hard?"

Kurt nodded in the imposter's direction. "Him. Something isn't right. I am convinced he is not German."

"Why would you say that?"

"Did you hear him shouting before? That was not German shooting from his mouth."

Audra shook her head, her blond hair falling in waves from under her gray scarf. "I didn't pay much attention. But you are sure he is foreign?"

"I would bet my vater's house on it."

She giggled. The sound produced a warm, comforting feeling in him. It just wasn't the aria that Gisela's laugh was.

She stopped mid-chuckle. "You don't think he is Russian, do you?"

"Nein."

They tramped through the snow for a while. Clouds scuttled across the sky and hid the moon for a moment.

Kurt tugged on her arm and halted. "Like I said, you need to talk to him. Imagine how famous you would be if you broke up a spy ring. Marlene Dietrich would have nothing on you."

Gisela and Audra sat together on the worn red-velvet train seats. The carriage stunk of unwashed bodies. Gisela wanted to hold her nose and gag, even though the wind howled through the broken windows and chased away the worst of the odors.

The old sisters occupied the seat in front of them. Renate sat on Audra's lap, clapping her hands and chattering away about the monkey in her book at home. Annelies snuggled against Gisela and dozed.

The men had gone out a while before to try to glean information about the engine. She wished they would return. Soon.

Audra bit her lip, then crossed and uncrossed her legs. "Josep didn't speak in German when the plane came. What language was that?"

Gisela shifted, Annelies's bony backside digging into her thighs. Had he slipped and spoken English? "You're mistaken. Perhaps you didn't understand the dialect since he is from the west."

"Really? Where?"

Once again, that speaking before thinking problem flared up. "Oh, um, Mannheim." She would have to tell Mitch as soon as possible about his hometown, to keep their stories matching.

"Why aren't you headed there?"

"We are. First we must stop in Berlin and get my mutti. With all the bombing going on there, I'm worried about her. My vater is off fighting with the *Volkssturm*."

"Is Josep your husband?"

Audra asked too many questions. "Ja, of course. Why would you ask such a thing?" How many other people suspected the truth about Mitch? They would have to be more careful.

Renate patted Audra on the cheek. "Listen, Tante, listen."

"I am listening, little one. Tell me another story." Audra shifted her attention to the child and Gisela breathed a sigh of relief.

She stared out of the window, no dirty pane blocking her view of the groups gathered outside of the carriage. Those still too afraid of another attack to come in from the cold. At last Gisela must have dozed, because the shouts from outside startled her.

"The engine is here. Send word to the farm."

Sure enough, the engineer blew a brief toot-toot from his horn and cheers erupted from the crowd. People scampered about, collecting items and family members. A mad dash ensued. Gisela was glad they had returned to the train when they did.

The engine from Danzig had been pushing them. This locomotive came from Stettin and would pull them the rest of the way there. All that remained to be done was to unhook the damaged cars and couple the engine.

Women shoved their way inside, bumping against Gisela and Audra as they worked their way down the aisle. The few empty seats filled in short order, as did every available space in the carriage.

Audra stiffened. "I have to get out of here."

Gisela gripped her wrist. "You need to stay. If you leave, you will never escape the Russians."

The color fled her face like the German troops ahead of the Red Army.

"This is the way to go."

"The only way?"

Gisela couldn't let her get off. It would be like that American saying—throwing her to the wolves. "The only way."

"I can't. Breathing is hard. I need to go."

"Tante Audra, you must be brave. That is what Mutti and Tante Gisela tell me."

Audra kissed Annelies's cheek. "You are right. These are times when we all must be brave."

"And pray that God will take care of us too."

"Ja, that too."

Gisela worried at Audra's continued pale countenance and uneven breathing. "How are you doing?"

"I'm trying not to think about it."

"Annelies gave you good advice."

Audra nodded.

A woman with several young, coughing children stopped beside them, unable to go any farther. Lines of weariness emanated from her soft blue eyes. Gisela climbed over Audra and motioned for the woman to take the seat. "You need it more than I do."

"Danke, danke. Come, children. We can sit this time."

Audra, too, rose and they cleared the seats. Gisela would miss the luxury of the bench for the remainder of the trip. She hoisted Annelies and positioned her so she sat on the top of the back of the seat. Audra did the same with Renate on the seat in front of them.

Where could the men be? She hoped Mitch wouldn't have to hang on to the outside of the train this time.

Bettina turned and kneeled on her seat, much the way a child would, and flashed a gap-toothed grin. "Dearies, this is such an adventure. What a wonderful trip we will have to the seaside. I hope you brought your parasols so you don't get freckles."

Annelies pointed to her own face. "I have freckles."

"Then see, you should have stayed out of the sun."

"But I don't have a parasol."

"Then your mutti should get you one. I am sure there is a shop in the village that sells them. You tell her, you hear?"

Annelies scrunched her eyebrows, her words hesitant. "I will."

Though there were fewer passengers now on the train, there were also fewer cars. Nothing like being stuffed into a train carriage like meat into a sausage casing.

Two wounded German soldiers squeezed their way in and stood beside the women.

With a sudden lurch and a hoot of the whistle, the locomotive crawled forward, halting at first, then gaining momentum.

Where had the men gone?

Lord, let there be space for Mitch. Let him be inside with us.

They hadn't gone more than a few kilometers before her legs grew tired. The sick children cried and coughed and sneezed. Audra swayed on her feet, and not in time with the train's motion. She clutched the back of the bench, her knuckles white.

Gisela's stomach grumbled in protest of the lack of food. Wriggling her sack from her back, she produced a little bread. She broke off a chunk and handed it to Audra. "Here, you look like you could use this."

Audra gave a weak smile and shook her head. "I am not hungry. You should eat."

Gisela offered the bread to Bettina. "God bless you, dearie. I must not have packed a sandwich for us." Katya, too, took the chunk Gisela offered to her. She broke pieces from the loaf for both of the girls and for herself.

She didn't want to let the other members of their party know, but her food supplies had dwindled. The trip had taken longer than they had anticipated. She did have some cigarettes still sewn into the hem of her dress. If they could make it to Berlin, at home with Mutti, they would have plenty of rations.

After their exhausting ordeal, many of the car's passengers slept, even those who stood. The soldier beside Gisela, a scar running the length of his face, shifted his weight and maneuvered closer to her. They stood shoulder to shoulder. He had said nothing for the short time they had been underway.

She couldn't move far because she held Annelies, but she pressed closer against the seat. He rubbed his thigh against hers.

Her knees shook. What was he doing? She clutched her charge closer to her chest and pulled her coat tight.

He pressed his body to hers. Her hunk of bread sat hard in her stomach. The cold metal band around the back of the seat dug into her midsection.

His hand came around her.

SEVENTEEN

In the stillness of the night, the train's wheels clacked along the track. The soldier's hand moved below Gisela's waist. She stiffened, then a tremor passed through her.

Thwack. Without a thought, she smacked the soldier in the cheek, hard. He winced.

"Dearie, what did you do that for?"

Stunned, Gisela stared at Bettina. "He was trying to assault me." She grew warm.

Beside her, Audra stiffened.

The soldier now grasped her arm, twisting it.

She turned and spit on the man. Words eeked out between her clenched teeth. "You vile, filthy pig. Can't you keep your hands to yourself? Nein, you are not a man. You are a beast, no better than those Soviet soldiers."

Audra touched Gisela's arm. She shook it off. "I will not calm down. We are putting our lives at risk to flee from men like you. And we have to endure this now? Don't ever touch me or another woman again."

Katya patted Gisela's hand. "There, there, dearie, it can't be as bad as that. This man fought for our country."

"What is going on here?"

Kurt. Gisela's muscles released some of the tension they held.

The crowd fell back as much as possible in the cramped conditions.

"I said, what is going on here?"

The soldier beside her moved away. "Nothing. This woman thinks I did something wrong. But in this crowd, who can move? How does she know it was me who touched her?"

"You are a disgrace. Leave this woman alone." Kurt clasped his hand around the man's neck. "Do you understand?"

Mitch threaded his way through the crowded car in time to witness Kurt's hands around another soldier's neck. "What are you doing?"

Gisela shrugged deeper into her coat. "That man had his hands on me."

His vision narrowed so he saw nothing more than the man's beady, cocky black eyes.

Mitch lunged forward, landing a fist on the side of the man's head. Kurt released his grip and the man swung back. Mitch ducked, then, while still low, punched the perpetrator in the stomach. He came up and Mitch chopped him on the back of the neck.

"Josep, stop it. Josep." Gisela's words penetrated his fog.

Kurt kicked the man in the groin and he staggered backward.

Someone grabbed Mitch from behind and held his arms behind his back. He struggled to free himself. "Let me go. Let me have at him."

"You have done enough damage." Another wounded soldier held him fast.

The man who had assaulted Gisela melted back, holding his midsection with one hand and the side of his head with the other.

"What on earth did you do that for?" Gisela stroked Mitch's tender knuckles.

"Did he hurt you?"

"Nein, I'm fine. He tried to, but I hit him and then spit in his face."

"That's the spirit. Like Xavier said, you are a plucky bird." He rather liked this side of his "wife."

"But why did you fight him?"

"You did."

"I slapped him in order to stop him."

"What's the difference?"

"First of all, to start a brawl on a crowded train is the worst idea I have ever heard. Second of all, you spoke in English."

Even though the compartment was warm, goose bumps rose on his arms. "I did? I was so angry."

Gisela said no more. She didn't have to. The stares of the entire car bore into him.

Kurt turned to face him. "You are British."

Mitch's heart pounded in his ears. Should he verify or deny it? He looked to Gisela.

"His mother was British, but his father is German and he grew up here. They spoke both languages in the home. When he becomes frightened or angry, he slips into English."

He flashed her a grateful smile. He wished she didn't have to lie on his behalf.

By Kurt's slight lift of his eyebrows and narrowing of his eyes, Mitch knew he was dubious. Gisela was right. In order to continue this charade and have any chance of getting back to his regiment, Mitch would have to be terribly careful.

"There was no need for you to get involved, Cramer." Kurt wasn't going to let this die an easy death.

"She is my wife. Of course I fought." He turned to Gisela and brushed a bruised finger over her cheek, pleased to watch the color wash over her face. "You are not leaving my sight."

"Danke." She spoke the word as a sigh. At least she didn't protest.

The squeal of the train brakes preceded the jerking halt by mere seconds. Another plane? *Dear God, no. We've had our share of them.*

All of the passengers held their breath. Whatever conversations there had been ceased. Mitch strained his ears but didn't hear the whine of a plane. The skies remained silent. Off in the distance, a dog howled.

Beside him, Gisela trembled. "What is it? Why did we stop?" A general din rose in the carriage.

"I don't know. I don't hear any planes. I'm not sure if it would be better to stay put or to get off." His thoughts bounced back and forth in his mind like a tennis ball at Wimbledon.

"What should we do?"

A weight pressed against his chest. He took a deep breath. "Stay put. For now." *Lord, I hope I'm not making another mistake.*

A buzz stirred the air of the compartment. A few left the train. Most didn't. At least the majority reached the same decision.

The children on the seat next to him coughed and moaned. Renate began to cry and Annelies whimpered in her sleep. Mitch reached out and rubbed the child's back.

They sat without moving for about ten minutes before the hulking beast lurched forward once more. "It must have been an animal on the tracks." He tried to soothe himself as much as Gisela.

She rested her head on his shoulder.

He wanted to do more for her, so much more. He wanted to whisk her away to the British countryside, to hear the peaceful lowing of cattle on the green hills, to see the riot of color in a cottage garden in the summer.

He wanted to take her in his arms and cradle her, protect her. His hand throbbed. "When this is over . . ."

"Will it be? Will it ever be?"

"Yes. By the spring, perhaps."

"I want to go home."

"You are on your way to Berlin."

"Not Berlin. America. Vater is the one who insisted we return to Germany. Mutti and I didn't want to leave. But what Vater said, you did."

"Is that why you joined the Hitler Youth?"

"In part."

They rode in silence for a while. He had yet to figure out who she was—an American or a German. Where did her loyalties lie? Did she have any?

She was the first to break the silence. "Was it cold in the camp?"

"There were warm coats and heated barracks. But I hated it." He tried to keep the conversation neutral, as if he was talking like a guard at the camp.

"At least you were safe, away from the front lines."

"I should have been fighting. I'm a coward for hiding out in a POW camp."

"You didn't have a choice."

"But I did. If not for me, we might have made it to our destination. To home. We fought in one battle. One, all war. That's it. And when the fire got too hot, we ran. The whole lot of us. What would you call it but cowardly?"

"I would call that war. I would call that God's protection over you."

"I didn't fight for my country's freedom. God could have protected me on the battlefield."

"He could have. He chose not to. Was it cowardly of me to go to East Prussia and stay there, away from the bombings in Berlin? There were things I could have done but didn't do."

"You're a woman. Another matter entirely."

"No. My friend stayed in the city. She works the air-raid search-lights. I chose to leave."

"The smart thing to do." She didn't understand. Not at all. It was a man's job to protect his family, his home, his country.

In this, he failed.

Mitch was running, running, running. No matter how fast he moved his legs, no matter how fast he pumped his arms, he never made any progress. The Germans were always right behind him and Xavier and the four others with them.

They shot in front of them, they shot behind them, they shot all around them. The trees always looked the same. The same farmhouse. The same hedgerows. Try as he might, he never made progress.

He couldn't catch his breath. He ripped off his pack, but his lungs refused to suck in air. And still, he didn't get any farther than when he had started.

He spun around. The men behind him cursed as they were hit. They fell like ants in front of a bulldozer.

And then he faced forward. Right in front of him were five German panzers.

With a start, he awoke.

Gisela was shaking him. "Josep. Josep."

"I'm up."

"You were having a nightmare. Calling out in your sleep. In English."

Around them, Audra snored a little, her head on Kurt's shoulder, Renate cuddled close to her. Annelies lay across the back of the seat.

"A nightmare?" Sweat beaded above his lip.

"Ja. Do you care to tell me about it?"

"Nein."

"But it haunts you."

"Only at night."

"Do the nightmares happen often?"

"Too often."

"You were screaming about the Germans coming."

"Yes." He didn't want to relive it. It was bad enough that it happened over and over again in his dreams.

"Is it about when you were captured?"

He nodded. "We met up with a panzer group."

She wrapped her arm around him under his coat, though his shirt was damp with perspiration. "Getting captured is no sin."

"It cost many of those men their lives. Because of my decisions."

She bowed her head. "It's hard in these days to know what is right and what is wrong."

For once, she didn't fight him but nestled into his embrace. Her head came to his chin, her ear against his chest. The feel of her in his arms soothed him.

When she spoke again, her voice was low. "When I was afraid of the dark, Mutti told me to think happy thoughts. Then I would dream of the beach, the seagulls calling as they wheeled overhead, the taste of salt water on my tongue. What makes you happy?"

"The wind in my hair, the earth underneath me, the sun on my face."

"I've been wondering that. Why join the army when you want to be a pilot? Why not the air force?"

"I wanted to, but Father forbade me. He thought he'd won that battle, that I'd stay in England and pick a sensible career, like a solicitor. Xavier dared me to join the army instead. Father got his way. I didn't join the RAF."

"Why do something like that?"

"You know how crackers young men can get. It sounded good to me at the time. He couldn't accept that I hadn't any desire for law. I would do anything to get away from his plans for me to go to university and join his firm. Xavier was always getting me into trouble. Father did not approve of our friendship." His grief gripped him fresh once more, and he rubbed his watery eyes. His chum would have found a way to enjoy this adventure.

"I'll dream that same dream, the dream about England, with you."

He relaxed against her and they melded together, sleep claiming him as visions of a woman with amber-brown hair and eyes to match invaded his slumber.

EIGHTEEN

February 22

Gisela's neck ached, along with her back, and her legs cramped. Hunger clawed at her stomach. The trip that should have taken them mere hours had lasted several grueling days as the train moved slowly, stopping and starting in fits, darkness wrapping its long fingers around them.

She peered at Mitch, standing in the aisle, his head bobbing on his chest. She tilted her head to the right and then to the left. If she had a stiff neck, she had no idea how sore his would be when he woke.

The first rays of the morning sun peeked above the horizon. Soon the sky was ablaze with red and orange, purple and navy. White stucco cottages with red roofs flashed by. Fields lay stark against the pine trees. The amount of snow on the ground dwindled with each passing kilometer as the weather warmed.

People in the carriage yawned, stretched, and wiped the sleep from their eyes. Gisela rubbed her neck, attempting to loosen the kinks. She would never take a duvet-covered bed for granted again. To sleep on a mattress would be a luxury.

Annelies awoke and sat up. "I'm hungry, Tante Gisela."

"In a little while, when everyone is awake, I will get you some bread."

"I'm awake." Mitch raised and lowered his shoulders several times. Her stomach fluttered at the sight of the crinkles around his eyes. "What would you like for breakfast, princess?"

"I don't know."

"Me neither." Renate had awakened.

"Let me see." Mitch tapped his pointer finger on his chin. "What about stollen?"

"Ja, ja. That would be good." Annelies clapped her hands together and her sister followed suit.

Gisela sighed. "And where do you propose to get these pastries?"

"How about bacon and eggs?"

"Ja, I would eat that."

"Quit teasing the girls. They will only be disappointed."

Audra's stomach rumbled. "You are making me hungry." The girls giggled.

Katya fluffed her hair with her fingers. "Sister, did you hear that? Eggs and bacon and pastry. What a fine meal. With some coffee to wash it down."

Bettina smacked her lips. "We can sit at a table on the Champs-Élysées and watch the couples stroll past."

"Now, Sister, do tell the truth. Is Paris not the most romantic place in the entire world?"

"I beg to differ, Sister. The beaches of Majorca are even better."

Gisela shook her head. "We're getting close."

Audra nodded. "Does anything look familiar?"

"Ja." A lump rose in her throat. "We are approaching Biesenthal. See the church steeple?" A dark roof and cross topped the white stone building that towered over the rest of the red-roofed town.

Audra touched her shoulder.

Gisela could say no more. Greta Cohen, her best friend in school when her family first came to Germany in 1936, moved to Biesenthal two years later. They were the "Two Gs" and Gisela often took the train here to visit Greta. In 1941, her friend disappeared. Gisela had no idea whether or not she was still alive.

And she had done nothing to help. She had known life was getting dangerous for the Jews, yet she never thought anything would happen to Greta. Then it was too late.

The stations rolled past. Even with the cracks in the windows distorting the view, they revealed brick buildings, trees against stark skies, tired people rushing through the streets. She sat a little straighter with each one that went by. Familiar landmarks stirred a wave of homesickness she didn't think she possessed. Had Berlin become a home to her?

Yet the destruction appalled her. In some neighborhoods, no more than one in twenty houses stood. Entire blocks had been reduced to piles of rubble. The barren trees, burned black, would never leaf. The Nazi regime was crumbling.

And what had become of their home? She hadn't been in contact with her family since before she fled Heiligenbeil. Would she find Mutti amid this destruction?

The train slowed and she recognized the buildings around the Berlin-Stettiner Bahnhof. The brakes squealed and the platform came into view. Two years ago, she had stood in this very place while Mutti wrapped the daisy scarf around her neck, then Gisela waved good-bye to her parents. She bit back a sob and squared her shoulders.

The crowd flowed down the aisle and poured out the doors.

Bettina pressed her nose against the cold windowpane. "I didn't think Paris would look like this."

"It's the war you know, Sister. Those French would burn down their entire city to spite us."

Gisela believed it would break their hearts to know the truth about their glorious fatherland.

The group waited to disembark until the last for the children's sake, though Gisela's feet itched. At the same time, her heart hitched. She didn't want to think about what she might find at her old address.

At last they walked down the aisle, her right fingers entwined with Annelies's, her left dragging across the crushed-velvet seats. She was glad to leave this stinky, filthy carriage.

They exited the building with its soaring, arching roof and began the next leg of their journey.

Gisela gasped the moment they left the station and walked out on the *strasse*. Rubble littered the city. In some buildings, windows were blown out and the buildings' facades damaged.

It wasn't the city she had once known.

Without familiar landmarks, she couldn't remember which direction to turn. It had been so long and the place had changed so much. She swallowed and tried to catch her breath.

Mitch's hip bump startled her. "I said, which way do we go?"

Panic strangled her. "I don't remember."

"Not again. Lord, not again." He tugged on his coat.

She took a deep breath, trying to recall. "Left. I think we go left." She glanced in both directions as people went about their lives among the rubble.

"But you aren't sure."

Was Mitch trying to confuse her? "Turn left. I'll know soon if that is correct or not."

"Be sure."

"There is nothing sure now."

He huffed as she struck out. "Bettina, Katya, are you coming?"

"I thought Paris would be cleaner than this. Sister, we should have stayed home. These people need to learn to be neater." Katya tsk-tsked but drew even with Gisela. "Dearie, I do believe the Eiffel Tower is to the right, not to the left. It may have been years and years since I was here, but I remember that much."

Gisela handed Annelies to Kurt and took the woman's suitcase from her. "I thought you told me you have never been to Paris."

"But I have been. In '26, Sister and I spent a glorious summer here. I fell in love with a painter and my parents rushed here to prevent my marriage to the man. They wanted better for me. He was better for me."

Gisela's gaze wandered to the handsome man beside her, his dark eyes framed by his wavy hair. His beard had thickened during the trek.

"Who are we going to tell Mutti you are? My husband?"

Mitch scratched his chin. "We have to keep up the charade as long as Kurt and Audra are with us. You will have to introduce me as your husband. Perhaps you will get a moment alone when you can tell her the truth."

She had lied easily enough throughout the trek, but never to Mutti. That is one person to whom she never told a falsehood.

"Careful."

Mitch's command brought her to an abrupt stop. A pile of rubble loomed in front of her. Best to keep her eyes on the road and not on the distracting man beside her. Between what had been two bricks, a little doll's face peeked out.

In the midst of the hustle and bustle that was the city of Berlin, air-raid sirens blared. Mitch's heart jumped as weakness surged into his arms and legs. Where were they supposed to go? He clasped Renate's tiny hand in his and squeezed it.

"Dearies, dearies, what is happening?" Bettina's words whistled out between her teeth.

"Why, Sister, the place is on fire."

Gisela's spine stiffened as she continued forward. "Nein, not on fire. It's an air-raid warning. We need to get to the shelter. Everyone to the *luftschutzbunker.*" She pointed to a building with a white arrow painted on the side with a sign. *Zum Öffentlichen Luftschutzraum.* He assumed it showed the way to the public air-raid shelter.

Berliners of all shapes and sizes followed the arrow as if they were headed to work or church. Of course they would be prepared for this. They had been dealing with Allied bombings since the very beginning. And Gisela would have experienced many of these terrifying raids.

The shaking in his legs subsided and he followed her down the street. Her momentary lack of confidence had fled and she marched forward with a sure step.

The huge crowd filed toward the shelter in a remarkably orderly fashion. A few, perhaps as newly arrived as he was, glanced around, terror in their eyes. Most Berliners continued with their conversations, unfazed by the howling of the sirens.

Off in the distance came the unmistakable humming of many, many bombers. Mitch craned his neck toward the sky. "My countrymen." How he wished he could be on the other side of this war. He needed to be on the other side of this war.

Gisela shook her head. "The Americans bomb during the day, the British at night."

He had missed so much while in East Prussia. "I know next to nothing."

She gave him a tiny smile, one that soothed him. "You know all you need to know for the moment. Each Allied bomb brings Germany one step closer to destruction."

"And one step closer to liberation."

She nodded.

The Germans bombed British civilians early in the war. Was

this their retaliation? Did that make them any better than the enemy? He pushed away the reviling thought.

Renate tugged on his sleeve and he stopped and lifted the child. She covered her ears with her hands and snuggled her face into his neck. The two old biddies cackled beside him, Audra and Kurt next to them.

Antiaircraft guns began their steady *rat-a-tat-tat* as they approached the entrance to the concrete bunker. The crowd pressed inside, creating a bottleneck at the doorway. Many either going about their business in the area or those who had no shelter in their homes crammed into the bunker with them.

They found seats on the wooden benches built into the concrete walls. The cement rose above them in an arch and large oxygen tanks squatted in the corners.

The noise of the planes above them became a constant roar. The stream of those seeking refuge continued unabated. As many as could manage it packed the bunker to overflowing.

Audra turned as white as a summer cloud. "I can't breathe." She rose from the bench. "Bitte, let me go outside. We will be crushed to death in here."

Mitch took her by the shoulders and pressed her into her seat. "You will be blown to bits if you leave."

"I would rather have that happen to me than to have every bone in my body broken by the crowd and have all the air sucked out of my lungs."

Kurt held her hands. "You have to stay here. Don't let the enemy take you."

She nodded, but her face remained devoid of color.

The air-raid warden closed the heavy metal door with a great clang.

A short while later, above them came the whistling of bombs. The building shook but stood. In the event of a direct hit, the tons of concrete above them, meant to protect them, would surely collapse. They would be crushed.

He forced himself to take deep, steady breaths. Not normally claustrophobic, he understood Audra's fear.

And shared a measure of it.

Gisela rubbed Audra's shoulder. "Don't worry about the bombs you can hear. They may break windows or loosen bricks, but the building will stand. The ones you don't hear are the ones that are dangerous."

If you couldn't hear them, by the time you realized what was happening, you would be dead.

What kind of place had they come to?

NINETEEN

Despite his brave front, Gisela read the fear in Mitch's eyes, even in the dimly lit interior of the luftschutzbunker. Air raids were terrifying. The ones early in the war had knocked the heart out of her. Then several quiet years passed before the bombings returned in earnest.

The ground beneath them rocked as another bomb exploded in the area. Annelies stiffened in her arms. Gisela had been fifteen when the first raids came in 1940. She couldn't imagine enduring this at the tender age of five.

Audra was more nervous than the kinder, playing with the hem of her faded purple sweater. A muscle jumped in Kurt's jaw but his eyes revealed nothing.

Mitch leaned toward her and spoke English in her ear. "Is it always like this?" He stiffened as another bomb hit its mark not far from them.

"They seem more intense now than two years ago. Like the Allies are dropping all they have in hopes of ending the war soon."

He leaned back against the concrete wall. "How long do they last?"

"Some raids go on longer than others. They all last too long."

Mothers clutched their children . . . old couples leaned on each other for support. Gisela remembered the almost party-like atmosphere that had marked the first raids years ago. Those days had vanished.

"When we were on the street and I didn't know where to go, you said something very strange."

He looked at the ceiling.

"You said, 'Not again.' What did you mean by that?"

"I have a reputation for getting lost." He flashed a very brief smile, but his words were underscored by a nervous laugh.

"We all get lost from time to time."

"Not like me."

"Does this have to do with France?"

He tented his fingers and sighed. "Do you always ask this many questions? Xavier would call you a nosy bird."

"You don't talk about it."

"What's to say." He held his palms upward and shrugged. "My chums followed me around Belgium and France and I led them straight to a group of panzers. Are you happy now?"

"You got separated from the other troops?"

"Retreating. Most of them went one way. We went another. I thought it would be easy to find our way west into France. We'd have a jolly good time along the way. But it turns out I was daft."

"Don't blame yourself. Getting lost in a strange country is no sin."

"But it is."

"I'm sorry. I didn't mean to pry. We all . . ." Well, she wouldn't want to talk about Goldap and her cousins. "Forgive me."

He nodded, then closed his eyes. She wondered if he was praying or remembering.

With ever-maddening slowness, the American bombers wheeled

around and headed west. An even longer time passed before the all-clear signal sounded and the heavy shelter doors were opened.

Audra pushed and shoved her way through the throng, ducking under arms, stepping on toes, and was among the first on the street. The rest of the their group joined her some time later and continued their journey toward home.

Home. Mutti. Gisela couldn't wait.

Then they came to the Unter den Linden, a wide boulevard, the main street of Berlin.

She spotted the lampposts.

A terrific scream rose in her and ripped from her chest.

She couldn't stop it. From each lamppost down the street, a man or woman or child swung from a noose, legs dangling in the wind, faces and bodies bloated. Her empty stomach protested violently. She covered Annelies's eyes and closed hers. "Nein. Nein. What have they done? Oh nein."

How could she ever erase these images from her memory?

Mitch pulled her close, Renate's hand still clasped in his. Gisela leaned into him, wanting him to hold her and make this horror disappear. He said something to her, but she couldn't hear him over her screams.

Mitch released her, then caught her upper arm and squeezed hard. "Stop. Stop. You are scaring the girls. No more shouting."

She quieted at his command and became aware of the kinder crying. She looked down and opened her eyes so she wouldn't see the horrible scene. "I am sorry, girls, so sorry. Please don't cry. You are fine and safe. Nothing bad will happen to you."

Annelies, free of Gisela's hold, peered at her through long eyelashes and golden bangs. "Why are those men hanging there?"

Gisela squatted beside her and took Annelies's face in her hands. "They are men who ran away from the army. They didn't want to fight for their country."

"They are bad men?"

"Nein, not bad men. Just men who didn't do the bad things they were told to do. The bad men are the people who told them to do wrong. When they didn't listen, this is what happened to them."

Annelies's gray eyes grew large and solemn. "Will it happen to me? Or to you? To Mutti or Vater?"

"Nein, never. Do you understand? You need not be afraid. God will take care of you."

In her heart, Gisela believed this truth. But how much did He care for them? When would this terror stop? The gruesomeness of war, the unimaginable need and uncertainty—how could this continue?

And then she stared at Mitch in his SS officer's uniform.

He could be strung up as a deserter.

He played a dangerous game.

The sight before Mitch's eyes—traitors and their families hung out like laundry to dry—drove home what he knew. The Germans were brutal beasts. No better than the Russians they were fleeing.

His stomach churned.

Traitors and deserters had to be punished. But not like this. Was every infraction worthy of the death penalty?

He pulled Annelies against his legs, shielding her from the grisly sight. No little girl should have to see this. No one should.

Gisela leaned against him, her entire body shaking. He wrapped one arm around Annelies and one around Gisela.

"You have to be careful." Her brows knotted together.

"Why?"

"That could be you. You don't have papers. They won't believe your story and you'll be the next one to swing from a lamppost."

His knees went weak. Kurt was suspicious already. What

would keep the German soldier from turning him in? "We need to get out of here."

Gisela nodded.

Had God deserted them? Did he believe what Gisela told Annelies? Right now he didn't see how any of them could survive.

Kurt held Renate who burrowed her head into his shoulder. Audra stood with her head bowed. The two elderly sisters huddled together.

"Do you see what I see, Sister?"

Katya spun around in a circle. "They have the oddest decorations here, don't they? Hanging dummies from the lamps. Who thought up that idea?"

Oh, to be senile for a while. The pleasure to not understand the brutality of the human race. If the Lord had any compassion for them, He would return at this moment and take them all home.

Mitch stood silent for a full minute, waiting for the Second Coming. It didn't happen. He spoke in English, softly, to Gisela. "Let's go home."

Gisela nodded. "Ja. Mutti will be there and you'll see, everything will be fine."

Was she trying to convince him or herself?

Kurt had a difficult time making his legs obey the commands his brain sent them. He didn't want to see that sight. Men, traitors, strung up as banners to all.

Men who didn't want to fight. He didn't understand them. He fought. He gave an arm for his country. His dream to Hitler.

He just wanted it to end. Wanted it to be over. The nightmares. The panic. The terror. The memories. If only he could forget. All of that drowned out the sweet music.

If only he could hear the melodies again.

Renate squirmed in his arms. He set her down and let her walk for a while.

Gisela strode ahead of him, her swaying hips the rhythm he missed in his life. It began with that. Rhythm led to notes and notes led to music. He needed to be close to her so he could recapture even a small part of what he had lost.

Audra walked next to him, Bettina and Katya trailing her. She said something to him, but he couldn't make sense of the words. Couldn't get the noise of whistling bombs and ricocheting bullets out of his head.

He would never purge the sight of those men hanging from the lampposts from his memory. He knew, just knew, they would haunt him forever.

They robbed him of the few notes dancing in his head.

They arrived at the cross street and turned into the familiar neighborhood. The bakery still stood, the line of housewives stretching down the block as they waited for their bread ration. The café where Gisela sat with her girlfriends on a carefree summer's afternoon and drank coffee sat silent, its bright awning rolled away. The butcher sported a line almost as long as the baker's. Inside the dress shop, its dirty display window bare, the seamstress bent over a ragged pair of men's pants.

The neighborhood became more residential, rows of old apartment buildings lining the narrow road. Before she moved, Greta had lived in the one across the street, one side of it now ripped away, the rooms exposed to the public.

On her left rose the most familiar of all the buildings. Red bricks covered the outside. Arched windows, framed by cream-colored stone, looked over the scene below.

Gisela couldn't contain the tears that began to flow. "This is it. We have made it home."

Mitch saw the joy and the sorrow mingled in the tears coursing down Gisela's heart-shaped face. "You are home." How wonderful it would be to walk through your own front door. He set Annelies down.

Audra rubbed Bettina's hand in hers. "You have a very nice house."

"Ja. Mutti plants flowers in the garden in the summer. Now vegetables too." Gisela climbed the three steps to the front door and entered, the rest of the band straggling behind her.

The interior was lit by a single, bare light bulb. The green Oriental rug covering the hardwood floors in the entrance bore the signs of many years of footsteps crossing it. One door was on their right and a stairway on their left, its banister worn down by many hands.

Gisela bounced up the steps, dragging Annelies along with her. Up two flights they went before they arrived on the landing at the top. Gisela stopped short, hesitated a moment, then knocked.

Her timid rap brought no response. She banged louder. "Mutti? Mutti?"

The door opened a tiny crack. "Who is there?"

"It's Gisela."

The woman flung the door open so it banged against the wall. "Oh, Gisela, my daughter, my daughter." She gathered her child in her arms. "You have come home, my daughter. You are alive."

Mitch bit back his own emotions as homesickness caused his arms to ache. He imagined his own homecoming, when he would see his parents for the first time in more than five years. Would he get this warm of a welcome? Would Father be happy to see him?

"And who is this with you? You brought a caravan." Frau Cramer released Gisela and stroked Annelies's cheek.

"This is Annelies, Mutti, and Renate here. Ella's girls. She stayed in Heiligenbeil with Opa."

Frau Cramer nodded, her long brown hair caught in braids in a crown on top of her head. Tears filled her eyes. "My vater, my vater."

Gisela drew her mum to her and for a while held her while they both cried.

Then Gisela turned to him and touched his arm. The heat of it radiated to his fingers. "This is Josep Cramer. My husband."

"Your husband? Truly?"

"Ja, Mutti. It was a whirlwind romance and we were married not much before we left Heiligenbeil."

"But he has our last name."

"There are Cramers all over Germany. It is a happy coincidence."

Though he knew Gisela didn't want to lie to her mum, she did a good job of thinking on her feet. He had never considered the last name business.

Frau Cramer embraced him. "Welcome to the family. My husband would say you need to treat our daughter well."

"I will." And he realized he wanted to.

Gisela continued her introductions as her mother drew the group into the tiny apartment. Plants hung in pots in front of the sunny window. A comfortable-looking red three-seater couch sat against one white wall, two matching armchairs flanking it. All were fashioned with scrolled wood arms and lovely carved wood bottoms and legs. A *Volksempfänger*—people's radio—occupied the space between them, its polished walnut cabinet gleaming, the plaque visible on the knob warning against listening to enemy stations.

Gisela shed her coat and flung it on the sofa. She began unbuttoning Annelies's. "What have you heard from Vater?"

"Nothing. Not a word since he was called up by the Volkssturm. His beloved Reich is crumbling. He is trying to stave off the bleeding with a handkerchief."

What Mitch suspected. This family was loyal to the Nazis.

Gisela stopped mid-button. "But not a word in all these months? I was sure when I got home you would have a stack of letters from him."

Frau Cramer worried the hem of her pale green apron. "Things are chaotic. It's not surprising that no letter has come. We will wait until the war is over to hear from him."

Gisela swayed. Mitch reached out and caught her halfway on her descent to the floor. The lack of food had caught up with her. With all of them. "Frau Cramer, she hasn't had a meal in more than twenty-four hours. Could you fetch some, bitte?"

"Oh, the shock of seeing my daughter and I forgot my manners. Are you all that hungry?"

Annelies nodded, her golden curls bouncing. "Ja. I could eat a whole knockwurst by myself."

Frau Cramer laughed, a sound of pure music, much like his mum's chuckle. On one hand, a nurturer; on the other, a Nazi. "You are a hungry girl, then. Shall we find what we can to feed this crowd? Knockwurst I don't have."

"Do you have bratwurst?"

Their voices faded as they left for the adjoining kitchen.

Audra struggled to shrug off her coat, her arms caught in the sleeves. Mitch helped her pull it off.

"Danke." She blinked several times.

"Do you have something in your eye? Let me take a look."

Her face flooded with red. "Nein. It is nothing." She swiped her finger across her eyelid.

Katya nudged Bettina. "Sister, you have done it again. What a charming flat for us, right on the Champs-Élysées. A remarkable find."

Mitch shook his head. The women prattled about the fine weather and admired the lovely view of the Louvre.

He studied the pictures on the far wall, between the two narrow windows overlooking the street. He stopped short. In many of the images, there were two faces staring at him. Two little ones in a pram, two little girls on a tire swing, two children with their knapsacks on the way to school.

Suddenly, there was only one girl.

Gisela had a sister.

One who must have died.

Audra settled on the couch. She didn't know if she had ever seen such a nice home. It was small, much smaller than her family's cottage, but so lovely inside. Colorful rugs covered the wood floors. What a blessing in the winter. She longed to remove her shoes and dig her toes into the pile.

And when she became as famous as Marlene, she would have an even nicer home. Just think of it. Some of those movie stars had swimming pools in their yards. Imagine that.

A coal stove warmed the room. Such a pleasure not to be cold, not to be jostled, not to be moving. A picture of a little girl in front of the strangest-looking house Audra had ever seen sat on the polished round table beside the couch. There was no mistaking the girl was Gisela. She stood under a kind of tree Audra had never seen before.

Kurt sat beside her on the couch and she felt him relax. "Interesting. Josep speaks both English and German. Gisela's mutti knew nothing of their marriage."

"What are you saying?"

"That I question everything they have said."

"And why would it matter to you?"

He hesitated, chewing his lower lip.

"Never mind."

But the question plagued Audra.

"Keep talking to Josep. See what you can find out."

Audra shrugged. Her stomach rumbled as she smelled sausage and potatoes. Her mouth watered.

A short time later, Annelies bounded into the room. "Oma says *essen kommen*. It is time to eat."

Bettina was the first to shuffle to the kitchen. "If the food here is half as good as the apartment itself, we shall have ourselves a fine stay, Sister, a fine stay."

Frau Cramer showed Audra her chair, one of several mismatched pieces crowding the small table. A narrow stove and oven and a small counter with a shelf above it took up much of one wall. "Danke for having us."

A smile lit the woman's lined face, marred by the hardships of the years. "It has been quiet in this house far too long. And to what other place would you go? It is a miracle we have no others living here. With so many losing their homes to the Allied bombs, families upon families squeeze in together."

While not a huge meal, it was better than any they had since leaving Heiligenbeil. Even while growing up, Audra would have been happy with a meal with meat like this. And she would have many more like this to come.

The two old ladies dug in even before grace had been said. "Sister, what a wonderful meal." Bettina pulled Frau Cramer to her level. "Waitress, please give our compliments to the chef. Excellent in every way. You French have a way with food. Don't they, Sister?"

Confusion filled Frau Cramer's eyes until Gisela explained.

The women had still been in their right minds the last time she visited her vater. She played along with them. "Danke, I shall tell the chef you are pleased." She choked back a laugh.

The ravenous crew devoured the meal in short order. No one, not even the girls, said much.

No sooner had Audra drained the last of her ersatz coffee from her cup when yet another air-raid siren sounded. Her heart leapt like a pole vaulter as the sirens screeched once more. "Another one, Frau Cramer? There was one a mere few hours ago."

The creases around the woman's eyes deepened. "The raids are almost constant now. Many don't bother to go to the shelters anymore. What good would it do? If you take a direct hit, there is nothing to be done for you. You saw the damage."

Audra could only nod. The war was lost. How many more innocent civilians would Hitler sacrifice to his pride?

Josep threw his napkin on his plate. "I am going."

Gisela pushed her plate back. "Come on, girls and ladies. Time to go downstairs."

Frau Cramer shook her head. "These dishes need to be washed. I will stay."

TWENTY

ein. That's foolish. You have to go." Gisela scraped back her
kitchen chair and stood, unable to believe that Mutti said she
wouldn't come to the air-raid shelter.

"Now that you are married, you think you can tell your mutti
what to do? We have time until the bombers get here. You go now
and when I finish the dishes, I'll come."

Gisela picked up the frayed dish towel. "Josep, take the girls
and everyone else. I'll help Mutti."

A stern glint lit his dark eyes. He didn't have to say a word—
she sensed his disapproval. "I promise to come."

He huffed.

Annelies tugged on her arm. "Tante Gisela, you have to come
with us. I don't want to go down there. I might see a spider."

"Josep will be there. He can kill the spiders for you. My mutti
and I will come very soon."

Her gray eyes filled with tears. Mitch bent down beside her.
"You can ride the horse downstairs."

Gisela questioned his sanity, carrying a child down three
flights, but Annelies didn't hesitate.

"Hold my neck," Mitch said as she adjusted her grip. "What do you say to make the horse go?"

"Giddyup," she shouted and Mitch galloped out of the apartment, Renate holding on to Audra's hand.

Katya clapped. "Off to the Louvre, Sister. The sights we will see. Isn't this exciting?" Her blue eyes shone. Then the door shut behind them. For a moment, Annelies's giggles hung in the air.

Gisela returned to the kitchen. Mutti had a few plates washed already. She picked up the gold-rimmed china and wiped the first dish.

"Why won't you go to the shelter?"

"I never said I wouldn't go to the shelter." Mutti scrubbed the dish harder than necessary.

"You are being stubborn."

"Don't upset this day. You are home, safe and sound, and a married woman. Can we celebrate that?"

"You are concerned about Vater."

Mutti scrubbed so hard Gisela worried she would break the plate. "Shouldn't I be?"

"Of course. I am too."

"You call me stubborn, but I am no match for your vater. Off he goes to fight as soon as they say they need him. Like he has no care in the world. And me, alone." She stopped her scrubbing. "I am so happy you are here. One of my own has returned. At least I have you."

How many times had Gisela heard those words?

"Vater is at work. At least I have you."

"I miss my sister in the States. At least I have you."

"Margot is gone. At least I have you."

They worked in silence for a little while. The sirens fell silent. The first warning had sounded. They would wait until the fighters were a certain distance away until the hurry-up-you-must-take-shelter-now alarm blasted.

Gisela set a tin cup in the cabinet. She remembered drinking milk fresh from the farm in that cup when they lived in America. "Do you miss home?"

"This is my home. Why would I miss it?"

"California, I mean. Do you miss it?"

Mutti stood and stared straight ahead for a moment. "Ja. We breathed free air and lived without constant fear." She paused, swallowing. "And we had Margot."

"Why did we leave the States, then?"

"Your vater wanted to come back to Germany. The Great Depression was hard on him, and he heard from your onkle that things were good here. Hitler had turned the economy around. Germany again would be the power God intended for it to be. The Allies had hamstrung the country after the Great War, but Germany would rise to be a glorious state once more."

"But you didn't want to come?" Vater took her away from the place where she had been happy. If only he hadn't . . .

"Nein. But I love my husband. God would have me obey him, so I followed him here." She handed Gisela a glass. "That is what you do when you are married. My first lesson to you as a married woman."

Should she tell Mutti the truth? She wouldn't turn in Mitch. There was no one in the apartment to overhear.

Mutti wiped the counters. "God wants you to honor your husband even when you may not agree with him. But never did I think things would get this bad. The shelling doesn't stop, day or night. You are lucky if you wake up in the morning in one piece."

Gisela wrung the dish towel in her hand. She shouldn't lie to her mutti.

"You are home. I am happy about that. I didn't know where you were or what had become of you."

"I am safe." She didn't want to think about the Russian planes or the cruel woman or the overzealous German soldier. She didn't share with Mutti how they slept on filthy straw or how the girls hung out of the back of the truck to use the bathroom. Those all were experiences she would rather forget.

"And you are fine? No one hurt you?"

"Nein, no one did."

"Tell me about Josep, your husband."

She couldn't keep up the charade. Not with her mutti. "He isn't my husband."

Mutti stopped mid-wipe. "Not your husband?"

"Nein. I met him on the trip here. Mutti, he's English. An escaped POW without papers. A woman was badgering him about who he was, so I stepped in and told her he was my husband. Too many people heard and we've had to keep up the cover."

Mutti wrung the dish towel in her hand. "That is dangerous. Why would you do such a thing?"

"I don't know. Because I didn't want her to turn him in to the authorities. I didn't want to see him hurt."

"And so now, what will you do?"

The floor behind them creaked. She froze, but heard nothing more. Most likely the old building creaking with the cold.

Gisela lowered her voice. "With Kurt and Audra along, we have to continue acting like we are married. At least until Mitch is out of danger."

"That is his name?"

"Ja. Mitch Edwards. But call him Josep. That is the name we told the others."

Mutti shook her head. "I don't like it. Not one bit. How long were you going to wait to tell me?"

"I didn't wait long. We needed to be alone so none of the others would overhear."

"You have changed since you've been gone." Mutti patted her cheek. "You aren't the shy little thing I sent away."

"Things have happened that have changed me."

"What kind of things? Don't tell me those Russians in Goldap hurt you after all."

"Nein. But I've had to be on my own. Had to struggle to survive and to get all of these people here in one piece."

"What happened along the way?"

She couldn't speak of these things yet.

Mutti put her arm around Gisela. "I know. I lived through war too. It does change you."

They slid the chairs back into place and Mutti began sweeping the floor. "But you like him?"

Gisela set the pot in the cupboard with a little more force than necessary. "Why would you say that?"

"Your eyes soften when you look at him. Your voice changes. It's almost wistful."

"We don't even get along." Gisela laughed. "Wait long enough and you will see."

"Be careful. You are all I have left."

"We have been. We will be."

Mutti dried her hands on her apron. "There, you see. Now I can leave knowing I have a clean kitchen. If the soldiers search the place during the air raid, they will not find a messy house."

Gisela wrapped her mother in a hug. "I missed you."

"Ach, I missed you too, child. You are a gift from God."

"How long until you'll be ready to leave?"

"Now. I told you I would go down and I will."

"Nein, not leave for the shelter. Leave Berlin. Head toward Munich. Toward the Allies and safety. That is where Josep wants to go, to return to the Allies."

Mutti untied her apron and laid it across the back of the kitchen chair. "Until your vater comes home, I will not leave. I am staying in Berlin."

Mitch put his hand to his heart when Gisela entered the basement. He had worried her mum would refuse to come, and she would insist on staying upstairs. He shouldn't care what happened to her, but he did.

The musty basement had an arched concrete ceiling, as if that might stop an Allied bomb from penetrating the area. An oxygen tank stood tall in one corner. They could breathe if they were buried in rubble. What a thoughtful touch.

Benches and chairs occupied much of the space. There were three beds down here, as well as shelves lined with food and water. Cobwebs decorated the corners. A mother and her five children huddled on kitchen chairs in one corner. Annelies and Renate wanted to play with them, but the mother shook her head. The girls came back to him, asking him why they wouldn't play. Having no other explanation, he told them they were tired. Two older couples mingled with them and now sat chatting with Bettina and Katya about Paris. Audra and Kurt sat silent to his right.

Gisela slipped in on his left. He squeezed her hand. It was warm. "You got your mum to come down."

"She doesn't want to leave Berlin." Pain and fright drew lines across her brow.

"Why not? If this ghastly bombing happens all the time"— the racket of antiaircraft fire interspersed his words—"you would think her eager to leave."

"She won't go because of Vater. She wants to wait for him to come home." The unspoken words *if he ever does* echoed in the room. He didn't blame her for not wanting to say them.

"How old is he?"

"Sixty-five."

"Why didn't you tell me about your sister?"

Her eyes clouded. "We don't talk about her much. It's too hard, even after eight years."

"What happened?"

She stared at the ceiling for a long moment. "Scarlet fever. I lived. She died."

For a moment, Mitch didn't know what to say. He stroked her fingers. "I'm sorry." This was why she was so eager to get to her mum.

"So am I. And now Vater is gone."

"Is Hitler out of his mind, recruiting old men to fight this battle he will surely lose?"

"Hush. Don't speak against the Führer. The POW camp will look like a summer holiday compared to a Berlin prison."

"It will be hard for you to leave your mum."

"I won't go. I refuse to travel on without her." She set her mouth in a firm, straight line.

Had she gone crackers? "You won't leave?"

"Nein. I'm all she has left. She lost one child already. Now with Vater gone, I'll stay. Try to understand. I'll work on persuading her to come, but I understand why she won't. What if he comes back and we aren't here? He would have no idea where to look for us."

"Leave him a note. Write him a letter."

"What if he never receives it? Nein, we can't leave. That is what Ella did for Opa." A single tear trickled down her cheek. "It is what I will do for Mutti. I will keep the girls with me. You take the others to Munich."

Munich would be in the direction of the Allies. If he stayed with her, by the time the British or Americans reached the city, the war would be over.

Planes droned above them. Soon the earth rocked beneath them.

Annelies and Renate continued playing with the little dolls Gisela's mum had given them. Either they were innocent about what was happening in the skies, or they had become so used to the sound of planes and bombs that it no longer affected them. He studied their golden heads, bowed over their dolls.

He watched Gisela watching them. She had a lovely profile, a little upturned nose, a strand of amber-colored hair sweeping her shoulder.

Yes, her Reich was on the verge of collapse. She shouldn't stay. He couldn't.

She must come with him.

Mitch tossed and turned the entire night. At least the part of the night they didn't spend in the bomb shelter. To be honest, he didn't know why the decision he faced was so difficult, why it kept him from sleeping. True, Gisela saved his life—twice—and he was grateful. But the time had come to walk away. He had to rejoin his regiment, wherever they might be. While the war was winding down, perhaps he could still fight. Still defend the honor of his country. So Xavier's death wouldn't be in vain.

Sitting in Berlin would accomplish nothing.

Yet the thought of not seeing Gisela or the girls tore at him.

He didn't know her well, so it was madness for him to be thinking this way.

Mitch slipped from under his blanket on the couch. The bed in the guest room wouldn't accommodate Frau Cramer, Audra, and the two old ladies, so Mitch insisted on sleeping on the couch so Frau Cramer could share her bed with her daughter and the Reinhardt girls.

He found Gisela sitting at the small kitchen table sipping her ersatz coffee. "How did you sleep?"

"I didn't. I hope you did."

"Not really." He pulled out a wobbly kitchen chair and sat. "We have to talk."

"I know." She traced the rim of her cup with the tip of her finger. "I know what you're going to say."

"After all those years in captivity, I'm free. Free to fight for my country."

She got up to pour him a cup of hot coffee. "I understand."

"I need to rejoin my regiment."

"You don't need to tell me these things. I know. How will you get back?"

Funny, in all of those hours of wakefulness during the night, he hadn't developed a plan for that. "It should be easy enough. If I get stopped by the Germans on the way, I'll say I'm returning to my post after an extended illness."

"You have no papers."

"Do you think they care about that now?"

She nodded. Her hair hung loose about her shoulders, tangles knotting the curls. "They always care about things like that."

"Then I'll pretend I've just lost them."

"And you'll say all of this in your flawless German?"

"Ja." He smiled but couldn't get her to crack a grin. "Perhaps I won't get stopped."

"And when you reach the line, you will be shot on the spot by your countrymen because of the uniform you wear."

"I don't have that anymore, remember?" Gisela's mum had spent a long, long time combing the nits out of his hair. His uniform, they burned, and she gave him a couple of her father's pants and shirts.

"You are out of your mind. Crackers, as you say. Your plan will never work."

He downed the contents of his mug in one gulp and stood to put it in the sink. "Thank you for the vote of confidence." The view from the third-floor window was dismal. Much of the grand city lay in smoldering ruins. Why would anyone want to stay here?

"Mutti knows that you're British and that we're not married."

"Will she keep the secret until I leave?"

"Ja. I had to tell her. I wasn't going to keep lying to her."

He hoped she was right. At this moment, he had no other choice but to trust her. In a little while, he would be gone. He turned to face her. "And what about you? What are you going to do?"

She stared at him, her light brown eyes searching. "About what?"

"Your mum."

"There is nothing to do. She won't leave."

"Are you sure?"

"I know my mutti. Once she makes up her mind, she will not change it. Ever."

"Your Führer won't save you."

"My Führer?"

"Yes. Your Führer."

"What makes you think he's my Führer?"

He sat up straight. "You were in the Hitler Youth."

"So was everyone else in my class. It was a club. We got to go to the mountains."

"What about your father?"

"I don't know. He is a difficult man to figure out. I believe he came here hoping for better than what America had brought him. He's fighting not for the Germany of today, but for the Germany of his youth."

He clasped her hands. "Then come with me."

A small cry came from the back of the apartment.

"I think the girls are waking." She rose and left her coffee on the table. He followed. Just when the time had come to leave, he discovered her to be different than he thought.

Gisela's mum sat in bed, cradling Renate in her arms.

Gisela stepped forward. "Is she frightened?"

"Nein. She has a fever."

TWENTY-ONE

M itch leaned against the doorjamb, his fingernails digging into the trim, watching as Gisela took Renate from her mum's arms. The child's cheeks were red. Annelies stirred in the bed and whimpered. The color in her cheeks matched that of her sister's.

He took two steps toward the bed.

Gisela turned to Annelies and touched her forehead with the back of her hand. "They must have caught the sickness from the children on the train. We should have found somewhere else to stand."

He sat beside her and pulled Annelies into his lap. Heat radiated from her small body. "What can I do?"

Gisela bowed over Renate, her brown hair falling about the child. She kissed the little girl on the forehead. "We have to fetch the doctor."

Frau Cramer nodded. "Dr. Liebenstraum will come."

Gisela stared at her mum, eyes wide. "Dr. Liebenstraum is eighty years old—at least."

"Many of the other doctors are off fighting or are so busy with the casualties, they cannot take care of the kinder. He will know what to do. He took care of you."

"And Margot. Even then he was old."

"He was around before this medicine that we cannot get now. He knows how to deal with having very little. I trust he will take care of them. They only have colds. It's not like with your sister."

Gisela massaged her hands together. "We don't know that. Maybe we should take them to the hospital."

"Is that necessary? If your mum thinks they have colds, there is nothing to worry about."

Frau Cramer shook her head. "Many of the hospitals have been bombed. Every available bed is taken with the injured. Unless you are missing an arm or a leg or have a hole in your body, they will tell you to go home." Gisela's mum wrapped her in a hug. "Trust me. Ella's girls will get the best care available from Dr. Liebenstraum."

Gisela looked at him, her mouth pinched.

"I don't know much about sick children, but your mum is far more experienced than either of us. Take her advice." He held her hand.

"We have no idea what is even wrong with them. And how contagious it might be."

Mitch hadn't thought about the possibility that others might become ill as well. "First things first, then. We will get the doctor and see what his diagnosis is. Tell me where he lives."

Frau Cramer shook her head. "Gisela told me who you are. To me, you sound very British. Stay here with her. Keep her calm. I will fetch Dr. Liebenstraum." She stepped from the room and latched the door behind her.

Gisela nodded. "Let me get some cool cloths. I'll wake Kurt and Audra. They can ask the neighbors if they might allow the sisters to stay with them for a few days. If it is contagious, we should keep them from being exposed."

Did every woman have this innate maternal sense, always knowing when to send for the doctor and how to care for an ill child?

Gisela laid Annelies beside her sister and pulled the blanket to her chin. "I should have never let them anywhere near those sick children. And we were in such cramped quarters. If I had thought, if I had thought at all, I would have moved to a different part of the train. But I didn't, and now they are sick. Ella trusted me to keep her children safe, and this is what happened."

He caught her upper arm. "Children get sick. They get colds. You can't blame yourself. Much as you want to, you can never keep children from every illness. There may have been even sicker children elsewhere. And you don't know for sure they caught this from those kids."

Tears shone in Gisela's eyes. "If anything happens to them . . ."

He pulled her close to himself, whispering into her hair. "Your mum said this isn't like what your sister had. We'll pray and trust the Lord to watch over them."

She buried her head in his chest and clung to him. "Everything I do, I mess up."

"That isn't true. You got them here. So far, you kept them safe. And it's not your fault they got sick. You could no more stop that than you could stop the rain."

She melted against his chest, and he never wanted to let go. "Thank you."

"I haven't done anything."

"You have just by being here."

Her heart beat in tempo with his. "There's nowhere else I would be."

"So you will stay with me?"

Audra stood at the Cramers' tiny kitchen window overlooking the destruction of this once-great city. Much of it had been reduced to rubble. The fronts of many buildings had been sheared away.

Entire blocks were flattened. Smoke rose from several spots along the horizon, places where the Allies had recently unloaded their deadly payloads. If the bombings continued much longer, there would be nothing left.

"What is so interesting out there?" Kurt's voice at her elbow startled her.

"What little is left of this city. I had always heard about how grand Berlin was. What a proud metropolis. There is nothing proud remaining."

"I wonder if it will ever be the same. I have been here several times, but I recognize nothing."

Audra turned from the window. She had not noticed the fine lines marring Kurt's almost-too-perfect face.

"I heard the most interesting conversation yesterday."

He had her attention. "Ja?"

"It's as I suspected. There is no German in Josep at all. He was a British POW. The marriage is fake, thought up by Gisela on the spur of the moment to protect him."

Audra's mind whirled. "Are you sure about this?"

"I heard Gisela tell her mutti when I came up to use the washroom. There is no doubt. And she's at least part American."

"American? She could help me get to Hollywood."

"But not if she truly comes to love Josep. Then she will go to England with him. And your chance at being the next Marlene Dietrich will be lost."

"You're sure about this?"

"I am. I didn't hear the entire conversation. The floor creaked and I was afraid they would find me eavesdropping. But I know what I did hear."

"So, what does that mean?"

Kurt didn't try to hide his enthusiasm. "Gisela can be mine."

"You like her?" She didn't really have to ask the question.

"I need your help. They have been spending time together, pretending to be married. I am afraid their feelings for each other will become real."

"How am I supposed to help?" The situation could turn out well for her.

"I will work on wooing Gisela." His blue eyes had become hard. "You pretend to like Josep. Don't let on that we know about them. Do whatever you can think of to plant that seed of doubt in Gisela's mind about him. If she doesn't spend time around him, it will be easier for me to lure her."

"You sound like you are fishing." He didn't come across very much like a man in love. And if he caught Gisela, she would remain in Germany.

The small clock ticked on the faded yellow kitchen wall.

"Josep and Gisela are in with the kinder now. Frau Cramer has gone for the doctor."

Kurt's jaw clenched. "This is just the crisis that might bring the two of them closer. We can't allow that to happen."

Nein, she couldn't allow Gisela to fall for him.

"I will do what I can."

Gisela and Mitch sat on the bed beside each other, the girls sleeping. Their breathing appeared to be deep and even, but she didn't dare relax. Not until they bounded from under the sheets and came to hug her legs.

"I'm scared," she whispered, not wanting to wake them, not wanting them to hear her trepidation.

"I know." Mitch's voice was as soft.

"What if I have to tell their mother . . . ?" The thought turned her stomach.

"You won't."

"How do you know?"

"They have colds. Nothing more. The trip tired them. They won't die or anything."

"And you pretend to know the mind of God?"

"No. But I trust Him."

Gisela wiped a stray hair from her eyes. "I want to believe. To trust. But what if God is punishing me for leaving Heide and Lotta?"

"Who are they?"

Though unable to put back the words that had come uncorked, Gisela slapped her hand to her mouth. Her legs trembled.

He caressed the back of her hand. "You can tell me."

"I would rather not."

"Who are they?"

Gisela stared at the worn toe of her brown oxfords. "My cousins. The ones I left in East Prussia."

"I thought you only had the one cousin—Ella."

"Before I went to live with Ella, I stayed with my aunt and two younger cousins, Heide and Lotta, in Goldap. It was supposed to be a German stronghold and Mutti and Vater thought I would be safe there." Still the screams echoed in her head. She would never be rid of those sounds.

"The Russians came last October. I ran away. Heide, Lotta, and my aunt did not." She closed her eyes, but the darkness only magnified those horrific memories.

Mitch pulled her close to himself. "Running away can be a very good thing. If I hadn't run, we wouldn't have survived the fighting in Belgium."

"In these days, how do you know what is right and what is wrong? One bad decision can affect you for the rest of your life. Might even shorten it."

"You're right."

She sat still for a while, her ear pressed against his chest and listened to his heart beating.

"Tante. Tante." Annelies stirred, and Gisela left his embrace to give the girl a drink of water.

"How are you feeling?"

Annelies shook her head. "Yucky. When is Mutti coming?"

That was a question Gisela wished she had the answer to. "Soon, very soon. After you sleep and feel better, then perhaps she will be here."

Annelies's blond eyelashes fluttered and she drifted off. Gisela stroked her glistening hair.

"Look at what your running did. You're alive. The girls are here, out of the clutches of the Russians."

"For now. What if staying here is the wrong thing to do?"

Audra gave a tap at the bedroom door before entering the sickroom. Both kinder slept, their faces pale, their cheeks rosy. Josep and Gisela sat together on the edge of the bed, his arm around her waist.

Kurt was right. If they didn't act now, Josep and Gisela might form a bond that would be difficult for him to break.

"Excuse me. How are the girls?"

Gisela nodded. "Resting well. I wish the doctor would hurry and come. Mutti left awhile ago."

"She will be here soon. Time drags when you are worried. You look exhausted. Why don't you go to my room and lie down for a while? I will let you know when the doctor arrives."

Josep released his grip. "That's a terrific idea. You go."

Gisela came to her feet. "Danke. You are a true friend."

Audra didn't relax until the door clicked shut behind Gisela. Then she slipped into the spot the other woman had vacated. "I am worried about you too."

"Danke. I am fine. That is nice of you to help Gisela."

"Renate and Annelies have become special to me. I have known them for a little while. When they came into the dress shop where I worked, they chatted away and sat so well while their mutti shopped. They loved it when I snuck them each a piece of candy."

"Gisela is good to them. You are too."

She sat in silence for a moment, deciding on what to say next. The awkward pause dragged on too long.

Josep cleared his throat. "Are you staying here? In Berlin?"

"I don't know. I would like to go to America someday. People there are rich. I could be a movie star." She sat straighter. "You could teach me English. I will never be an actress if I don't learn it."

"Not everyone in America is rich."

"You've been to America?"

He bit the inside of his cheek. "Nein. But that is what I hear."

"But people have cars and jobs and plenty of food to eat. When I was growing up, there was never enough for me or my many brothers and sisters. I never want to live that way again."

"I understand. I hope you succeed. If you'd like to learn English, I could help with that."

She flashed her best before-the-war smile. "Thank you." She leaned into him, touched his cheek, and placed a feathery-light kiss on his lips.

And then the door scraped open.

Gisela stood on the threshold.

TWENTY-TWO

Gisela stood in the doorway, a dark silhouette against the light from the window. Mitch heard her sharp intake of breath, saw her cover her mouth, watched her turn and flee from the room.

"Gisela. Stop. Wait." He rose from his position on the sickbed. Audra pulled him down. "Let her go. She needs to calm down."

He tugged his wrist free. "Nein. I have to tell her."

"Tell her what? It was an innocent flirtation."

"She is my wife."

"She isn't." Audra narrowed her eyes. "You lied about being a German officer. You hid your British identity. What else have you been fibbing about?"

"How do you know?"

"Kurt knows. He heard Gisela talking to her mother. What is your real name?"

The situation just became very dangerous. "I think it's best you don't know." What would they do with that information?

He'd worry about that later. Right now he wanted to find Gisela. Had this crazy urge to locate her. This war would separate them, but he still wanted to find her. He stood once more.

"Bitte, Josep, don't go."

Had Audra lost her mind? "I have to." He ran out of the room and checked the rest of the apartment. Gisela was nowhere to be found.

Where might she have gone? She wouldn't leave the children alone.

Audra stopped him in the living room. "You will make things worse if you go after her now. She will be angry with you. I tell you, waiting a little while will be good. Let her come back when she is ready."

Audra clung to his arm as Kurt entered from the kitchen. "What is the matter?"

"She"—Mitch glared—"kissed me. And drove Gisela away."

Kurt's stone-like face was difficult to read. Was it shock, surprise, or glee Mitch saw in the other man's eyes? "She is a beautiful woman."

"Where did Gisela go?"

"I didn't see her leave, only heard the door shut. I thought perhaps the doctor had come."

"I have to find her." Mitch tore himself from Audra's clutches and left the apartment as fast as possible.

But when he got to the bottom of the stairs, he didn't know which way to go. Did she head outside?

He knocked on the door of the first-floor flat. Perhaps she had gone to visit Bettina and Katya. An older woman, rather stooped, her hands shaking, answered his knock. He recognized her from the air-raid shelter.

"Have you seen Fräulein Cramer?"

"Nein, nein. She is missing?"

He didn't want to concern this woman. "She is upset about the girls being sick. I wanted to check on her."

"Dearie, who is at the door? Is it Jean-Claude? If so, do let him in."

The woman shook her head, a few gray curls escaping from her pins. "That woman believes we are in Paris. I don't know why she thinks that."

"She is confused. They both are. Play along with the game. You'll have fun."

"She speaks to me in French." The woman held her hands high. "I don't speak French."

Mitch needed to hurry. If Gisela had gone out, by this time she would be far down the street. Perhaps even around the corner.

"If you see Fräulein Cramer, bitte, tell her Josep is looking for her. Danke."

He turned away and rushed to the street before the old woman closed the door. He gazed to his left and right. No sign of her. No telling where she might have gone.

He struck off to his left, stepping around rubble. No cars rumbled past on the street and very few bicycles. Most people walked. A few blocks down ran a streetcar line, but the tracks had suffered damage and the cars didn't operate on a set schedule, according to Gisela.

If she had gotten on the tram, he would never find her. He walked around the block, hoping to spy the pretty pink sweater she had been wearing this morning. He missed her easily identifiable green scarf.

No sign of her. No one frequented the cafés, the tables pulled inside for the winter. With all of the air raids, he doubted anyone had sat at the tables for a while.

He continued his circuit around the block but saw no sign of her. Without her, his heart was hollow.

Had that thought crossed his mind? How much he missed her when she was not with him?

Impossible. She was like a pebble at the bottom of his shoe.

Besides, a romance between a British soldier and a German

woman would be frowned upon for sure. His chaps would call it fraternizing with the enemy.

Then again, she was also American. Did that make a difference?

What did matter were the stirrings in his heart, unlike anything he had ever known. Most others in his platoon had girls back home. Even in the POW camp, they had received letters from their sweethearts.

His letters came from his mother and sister. No girl had ever caught his eye or held his attention for very long. He'd been too busy with rugby and cricket with his mates. And, strange as it was after having known Gisela for but a few weeks, she intrigued him. Perhaps this was what war did to you, made you realize what was important. Then again, he'd never known anyone as beautiful or as special as Gisela.

He searched the neighborhood for a good fifteen minutes without sighting her. Dragging his feet, he made his way back to the apartment.

He entered the lobby and stood with his hands on his hips for a minute or two, trying to think where else she might be, when he heard a soft mewing from below. Like a kitten crying.

He dashed down the wooden steps. Sure enough, on the bed in the far corner of the dark and damp shelter sat Gisela. She covered her face and cried a pitiful, heart-breaking cry.

Ten strides took him to her side. Not wanting to startle her, he settled himself beside her on the mattress. She continued her soft weeping. Her tears wrenched his gut. He pulled her close to him, but she didn't stop.

"Gisela."

Now she looked up, straight into his eyes. Unshed tears dangled on her golden lashes. "You came."

"Yes."

All of his senses were heightened—the pink of her sweater

more vibrant, the moldy odor of the basement more pungent, the cold of the bunker more intense. "I'm sorry."

"It's not about that."

"It's not?"

She sniffled. "Not entirely. If you are supposed to be my husband, you shouldn't have been kissing her."

"She kissed me." Though it sounded like he was making excuses, it was the truth. "And they know we aren't married. And that I'm British."

"How?"

"They heard you talking to your mum."

Her last tear fell. "I did this. What if they tell? Now you have no choice but to leave."

His heart leapt like it might jump from his chest. "Not until the girls are well."

"Does it all ever get to be too much for you?"

"What?"

"For years, our lives have been in constant danger. We run from one place to another, never safe. I ran away from Heide and Lotta. Then Ella entrusted her precious children to me, and Herr Holtzmann died, leaving me to care for his senile sisters. Now the girls are sick. How much more does the Lord expect me to bear?"

Her tears were for more than the incident with Audra. What answer did he have?

"Will the Lord forgive me for all the wrong?" She gazed at him with such expectation in her eyes.

"You have done nothing wrong."

"So many have depended on me."

He gave her a sideways hug and she leaned on his shoulder. "You have your mum to help you, and you have me. I don't think you want Kurt's or Audra's help."

She chuckled just a little under her breath. "No. Not if she's going to be kissing you."

"You aren't in this alone." He pulled away from her and caressed her cheek. "We will do it, you and I. We will get it right this time."

"Atone for our past mistakes?"

Could they? Could he? He'd made enough of them.

Above them, the lobby door opened.

Gisela wiped away her tears on her sweater's sleeve. The pink fuzz tickled her nose. "I think the doctor is here."

Mitch led her upstairs, and they caught up with Mutti and Dr. Liebenstraum at the apartment door as the old man was removing his thin black coat.

He smiled when he saw Gisela and kissed her on the cheek with his chapped lips. "My, my, you have grown up. What a fine young lady. You had a harrowing experience, I hear. Glad to know you are safe and sound."

"Good to see you, Dr. Liebenstraum. Bitte, tell me the girls will recover."

He laughed, his neat white mustache stretching wide. "Let me first examine them. Then I can give you my prognosis." He retrieved his doctor's bag from the davenport.

How stupid of her. She wanted to hear the news, to know if the kinder would survive; yet every nerve stood at attention, prepared for the worst.

Mutti led the way to the sickroom. If possible, the girls appeared even paler than when Gisela saw them before.

All this time, Mitch had been right behind them, and now he stood at her shoulder. He declared his intention of staying here, at least for the time being. Together. His presence comforted her.

The doctor opened his black bag and rummaged through

it. Mutti must have filled him in on the details of the kinders' symptoms because he asked no questions. Instead, he pulled out a thermometer and took their temperatures while feeling their pulses. He listened to the girls' hearts and to their chests and palpated their stomachs.

The doctor hung his stethoscope around his neck and stepped back. Gisela rocked forward on her feet. He ran his fingers through his thinning gray hair. "Just a cold. They need rest and in a day or two, they will be fine."

Gisela rubbed the back of her neck. "Are you sure that is all? Don't you have to run tests?" She had been right. Dr. Liebenstraum was too old. They needed another opinion.

"Even if I had the ability to right now, I wouldn't. It is nothing serious. Their lungs are clear and their fevers aren't that high. Fluids and aspirin are my prescription."

Gisela's head began to pound. "We should have moved far from those sick children on the train."

The old doctor shook his wizened head. "No harm done. In no time, they will be bouncing around like little girls do."

"Danke, Doctor." Gisela forced herself to unclench her hands.

He snapped shut his bag. "I will be back in a couple of days to check on them. In the meantime, if there is any change in their condition, let me know." He wagged his finger at her. "But I don't expect there to be. Stop worrying so much."

How could she? People died when they were entrusted to her. Too many people around her had died.

Mutti left to show the man to the door.

"How will I tell Ella that her children became sick?"

"She's a mum, so she'll understand. These things happen. She'll thank you for taking such good care of her girls and will be grateful you have brought them this far to safety."

Annelies stirred and muttered, "Mutti, Mutti."

Gisela bent over and kissed the girl on her warm forehead, holding her hand. "She will be here soon. Very soon."

Annelies opened her eyes, the usual sparkle missing. "I wish she would come."

"Me too. But she will be here before you know it."

She prayed her words were true. Reality told her they were false.

An air-raid siren picked that moment to screech.

She glanced at the two sick girls. She couldn't take them to the shelter and risk getting them sicker or infecting one of their other cellar-mates.

How would she protect them now?

TWENTY-THREE

Audra and Kurt sat beside each other on the hard kitchen chairs in the chilly air-raid shelter, alone for now. He expected the others to clatter down the stairs any moment.

He leaned forward in his seat. While Audra may have blown any chance she had with Josep, her blunder was all the better for him. She created the perfect opening for him to endear himself to Gisela. His missing fingers tingled to touch those smooth, familiar piano keys.

Now he needed to keep Josep and Gisela from reconciling. "What about that little tactical error you made this morning?"

Audra raised her chin. "I made no error, just created a problem between Josep and Gisela. You were supposed to go after her, though, and not let him comfort her."

"But you need to keep Gisela as your friend. Not that it matters to me, but she won't want to take you to America if she is angry with you."

"She won't take me to America at all if she falls in love with you."

A bit of a problem he hadn't thought of when recruiting her.

"In exchange for your help breaking them up, I will insist she go to America until am I able to get a job to support her and take you with her."

She gave him a dubious look.

"All is not lost. You keep flirting with Josep, and I will generate doubt about him in her mind. The longer those girls are sick, the worse off we are. Pray they recover soon."

"I disagree. This is the chance you need. The stress of having ill children will wear on her. When she breaks down and cannot handle more trouble, you will be the one to support her, to take care of her when no one else is."

Kurt couldn't help but admire this crafty, wily woman.

The roar of bombers thundered in the distance, rattling Gisela's bones. The sirens' screeches pitched up in intensity.

Gisela studied the two kinder now awake in the bed, their gray eyes large. She couldn't bring the girls to the shelter. And if they were contagious, she didn't want to start an epidemic.

But should they stay here, with bombs whistling to earth around them?

Mitch decided for her, scooping Annelies in his arms. "Can you get Renate?"

She nodded, lifted the girl from the mattress, and carried her downstairs.

Sudden cold, like a Russian winter wind, cloaked her. She rubbed her arms and sat on the edge of the mattress they had brought downstairs so the girls could sleep during the air raids. All around, the Allied planes emptied themselves of their cargo. The chattering of machine guns indicated a dogfight in the skies above them.

Annelies lay back on the pillows. "My head hurts, Tante Gisela."

With a touch she tried to make as tender as Mutti's, Gisela smoothed back her hair. "I know, sweetheart, I know. You will be better very soon."

She gazed at Gisela with pleading eyes. "Promise?"

"I promise."

"I hear the planes."

"Don't worry about them. They won't come here today."

But the droning grew louder. The sirens screeched. The building shook.

Annelies grabbed Gisela's arm and clung to it. Renate opened her eyes, glazed with fever. "Airplanes."

"Ja, I hear them too."

A bomb whistled as it streaked to the earth.

She threw herself over the girls.

An ear-splitting explosion deafened Gisela.

The floor beneath her shook. Or was that her shaking?

Ceiling plaster rained down on them.

When would it be over?

Booms continued to sound around them, at last becoming more distant. Little by little, the rumble of the bombers hushed.

A siren screeched again—all clear. The bombers had turned back toward Britain. For now.

Gisela sat, still trembling all over. That bomb could have struck them.

Mitch adjusted the blanket around Annelies and lifted her into his arms. "That hit nearby. But at least we heard the siren."

"We should inspect the damage." Kurt carried Renate in his single arm. "It might have been just down the block."

"Ja. That's good." Mitch lugged Annelies upstairs and tucked her into bed beside her sister.

Gisela went to the kitchen to rinse out the compresses. One of the cupboard doors had flung open and broken dishes littered the floor. Too much like the large earthquake that had hit California not long before they returned to Germany.

Before she could reach for the broom, Mutti and Audra returned from the shelter. Mutti's mouth fell open when she saw the mess. "Not enough plates to eat off of as it was and now this. Another hardship of the war."

If you weren't matter-of-fact about things these days, you might as well sit down and let a bomb end your misery.

Gisela swept the broom over the floor and Mutti held the dustpan. Every so often, she caught herself peering over Mutti's shoulder, hoping for a glimpse of Mitch in the doorway.

Audra took the pan to bring the shards of glass to the dustbin. "Who are you looking for?"

Gisela had been attempting to ignore Audra, the sting of her kiss with Mitch too fresh yet. "Where are the men?"

"They went out already to check on the damage."

So close. Like two years ago, when their neighborhood had sustained much damage and Mutti and Vater sent her east.

How long would it be until their apartment building was hit?

Audra almost danced out of the room with the dustpan. "I will bring Josep a drink of water when I get back. He is working so hard."

Gisela grabbed the washcloths hanging on the side of the sink where she had left them. She had no claim on Mitch, not now that their secret was out. If he wanted to pursue Audra, fine. He would be leaving soon.

Why, then, did the very thought of Audra with Mitch make her lonely?

Gisela dragged herself to the main bedroom, though she longed to split herself in two and go to Mitch. She gave each girl a drink and laid the compresses on their warm brows.

Renate touched Gisela's face. "You take good care of me, Tante."

"I do?"

Annelies stretched. "You do. Almost as good as Mutti."

"Almost?"

Renate bobbed her head. "Ja. Mutti has a 'sick book.' When you are yucky, you draw pictures."

"Is that so?" She had no paper or pencils. "You sleep for a while and you will see what Tante Gisela has for you when you are better."

Two somber little girls nodded, then lay against the pillows. Just as well, since she had nothing for them.

She sighed and stroked Annelies's hair before moving to the bedside chair. The late afternoon sun cast long shadows across the room. In the quietness, Gisela heard the noise next door as bricks were moved and cast aside. On the street, people shouted. The little clock on the nightstand ticked off the minutes. Each jerk of the minute hand brought liberation ever closer. How many more minutes would pass before they would be free? Until she could travel home?

The hard, angular kitchen chair provided little comfort. Still she managed to close her eyes and nod off.

The smell of burning gas, burning wood, burning flesh consumed her. Screams rattled in her head. She wanted to run, but her legs refused to move. She couldn't get where she needed to be. Something, someone held her fast. All her kicking and biting did no good.

And the screams faded into silence.

She woke with a start, her heart kicking like a bucking bronco in her chest.

"Gisela, wake up, wake up."

She slid upright and pulled her wrist from Mitch's grasp. His dark eyebrows were knotted.

"What's going on?"

"You had a nightmare. Or a daymare. It must have been a ghastly dream."

Wiping her eyes, she was surprised to find them damp. "It was."

"Care to tell me about it?"

She shook her head. "I'd like to forget it. I'm fine now, thank you." It wasn't until then that she noticed the streak of soot dashed across his cheek and the dirt down the front of his plain green shirt. "What happened to you?"

Mitch stared down at the mark on his shirt. He owned nothing but the clothes on his back, and Frau Cramer had been gracious enough to give him two shirts belonging to her husband. He was a bit shorter and stockier than Mitch, but he was grateful for the gift.

He hesitated, trying in vain to block out the scene he had witnessed a few doors down. "I don't feel much like discussing it."

"You went to the neighbor, that's what Audra said. Did they sustain a direct hit?"

He nodded, his head pounding as he attempted to stop the images of the carnage.

"Are they all . . . ?"

"I haven't any idea. We located a few, um, bodies. Those who perhaps didn't go to the cellar. We're digging now to see if there are survivors in the shelter." If he could shout to the bombers, the ones with the white stars or the ones with the blue circles with red bull's-eyes, he would tell them to stop. Stop bombing innocent women and children.

He clenched his fist and struggled to keep his arm at his side.

Gisela rubbed her bloodshot eyes. The light, the fire, the feistiness had been extinguished. "How much longer?"

"Not much."

"How do you know?"

"I can feel it in my bones. The German government won't be able to hold out much longer. Too much destruction, too much death. I wouldn't be surprised if they are working on terms of surrender behind the scenes."

"The radio keeps talking about German victories."

He stood and wiped the soot from his brown pants. "Propaganda. Don't believe what Hitler tells you."

"I never believed him. Not much, anyway."

"That's good. How are the girls?"

"The same."

He turned to leave the room.

"Does God still hear us? Or has the evil of our country—our world—caused Him to turn His back on us?"

He went to her and knelt in front of her, his hands on her knees. "You're exhausted. Mum always said things look darkest just before the dawn. In a matter of weeks, this will be over. Life will return to normal."

"Normal is unimaginable. But has God turned His back on us?" She pursed her lips, fine lines that had no business gracing such a young face marring it.

He didn't have a good answer for her. "I have to believe He hasn't. Life wouldn't be worth living if He had."

All the way down the stairs and out the door, Mitch thought about Gisela's words. He knew he should believe God hadn't abandoned them. He wanted so much to believe that God continued to listen to them. Yet he understood her doubts.

TWENTY-FOUR

Mitch returned to the demolished apartment house. Up and down the street, bricks and chunks of concrete littered the sidewalk and the roadway. Fires smoldered, women wept.

He wanted to forget every sight, every sound, every smell of this war.

Kurt lifted his head and acknowledged Mitch's return. "How is Gisela?"

Now Kurt was interested in her? "Fine. The kinder are resting well." He ignored Kurt's stare and the questions written across his face and got back to work.

They labored with as much speed as possible, careful about which bricks to remove first, not wanting the building to collapse on top of whoever might be down there. They dug until Mitch's fingernails were broken and his knuckles bled. Every little while, they paused, listened, prayed to hear sounds of life.

None came.

Darkness fell. Twice they had to stop because of air raids. No other bombers targeted this particular area today. If nothing else,

Mitch hadn't felt this useful all war long. At least he wasn't milking cows or mucking stalls. He was trying to save lives.

If there were lives to be saved.

Because of the blackout ordinance, they were unable to use floodlights or even torches to illuminate the ruins. They toiled in the thin light of the moon, alternating between digging and listening. His arms ached and his shoulders burned.

Kurt stopped and stretched his back. "Those British. They bomb innocent women and kinder. Hospitals too. What kind of monsters are they?" He pointed at his own empty sleeve. "We hit military targets and leave the civilians alone."

Kurt was trying to bait him. "The Germans killed thousands of Londoners at the beginning of the war. You expected that they would treat the Germans differently?"

His poor German was, in all likelihood, a good thing. If he could speak the language better, he would tell Kurt just what he thought of the Nazis and their war tactics.

A beam of moonlight illuminated the German soldier who scrubbed his face. "Gisela is very beautiful."

Now Mitch knew for sure Kurt was trying to get the best of him. "Ja." He bent down and lifted away another couple of bricks.

But it was true. Gisela was beautiful. The kind of woman a man wanted to shelter, watch over, provide for. Mitch wanted to take her to England, show her his favorite spot under the willow tree, take her flying.

But she wanted to go to California. He had been away from Britain for such a long time, he hadn't a thought of going anywhere but home.

"How did you meet her?"

"At a farm."

"You don't talk much."

"Nein. We have to work." Mitch put his head down and concentrated on the task in front of him. They would soon have to stop. Then he shifted a hunk of plaster.

He would never forget the gruesome sight that met his eyes.

Sleep eluded Audra in the few hours they were able to be upstairs when the all-clear had sounded. She should be exhausted. A few hours of rest here and there weren't enough. But she lay wide-awake.

She hadn't meant to make Gisela angry with her. This was going to be hard—being friends with Gisela while trying to make sure she didn't go to England. If she did, Audra might never make it to America.

She crept from the bed she now slept in with Frau Cramer, careful not to disturb the woman. Gisela's mother turned over and resumed her snoring.

The city lay in silent slumber. Blackout shades covered the windows, refusing any light entry to the apartment, but she imagined the fires burning red against the dark sky. For now, peace had descended.

Even with the destruction, she loved the vibrant heartbeat of the city. And imagined Hollywood. No more fighting every day to keep body and soul together. There were opportunities and she would take them.

She grabbed her sweater from the edge of the bed, wrapped it around her shoulders, and tiptoed across the creaking bare wood floors to the larger bedroom where the girls slept. Their breathing was congested but even. Gisela slumbered in the bed beside them. She hadn't left them since they took ill. That would have given Audra the chance to spend time with Josep, if he wasn't so busy digging bodies out of the collapsed shelter next door.

Audra leaned over Renate and felt the girl's forehead with the back of her hand. Still warm, but perhaps not quite as warm as during the day. Annelies slept with her mouth wide open.

The color of the children's hair, as fair as wheat in the fields, reminded Audra of her younger sisters. All of the girls in her family were blessed with that beautiful feature. You could pick a Bauer from a crowd because of it.

She padded to the living room. At home when she couldn't sleep, she would sneak to the barn and curl up in the hayloft beside the kittens. Their warm, purring bodies had a way of lulling her to slumber.

After all of the barns she had slept in the last few weeks, she never wanted to sleep in the loft again. From now on, it would be nothing but featherbeds and silk sheets for her.

She sat on the old, sagging couch in the dark. Kurt slept on the other davenport, the gray one, and Josep on the floor. With the lumps digging into her backside, she surmised the floor provided more comfort.

Josep stirred and thrashed about, moaning, then screaming, his breathing rapid.

She knelt beside him, touching his shoulder lightly. He calmed without waking, and his breathing returned to normal.

At last her eyelids grew heavy and she leaned her head against the back of the couch. Her body twitched as sleep claimed her.

Then the floorboards creaked and someone touched her arm.

Audra's eyes flew open and she clutched her chest. She scooted deeper into the dark-red davenport. Kurt hadn't meant to frighten her.

She stared at him. "What do you think you are doing?"

"I'm sorry. I thought there might be something wrong."

She ran her fingers through her long, brilliant white-blond hair. "Nein, nothing. I couldn't sleep."

"Those Americans and Brits don't want us to get any rest. They think they can break us that way."

"They are wearing us down."

"And what about Josep? Are you wearing him down too?"

"As much as possible. Today—yesterday—was more about planting seeds of doubt in Gisela's head." Audra sat straighter. "Have you seen the way he looks at her?"

Kurt lowered himself beside her, his hand on his knee. "You think he likes her?"

"Ja. Maybe he more than likes her. Like she is as vital to him as air."

"Then we have to work harder. More doubts. More questions in their minds." Gisela may be as vital to Josep as air, but she was as vital to him as his music. Without that, he had nothing.

She turned toward Kurt. "I admire you, you know. You don't quit."

How many times he had wanted to.

"You're the type of person who can do anything he sets his mind to."

"I couldn't be a typist. Or a trapeze artist." Or a concert pianist.

She giggled, pure and clean as a mountain stream. "Nein, I suppose I couldn't see you in a room full of women on their type-writers or swinging from the rafters. But you could be a banker. A preacher. A professor."

None of those professions held even a bit of appeal. Nothing but his fingers flying over the ivories.

She touched his empty sleeve. His missing digits tingled. "Oh, I know, you could be an escape artist. Can't you hear the ringmaster shouting now? 'Ladies and gentlemen, may I direct your attention to the center ring. The world-famous Kurt Abt is going to attempt to escape from this locked case, underwater, with one hand tied behind his back.'"

Her words stung. He knew she meant them in jest, but they hurt. Was that all he was good for? To be a circus act?

Audra backed away. "I'm sorry. That came out all wrong. I mean . . ."

She didn't understand like Gisela did. She would never insult him, would never belittle him. He guessed she never even thought about his missing arm. She didn't stare like everyone else did.

And most important, she brought the music.

He shook his head. Regardless of the careless words Audra threw around, he needed her. "Just remember the plan and stick to it. If we do that, both of us will get what we want."

Josep stirred. "Hey, quiet here. A man needs his sleep."

Kurt had forgotten about Josep on the floor. How much of their conversation had he heard?

What did he know of their scheme?

TWENTY-FIVE

April 16, 1945

Gisela couldn't stand being cooped up in the apartment one minute longer. The girls' colds had lingered for several weeks. She and Mitch had each caught it a week or so after they got sick. The cough stuck around. Finally, they were all feeling better. With the arrival of warmer weather, they would do well to enjoy it. She grabbed a sweater for each child. "Today we are going out."

Annelies's and Renate's curls bounced up and down as they skipped about the tiny, crowded apartment. "Where are you taking us? To the zoo? I want to see the giraffes."

Gisela shook her head. The zoo had been destroyed long ago. "Nein. The giraffes will have to wait until after the war. We'll take a short walk today."

Mutti buttoned up Renate's gray sweater. She had outgrown it and the cuffs had begun to unravel. "You will have fun, nein?"

"Ja, I'll run in circles."

Mitch laughed. "See, that is fun."

Gisela worked the buttons for Annelies on the sweater that

hung almost to her knees. At least she would grow into it. "Are you sure you don't want me to stay and help with the laundry, Mutti? That is so much for you to do on your own."

Mutti patted Gisela's cheek. "Look how pale you are. I think you need the sunshine more than the girls. And we need our rations. You can fold the laundry when it is dry."

Gisela hated to leave that work to Mutti. "We'll be back in time for me to hang it."

"Don't rush on my account. Have a good time."

Gisela kissed Mutti's wrinkled cheek. When had she started looking so old?

Kurt came in from the kitchen. "Going for a stroll is a splendid idea. If you will wait for me, I will come along. Would you like that, girls?"

Gisela shot a look at Mitch, then at Kurt. "We won't be gone long. We all still tire easily. Too much excitement isn't good for them. Or us."

Audra also joined them from the kitchen. "A walk in the fresh air sounds wonderful. As soon as I have my sweater, I will be ready to go."

Just that fast, she disappeared, Kurt following in her wake.

Mitch grabbed Renate and shoved Gisela toward the entrance. "Let's get out of here before they get back."

"But . . ." Annelies tugged at Gisela's sleeve.

Gisela slapped her hand over the girl's mouth. "Tell me later," she hissed.

Mitch nodded and winked, the gesture warming her more than the April sunshine. They didn't need Annelies to repeat what he had said.

Mitch hadn't left. Every day she expected to awake and find him gone, vanished. Out to locate his countrymen.

He had never said he would stay with her. Yet he didn't leave.

What happened to change his mind? He had been so anxious to leave earlier.

After they descended the stairs and reached the out-of-doors, Mitch flashed his dimples. "Whew, that was a close shave."

"Should we wait for them?"

"I say let's get going before they catch up to us. It's a lovely spring day."

"I smell fire." One part of the city or another was constantly burning now.

"Use your imagination. You're in a field of daisies, the breeze blowing the grass at your feet."

The image made her want to weep. These kinder deserved to have such a childhood.

"Why so sad?" Mitch stopped and invited Renate for a piggy-back ride.

Gisela shook away the disturbing thoughts and gave a smile she hoped wasn't too fake. "I'm not."

He galloped close to her. "At least I am enjoying myself."

"I never said I wasn't."

"Then enough with the doom and gloom. Today is a holiday from the war."

The corners of her mouth crept toward her cheeks. "I didn't realize the war took holidays."

"Of course."

"First, the bread. Perhaps today we won't have to stand in line very long."

Gisela's wish didn't come true. They joined the queue for the bakery before they even turned the corner to the shop. Another lengthy wait for a few meager rations.

Annelies and Renate chased each other in circles around Mitch's and Gisela's legs, drawing them closer to each other. He wrapped his arm around her waist. They fit together so well. Like God had made them for each other.

Had He?

She snuggled her head into the crook of Mitch's arm. "I wonder if Kurt and Audra are looking for us."

His dimples deepened. "I'm sure they are. Let's hope they don't find us."

"That's mean."

"Haven't you noticed the way they try to separate us? Get us alone with them?"

"Audra likes you."

"And who wouldn't?" He flashed his impish grin.

She jabbed him in the ribs. "Modesty doesn't become you."

"I wasn't trying to be modest."

"I know."

Annelies wriggled between them, pulling them apart. Mitch hadn't denied having feelings for Audra. She hadn't given up her campaign to win his heart. Every chance she got, she batted her long eyelashes at him and jumped to meet his every need.

Gisela supposed he liked it that way. A bit of the day's luster wore away. "When are you going to leave?"

"Sounds like you want to get rid of me."

"Don't you want to?"

"Yes, I would like to get back to the lines, to rejoin my mates. To fight for my country. If I don't hurry, I'll miss all the action."

"I'll miss you." And she would. More than she would admit, even to herself.

"You make it very hard for me to leave."

Conversation buzzed around them. The woman in front of them had rather a loud voice.

"I still can't believe the news."

The woman's companion leaned in, looking ready for a good bit of gossip. "What news?"

"Don't tell me you haven't heard? Don't you have a radio? Do you ever leave your house? The American president is dead."

Gisela clutched her stomach. They had heard the information on the radio a few nights ago. She had a hard time believing it. Mr. Roosevelt had been president for almost as long as she could remember. "America has peaceful presidential transitions, so perhaps nothing will change. Pray that it doesn't delay their soldiers' arrival. We need them."

The teenage girl behind them, wearing the very familiar Hitler Youth uniform—dark skirt, white shirt, kaki jacket with a diamond swastika patch on the left arm—chimed in. "Now the tide of the war will change. Watch and see. America will fall into disarray and their troops will lose the will to fight. Germany will be victorious again."

Gisela peered at the destruction wrought on Berlin by Allied planes. There was no way Germany would regain the upper hand. She didn't want the Third Reich to survive.

God, don't let it survive.

They inched forward, now far enough along to see down the side street to the main avenue, Unter den Linden. Gisela gagged and moved to shield the girls from the sight of traitors being punished.

The Hitler Youth member behind them strode forward and noticed the scene as well. "See what happens to those who do not sacrifice enough for their country, who run away and hide, shirking their responsibilities? It is because of people like them that we have allowed the Allies this close to the capital. They did not give all they had." She narrowed her eyes at Mitch, accusation in her stance.

Gisela clung to his arm. "He served the Fatherland well, so well that he has shrapnel lodged next to his heart. He can no longer fight."

Mitch stepped forward. "I man the antiaircraft guns."

Would he ever learn to keep his mouth shut and not speak German in public?

The girl nodded, but Gisela continued to feel her stare boring into their backs.

A low-flying Allied plane swooped overhead, its engine whirring. Gisela pulled the girls closer to her and held them.

The plane completed several loops before flying east. Russian reconnaissance, most likely.

Gisela blew out the breath she didn't know she had been holding. Once they had their bread, they walked the back streets to the Tiergarten, avoiding the gruesome scene on the Unter den Linden.

And for a few minutes then, it did feel like a holiday. The lawns of the beautiful park had been torn up, but the wide paths still existed. The girls squealed when Mitch swung them in circles. They couldn't contain their laughter when he got on all fours and pretended to be a mean old bear.

Nothing did her heart better than to hear the girls giggle.

Then the air-raid siren sounded.

The four of them froze.

Mitch swiveled around, searching in all directions. "Do we have time to get home? Or is there a luftschutzbunker around here?"

"We have plenty of time. Those planes probably haven't crossed the English Channel yet." Not wanting their day together to end, Gisela ran to him and gave his arm a playful slap. "You're it."

He chased her as she scampered away. "That wasn't fair. I didn't even know we were playing tag. Now you had better watch out. You have it coming."

The girls shrieked and joined the fun. "I'm going to get you, Tante Gisela." Annelies's little legs flew over the uneven ground.

"Me too." Renate did her best to keep up the pursuit, tripping and falling, then getting up again. After a couple of minutes, Gisela grew winded and slowed, then stopped, her hands on her knees, still weak from the illness. Mitch and the girls tackled her and they fell into a laughing, giggling, coughing heap.

The air-raid sirens screeched their second warning. Mitch stood and brushed the grass and dirt from his pants. "I guess that means it's time to go."

Annelies crossed her arms and frowned. "I don't want to. I want to stay here and play some more."

Mitch tousled her already tangled hair. "Sorry, poppet, we'll have to play in the shelter now. Time to go." He swept Renate into his arms and onto his shoulders.

"Giddyup, horsie," she cried.

He neighed and galloped off. People hurried in the opposite direction, toward a public shelter.

Mitch peered over his shoulder at Gisela. "Are you sure we have time to get home?"

His questioning made her wonder and her midsection tightened. No use in frightening the girls, though. "Plenty of time. You trot on ahead and we'll be right behind."

The sound of bombers murmured in the distance, growing louder, more ominous with each passing second. Antiaircraft fire shook the air. Gisela pulled Annelies behind her and fast-walked to catch up to Mitch. "We need to hurry. We still have several blocks to go."

The ground beneath them rumbled at the approach of the bombers. Gisela wanted to shout at them to turn around. Did they intend to kill her with everyone else in the city?

The earth shook as the first bombs struck.

"Hurry, hurry!" The roar of the engines drowned out her words. She couldn't tell whether her body shook or the land beneath her.

She tried to draw a deep breath but couldn't.

They would never make it to the shelter in time.

TWENTY-SIX

M itch's heart threatened to evacuate his body, along with his lunch. The whistle of the bombs grew louder, deafening. The Cramers' home was too far away. The planes would be upon them in a moment. He slid Renate from his shoulders and held her close to his chest.

Where should they go? What should they do?

He scanned the area for any possibilities, his mind whirring. Lying flat on the ground wouldn't help. Hiding behind a tree wouldn't protect them.

What now, Lord?

Then he spied it—a recessed door in a sturdy-looking brick building, the arched entrance as much protection as they would get. He broke off their trajectory, grabbed Gisela's hand, and sprinted up the steps.

He had never heard the antiaircraft fire so loud. Flak fell around them. Would they be killed by falling shrapnel?

They reached the doorway. Annelies whimpered and Renate sucked her thumb with passion. They huddled together as if that would provide protection should they take a direct hit.

Gisela stared at him, biting her lower lip, crushing Annelies in her grip. Her face was as white as his mum's bedsheets.

The American pilots wheeled their planes overhead. The air around them buzzed with the whistles of what sounded like a hundred bombs. Mitch covered Renate's head with his hands. Gisela slipped her arm around him.

No, dear God, no. Keep us safe.

The atmosphere filled with debris. Chunks of concrete crashed to earth in front of them, smashed on the walkway and roadway. Powdery clouds of dust choked them. Renate covered her ears and screamed at the cacophony. Gisela snatched a handful of Mitch's shirt and pulled him close to her.

One bomb blast was followed by another and another. Bricks fell from the building where they had taken shelter.

Would the entire structure collapse on top of them?

The stench of burning filled his nostrils while Gisela's hair smelled of roses. They leaned on one another for support.

Dear God, when will this be over? Will we survive? Lord, don't punish them for my wrong decision.

Mitch had no idea how long they stood in the entryway. After the pilots had carpet bombed the neighborhood, they directed their planes west. To his beloved homeland.

Silence descended.

Then screaming pierced the stillness. Screaming of women and children. Screaming of the dying. Screaming of those left alive.

Mitch didn't think he could push any sound through his vocal chords.

The all-clear siren announced the end of the air raid.

He set Renate on the ground and felt her arms and legs and head. "Are you okay? Is anything hurt?"

Her gray eyes stood out in her face. "That was loud."

"Ja, ja, it was. Annelies, how about you? Are you hurt?"

"I want to go home."

She bore no visible signs of injury. A little of the weight on his chest receded. He stroked Gisela's arm. "Any damage?"

She trembled beneath his touch. "I don't think so. I'm sorry. I'm so sorry. We could have been killed."

A well of tears marked the sorrow in her eyes. Her misery was his own. "Don't be sorry. I'm the one to blame."

As they scurried to the flat, he couldn't corral his galloping thoughts. They insisted on stampeding to Frau Cramer and the others. Many, many bombs had fallen on the neighborhood today. Did the building still stand? Had they come through unscathed?

They passed skeletons of homes, glassless windows vacant, staring silently on the scene. What trees had not been cut for fuel stood barren, stripped of their young leaves. Awnings, just unfurled, had burned, the charred metal framework forlorn.

Bleak. Desolate. Foreboding.

Gisela, clinging to Annelies's hand, willed her frightening thoughts away, pushing them to the furthest corner of her mind as she picked her way down the once-vibrant street. Her pulse pounded in her neck and her breath came in short gasps. Building after building in their neighborhood reduced to a pile of bricks. The glass in the streetlamps lay shattered on the ground.

She handed Annelies to Mitch and increased her pace.

No sound reached her but the whooshing of blood in her ears. Destruction flanked her to the right and the left.

Mutti's neighbor—she didn't remember the woman's name—approached them, her eyes distant, unblinking. Gisela grasped her arm. "What happened? Have you seen Mutti?"

The woman gave a quick shrug and hastened away.

Fear wrapped itself around Gisela like a straitjacket.

She sprinted now, her arms and legs pumping. The buildings, or what was left of them, were a blur.

She turned the corner onto their block. Screams burst from her burning lungs. "Mutti! Mutti!"

The home she had left this morning no longer existed.

Carrying Renate and dragging Annelies behind slowed Mitch's progress. He lost sight of Gisela as she rounded the corner.

He knew what the news would be.

Piles of red bricks and white stone were heaped where flats, homes, and small businesses once stood.

The buildings' residents would have been in the shelter. While they liked to pretend that would protect them from a direct hit, Mitch knew that wouldn't be the case. When a three-story building crumbled around you, it didn't matter whether or not you were in the bunker.

He continued down the street. People stood in the rubble. Bloodied. In shock. Terrified. He turned the corner and the sight confirmed his worst fears.

Every building on the block had been destroyed. The Cramers' garden had become a huge, smoldering crater.

A direct hit.

Gisela ran ahead of him, stumbling on the debris lining the street. Filling the street.

Her screams echoed the ones he suppressed. Echoed the cries of those in his regiment as they died on a field in Belgium.

He saw no sign of her mum. Or any of the others.

Gisela dropped to her knees and dug through the rubble. In a full-blown panic, she ripped her hands open against the jagged hunks of concrete. "Mutti! Mutti!"

Her cries pierced his heart. He sat the girls on the concrete step—all that remained of what this morning was a home. Mitch went to her and held her.

She shuddered beneath his touch, then pounded his chest. "Let me go. I have to find Mutti. She's not here. She's not here."

"We'll find her, love. Don't worry."

"We have to dig to the cellar. She might be trapped down there. She was in the basement doing the laundry. Why did I ever leave? I should have stayed and helped. A good daughter would have done her duty."

"You offered to stay. She wanted you to go."

She wrenched herself from his embrace and resumed her frenzied search. He joined her.

"And what about Audra and Kurt and the old ladies—where are they? Down there with Mutti?"

"Hey, hey, slow down. You have to be careful how you go about this. If you move the wrong brick, you could rain more rubble on them."

For a moment, she attempted to heed his warning, moving the remains of the building a little slower. That didn't last long. She soon resumed her frenetic search.

Blood covered some of the bricks she tossed to the side. Hers? A victim's?

Time crawled. Time flew by. He couldn't decide which. His stomach growled. The girls held on to one another. Shadows lengthened and the air held a distinct chill.

"Well, dearie, what is this? Why are people digging like that? I believe the shovel was invented years and years ago."

Mitch shot to his feet, the world spinning as the blood rushed from his head. Down the street and around the rubble, Kurt and Audra led Bettina and Katya. He slid over the pile of discarded bricks and hurried in their direction. "Look, Gisela."

She paused a brief moment, scanned the group, then resumed her work, her only goal reaching her mum.

He met them several meters down the street. "Where were you?"

Audra bit her lip. "You didn't wait for us like we asked. We've been looking for you."

Bettina patted Audra's hand. "Ja, she took us up and down the Spanish Steps and around the Piazza Venezia. Oh my, what fabulous Roman architecture. Don't you agree, Sister?"

Katya nodded.

Mitch pressed the matter. "What about Frau Cramer? Did she go with you?" Audra stared at the building's ruins, as if seeing the destruction and understanding what it meant for the first time. He reached out to steady her as she wobbled and she clasped his wrist. "She didn't want to come with us. When we left, she was down there, wringing out the clothes."

Just as they feared. The same cold in the pit of his stomach that had gripped him as he raced across France grabbed hold of him now.

Kurt scampered over the rubble pile and rushed toward Gisela. She turned at his approach, her eyes wide and wild. Tears traced a path through her dirty cheeks. "My mutti. Oh, my mutti."

She allowed him to hold her. A hot rage surfaced in Mitch, a jealous possessiveness he didn't know he had. He pulled Audra along with him and clambered over the debris to Gisela, almost tearing her from Kurt's grasp. "Let us not waste more time. Start digging."

The old ladies took their places beside the young sisters, offering them candy they didn't have.

Night fell. Darkness closed in until they couldn't see where to dig next. He knelt beside Gisela and spoke to her in English. "We have to stop. There's nothing more we can do tonight. We'll come back in the morning and see if we can locate anyone."

Gisela slapped Mitch's hand away when he tried to pull her from her digging in the demolished apartment building. Didn't he understand that she had to find Mutti? Had to help her? She was in that basement. That's what Audra said. She was down there, perhaps suffocating as they worked.

Why did she leave her? Gisela wouldn't make that mistake again. "I'm not going anywhere."

His voice was gentle but insistent. "It's too dark to see. We'll look more in the morning. You need to rest."

She couldn't. "Where will we go? We don't have a home. There is nothing to do but continue searching."

Mitch rubbed the top of his head with both hands, his dark hair sticking up in every direction. "I hadn't thought about that."

"Just a small problem."

"Dearies, there is a nice hotel not far from here. Classy. Attracts the right kind of clientele. Why stay here when we can go there?"

Gisela's skin itched in irritation. "Get them out of here. Take them all away so I can work in peace. By myself." She thumped her forehead a few times. Who did she know in the neighborhood anymore? "Mutti's friend Frau Mueller lives nearby." She gave him directions. "Mention that you know me and she'll take care of you."

Mitch persisted. "You have to come with us. Have a hot meal, wash up, get a little rest. You can't continue working at this pace. You'll be no good to your mum if you fall over."

Gisela leaned on her haunches. "I can't leave. What if she needs me? What if she did go somewhere and comes back? Then she won't know where to find us."

"If the first place you thought to send us was a friend of your mum's, then that's the first place she'll think to look."

Her exhausted brain attempted to comprehend what Mitch said. Did it make sense? Would Mutti search for them at Frau Mueller's? Perhaps she was even there.

"I don't know." She was giving in to her desire for a bar of soap and a warm bed and hated herself for it.

"Come on." Mitch pulled her to her feet.

She stopped before they took a single step. Held her breath. Detected a faint cry. "Wait. Did you hear that?"

"Hear what?"

She hushed him. "A noise. From downstairs."

They didn't move for a couple of minutes. She strained to hear that noise again, any little sign that Mutti was alive under this rubble.

Mitch dared not to breathe. A direct hit on a building meant death. Gisela couldn't have heard a noise there. Could she?

He didn't detect a single sound. Not a peep. Not a scratch nor a bang. "Gisela, you didn't . . ."

She turned on him, her light-brown eyes alive with fire. "I did."

Better not to argue with her. "We'll dig a little longer. But the night raids will start soon."

"Take the Holtzmanns to Frau Mueller."

Mitch climbed from the pile of rubble and nodded to Audra and Kurt. "That would be best." He lowered his voice. "I will stay and make her go soon."

Kurt puffed out his chest. "I'll stay with her. You take Audra and go."

Mitch looked at Gisela. Her thick brown hair, rolled on top of her head, had come loose from its pins and hung around her face, covered in powder. Dark circles shadowed her eyes. She radiated fear, longing, determination. He couldn't leave her.

He nodded at Audra. "We'll come soon. Take Annelies and Renate with you."

Gisela whipped around to face them. "Nein. You cannot take the girls. They have to stay here with me."

Annelies and Renate sat huddled together on the step, dust turning their pale faces ghostly white.

"Let them go. Audra can get them washed up and fed at least. You will be there in time to tuck them into bed."

She directed her gaze to the sky, then to the ground, then to him. "Fine. Let them go." Her voice was weak, raspy.

Kurt went to her side. "You come too. Let me take care of you."

"I know I heard a sound. I won't stop until I reach the person who made that noise."

Audra gave her a hug and whispered in her ear, then paraded down the street with the two sets of sisters. If not for the fact that they stepped around the remains of buildings, they might have been comical.

Kurt stayed at Gisela's side and held her hand.

"I won't leave Mutti."

He drew her closer. "And I won't leave you." He kissed her forehead.

Mitch clenched and unclenched his hands. He wanted to be the one to comfort Gisela. What hurt the worst was that she didn't draw away from Kurt. Instead, she leaned into him.

After a moment in silence, the three of them resumed their digging. Crazy, really, because they couldn't see their hands in front of their faces. Mitch moved bricks here and there, mostly listening to hear if he could detect the noise Gisela heard.

Nothing.

A sliver of moonlight cast pale shadows across what had been a building. His hands hurt, still not healed from the last search he had conducted, his one hand still not healed from the Russian's bullet. Blood ran down them, though they had been callused by the farm work he did during his imprisonment.

His calluses were no match for the sharp edges of glass from cups and mirrors mixed in with the debris. Nothing but adrenaline propelled him forward.

They must have worked for at least an hour. Clouds covered the moon in the thick darkness.

"Josep?" Gisela collapsed in a heap on top of the ruins. Her moan-like weeping tore through him like a bullet.

"I'm here."

"I don't think I heard anything. I don't think there is anyone alive. What am I going to do? What am I going to do?"

He let her cry for a while, Kurt adhered to her other side. Mitch had watched Dad with Mum a time or two. Gisela needed to weep.

When she had spent herself, he helped her sit and Kurt offered her his very dirty handkerchief. The air-raid sirens broke the stillness of the night.

"I can't go."

Hoping the family friend she mentioned did indeed live around the corner, he stayed by her side. They would have to leave in a little while. He didn't want a repeat performance of this morning, but they had a few minutes.

"Is Mutti even here?" She rubbed her eyes with her filthy hands.

"I don't know. I can't answer that."

"I'm afraid to dig."

"We should stop for the night." Who knew what they might uncover? He didn't want Gisela to see the ghastly sights he encountered digging through the neighbor's rubble. Didn't want her to find her mum like that.

Kurt helped her stand. "Let me look tomorrow while you stay

with the girls. Right now you need a little food in your stomach and a washcloth."

She allowed him to help her slide down the mass of bricks to the street. An acrid smell filled the air. Fires burned here and there.

The second alarm rang.

Gisela sprung to life. "Annelies. Renate. I can't be away from them during the raid."

She stared at the debris, now a coffin for how many? They had been so focused on Gisela's mum, they hadn't thought about the other occupants of the building. The mother with the gaggle of children. The old people.

She tugged at the sleeves of her sweater. "What do I do? Where do I go? Mutti? The girls?"

The sun had just peeped above the horizon, painting the world in red and orange, not yet chasing away the shadows. The streets remained quiet, an eerie silence, as Mitch, Gisela, and Kurt walked to the Cramers' destroyed building from Frau Mueller's place, a world holding its breath waiting to explode.

Mitch held his breath too.

Viewing the destruction at this hour, from this distance, brought the reality home to him. On block after block, not one stone remained on top of another. Other buildings were burned-out skeletons, dark against the radiant sky.

Twenty-four hours ago, this had been a thriving neighborhood. Today, nothing but ashes. In the distance, a dog barked.

Gisela stumbled as she picked up her pace, nearing what had once been her home. Mitch caught her elbow and prevented her fall. "You'll get there soon enough."

While Mitch had been able to tear Gisela away from the girls, promising to return to their temporary home the second the air-raid sirens blared, he could not prevent Kurt from accompanying them. He stuck like wallpaper to Gisela's side. Wallpaper Mitch wanted to rip away.

"We won't get there soon enough." Gisela continued at her breakneck speed. "It's chilly and Mutti had to spend the night down there, in the dark, in the cold."

Whether she was a glass half-full sort of person or an I'm-not-even-going-to-look-at-the-glass kind of girl, Mitch didn't know. She walked erect. Something fueled hope in her.

He wanted to warn her, to prepare her for what they might find today, but without deflating her. When the time came, they would deal with whatever they unearthed.

Digging in the daylight proved to be much more efficient than searching at dusk. They removed a large amount of debris in a short period of time, great chunks of plaster and smashed bricks.

Mitch uncovered a mattress, its top shredded.

And below he discovered a hand.

TWENTY-SEVEN

M itch stood in the rubble, unmoving beside Gisela. A strangled cry escaped his lips, his face as pale as last night's moon.

She followed his gaze downward. She gagged. Turning to the side, she fell to her knees and lost her small breakfast.

It was a hand. A human hand, fingers mangled and bloodied, blue and swollen.

He held her shoulders as she retched again, her hair clinging to her cheek.

At last empty inside, she sat back, trembling. She steeled herself for the answer before whispering the question. "Who?"

"It looks like an older woman's hand. The knuckles are too gnarled to belong to a younger person."

Mutti had arthritis in her hands, the result of decades of hard work. Her fingers bent and twisted in odd directions. She had been in the basement finishing the laundry . . .

Gisela shivered, unable to control the tremors. Her heart seemed to stop beating and she had to remind herself to breathe. "God, not Mutti. Not her, Lord."

Mitch kissed her forehead and wrapped his arm around her,

helping her to her feet. For a few moments, they stood together and her shudders calmed under his gentle touch.

Kurt arrived next to her and pulled her away from Mitch. She was bereft and reached out for Mitch, the man she knew without a doubt she loved, but the German soldier led her to the stoop. "I will keep digging. You don't need to see any more."

She agreed. Never would she forget the picture of those protruding fingers. Already horrific images bombarded her brain. The reality would be far worse.

As the men worked, she chewed on her broken fingernail. Others in the neighborhood came to dig, to try to find missing loved ones in the remains of their homes. She hid her face in the crook of her elbow. The nightmares of this day blended with those of a night not so long ago.

For a long while, she sat and tried not to think. The chill seeped through her bones, deep into her body.

The bricks and debris shifted as someone approached. He lowered himself beside her and rubbed her aching back. No comparison to the aching of her heart.

She didn't bother to lift her head, recognizing Mitch's touch. "I don't want to know what you have to tell me." If he didn't speak the words, it couldn't be true.

He smoothed her hair. "The hand belonged to the old man. His body shielded his wife's. We found the woman and three of her children. We don't know where the others are."

She shivered as if she had been in an icehouse for hours. "And Mutti?"

"No." Mitch's deep voice reverberated in the air.

She raised her head and stared into his compassionate brown eyes. "Not Mutti?"

"No. No sign of her. She wasn't home when the bombs fell."

"Then where is she?"

Mitch squeezed her. "You tell us. Think about it."

"I don't know." She forced herself to concentrate, to no avail. Her thoughts whirred too fast for her to catch them. "Are you telling me she is still alive?"

He nodded. "She isn't here. That much is for certain."

Across the street, wails rose up from the devastation. Another life snuffed out. And another. And another.

"I have no idea where to look. Her friends—but I'm not sure I remember where they live. Especially with so many landmarks gone, it looks like a different place. Did she go to the store? Which one? No one can give us those answers."

Mitch ran his hand through his scraggly dark hair and whispered, "You stay here. I'll see if Frau Mueller has some paint. We can leave a message for your mum so she knows where to find us. I imagine this will be the first place she will search for you."

Mitch and Kurt moved the bodies from the rubbish heap to the sidewalk and covered them with coats. Then Mitch left to get the paint. Gisela dared to move about, sifting through the rubble, not for her mother's body, but for anything salvageable.

Not much remained. She uncovered Annelies's doll and located a few pairs of socks. She gasped when her fingers touched the beautiful gold watch Vater had given her for her thirteenth birthday. The one that matched Margot's. With tears in her eyes, she slipped it on her wrist. Kurt handed her a pot and a pan along with a few spoons, a fork, and a knife.

He hovered over her as she sifted through their few worldly possessions. "I'm sorry about your mutti."

"Danke."

"I will do whatever it takes to find her. I will bring her home to you."

"If only you could."

"My uniform will help."

229

Gisela shook her head. "Your uniform means little now. The Russians will be here any day."

She turned her attention to her work. The corner of a book peeked out from underneath a smashed piece of furniture. The wood had splintered but hadn't caught fire. She tugged and it came free.

Her Bible.

Scars marred the brown leather cover, but the pages remained intact. She lowered herself to the step and flipped to Isaiah 43. The faded daisy lay in its hiding place in that passage. She touched the fragile paper. *Oh, Opa, I wish I knew what happened to you. But maybe it is best you don't know about Mutti.*

Mitch broke her reverie when he plunked down beside her, a tin of paint and a brush in his hand.

She showed him the watch on her wrist. "I can't believe it survived. My sister and I got identical watches. She is buried with hers. I thought mine had been buried too."

Mitch smiled. "I'm glad you found it."

"It's my last link with my sister."

He held out the brush to her. Kurt had moved to the back of the garden, searching the bushes for debris that had blown there.

Her hand quivered. "I can't do it. I'll make a mess of it and she won't be able to read where we've gone. And what if she doesn't come back? What if she was in another shelter that was hit?"

Mitch took the brush from her. "We'll find her."

"How do you know that?"

He slapped his thigh. "Listen, I haven't any guarantees. There are no guarantees in this mad world. Nothing is as it should be."

An insane mix of emotions surged through Gisela, things she couldn't explain. "I want you to make everything right again, to wake me from this nightmare, to take me away from here."

"I can't. These bodies over here—they aren't a dream or a

vision. They are reality. That's reality now. This is what Hitler has done for you." The words were harsh, but his tone soft.

"But I'm an American. I should be safe in our bungalow in California."

"You should leave Berlin for the west. We all should."

Screaming, shouting, crying came from up and down the block. The sounds reverberated in her head.

They echoed the sounds from another day.

Gisela and Heide and Lotta shared a bedroom upstairs. They were trapped, not knowing what to do. She wanted to shout for help but didn't want to draw attention to them. Heide and Lotta suggested hiding in the wardrobe or under the bed. But surely the Soviets would look in those places first thing.

"Gislea? Are you ill?"

Mitch. She wasn't there anymore.

"You were in a far-off place."

"In my head, I can still hear the Russians' heavy boots thunking as they made their way upstairs at my aunt's house in Goldap. I held my breath, afraid to make even so small of a noise as exhaling. I knew by the squeaks of the risers which step they were on. Any second they would burst through the door."

Her body trembled as if an earthquake rocked it. She couldn't stop. She drew a ragged breath.

Even as she spoke to Mitch, she felt herself drawn back there.

Without formulating a plan, she propped open the window and climbed to the porch roof. Her cousins closed the window behind her. What were they doing? Why didn't they climb out too? Without any other choice, she swung her legs over the edge and dropped to the ground.

She ran as fast as her legs could carry her, to the garden, where she hid under the hedge. It was cold, so very, very cold. The ground was damp and the chill seeped through her clothes. She stayed under there all night. No matter what, she couldn't shut out her cousins' screams.

The Russians found them.

When gunshots filled the night, their screams stopped.

Mitch gave her hand a squeeze, bringing her back to the present.

She rubbed her temples. "I ran away once. At the cost of two lives. No more running. Not for me. You go if you want. But leave me here."

Mitch wanted to shake Gisela. He hadn't left yet, knowing he could never talk her into coming west when the girls weren't well. And then he had fallen ill himself.

And now . . . Why didn't he leave? Just go. She was home. She would be fine here.

But that wasn't the truth. And he couldn't stand it if anything happened to this beautiful, headstrong, stubborn woman.

She fiddled with the gold watch on her wrist. "You see, if I had prodded Heide and Lotta out that window, we might have all survived. But I didn't. I thought only of myself."

If she hadn't, she wouldn't be here right now. "With the time it would have taken for all of you to get out the window, the troops might have caught them anyway. You don't know what would have happened. They chose not to come."

Just as his chums had chosen to follow him, all because of his bragging. Couldn't they have found a map or followed someone else? But they trusted him. That was the worst. He broke that trust.

"I will never forget that night. Those sounds."

And he would never forget the sight of those German panzers. "How did you escape?"

"I ran. When morning came, I ran and ran, until a stitch in my side forced me to slow down. A few hours later, I caught up with a group of retreating German soldiers. They took me to Heiligenbeil. Don't you see? I survived. They didn't. Just like with Margot."

"You have to know it's not your fault."

"If I could go back and change things . . ."

"No what-might-have-beens. If God says not to worry about tomorrow, I would think the same applies to yesterday. There's enough trouble in the here and now to worry about how differently things could have turned out. You're talking to an expert on the matter. I'm world famous on what-might-have-beens." He came to her, and though she attempted to push him away, he didn't allow her.

Despite her protests, he held her close. Close enough to stroke the curls at the base of her neck. She buried her head in his shoulder. "Oh, Mitch, what a muddle I have made of my life."

"We all make messes."

"You too?"

"Yes."

"France. That's what you're talking about."

"And East Prussia. How could I have done it twice? Walked in circles?"

She turned her head so her ear was pressed to his chest. "Do you think this will all end?"

"It will. It has to." Either there would be a truce or they would all die. Heaven became more real to him with each passing day.

He peered at her, a ray of sunlight falling across her head, the golden highlights in her brown hair shining through the grime.

"I'm not sure I can keep going. God is punishing me for what I did. For what my country did. He may never relent until He has purged us from the earth."

"I have to believe He continues to love us. How else could we get out of bed every morning?"

She sat in his embrace a moment more before she pulled away. "We must get this notice painted. The girls need me. They have to be so frightened and confused. I never should have left them this morning."

She held the can of white paint and Mitch traced the letters of the words on the red bricks. He couldn't spell in German worth a lick, so she helped him, and they painted the message. They set the brick on the steps where Frau Cramer would be sure to see it.

"That's all we can do for now."

Gisela shook her head, her wonderful stubborn streak rearing its ugly head. "There's more."

She may have failed her cousins, but she wouldn't fail the girls and she wouldn't fail Mutti. Along with Mitch and Kurt, she picked her way the few blocks to Frau Mueller's place.

Dear Lord, let Mutti be here. Bitte, bitte.

She climbed the three stairs to the house's front door, her legs heavy, stiff. Her hand trembled when she turned the ornate brass knob. Mitch opened the heavy wood door for her. Mutti, she just knew, would be on the other side.

Two little blondes ran to her and wrapped themselves around her legs. "Tante Gisela, you're back, you're back."

"Ja, I am that." She looked into Frau Mueller's lined face, asking the question with her eyes.

Frau Mueller shook her head.

TWENTY-EIGHT

A udra sat on the couch, twisted her hands, then traced the green scroll pattern on the cream fabric. She stared at Gisela first, then Josep as they entered Frau Mueller's small home. "Did you find your mutti?"

Josep shook his head. "Nein. She may not have been at home at the time of the bomb."

She did pity Gisela. The not knowing had to be terrifying. "I'm so sorry." She bustled to her feet and hurried to the kitchen, calling over her shoulder, "You look exhausted, both of you. I will get you coffee and a damp towel."

Audra walked the tightrope with care—not allowing Gisela to go to England with Josep while befriending her. Within minutes she returned to the living room and handed him the coffee, along with the towel.

His face crinkled in concern. "Where are the girls?"

Audra rubbed his arm. "Napping."

Gisela turned in the direction of the narrow stairway that led to the guestroom the girls occupied. "I'll go and lie down with them."

Audra staked a claim on the davenport beside him. "Have a good rest. Sleep for as long as you can."

She waited for the bedroom door to click shut. Josep stared into the depths of his coffee cup.

"Kurt didn't come with you."

"He went to look for Frau Cramer."

Ah, ja. Play the part of the hero. Perfect. She would take on the role of comforter. "You must be tired too."

"Where are Frau Mueller and the Holtzmann sisters?"

"Out on a search for more rations." Which meant they were alone.

Josep set his cup on the glossy walnut end table and stretched.

"Are you sore from so much work?" She grabbed him by the shoulders and began to rub them.

His muscles were taut under her fingers. She worked the knots and one by one they loosened as he relaxed. He groaned, then sat straight and pulled away. "I shouldn't have let you do that."

"Yes, you should have. You are so good to Gisela. She doesn't appreciate you enough. You need someone to take care of you."

"Like all of us, she is having a hard time."

In a flash, she determined the moment was right for a gamble. "But she's not your wife. That's a great sacrifice on your part. You would be back with your countrymen now if not for her."

"I wouldn't be alive if not for her."

"I think you would have been fine."

He rose. "I want to peek in on Gisela and make sure she is sleeping."

She wanted to shout at him. What did that woman have that she didn't? Why was he so devoted to her when she didn't deserve it?

Instead, she bit her lip.

Near noon the next day, Mitch held Gisela's elbow to keep her steady as they walked among the ruins of what had once been one of Europe's grandest cities. Hitler had brought her to her knees. Parks had been turned into gardens, homes into graveyards, a city into a wasteland.

He had waited until the usual morning air raid was over to venture out. Both the Americans and the Brits had become systematic in their bombings. They learned to plan their days by them.

Yesterday had been different, though. The air raids had been more frequent. Last night the eastern sky had burned red. The Soviets crept ever closer. Almost close enough to touch.

Gisela struggled over the decision to leave the girls while she conducted the search for her mum. He promised her they would be fine for a while and she consented with great reluctance.

She stopped and massaged the back of her neck. "I don't even know where to start looking for Mutti. My landmarks are gone. Even if I knew which friends to inquire of, I have no idea how to get to them."

"Then ask. Just step up to any of these people on the street and question them."

She pressed her lips in a thin line. Fear and hope blended together on her face, tiny lines accenting her wide eyes.

"Do you want me to do it?"

"You shouldn't be out, much less speaking. You could be hanged as a coward for not fighting for the Fatherland."

Wasn't that what he was? A coward for not fighting for his fatherland?

He slid his right arm from his jacket's sleeve and pressed it against his side. "Now I'm a hero. No one will question me."

She flashed him a dubious look, her brow furrowed. "Just don't say anything."

A scouring of area hospitals turned up nothing. No one matching her mum's description had been admitted at any medical institution.

They spent the waning hours of the afternoon knocking on doors. Many of the places they went to look had also been bombed out. So many displaced.

At each residence, the answer was the same. No one had seen Gisela's mum.

Now they stood listening to bad news for the tenth time that afternoon from a plump hausfrau. "I'm sorry. She isn't here. If she should come, I will tell her you are looking for her."

Gisela turned away, her shoulders humped. "I have run out of places to look. I can't think of where she might be."

"Probably either at Frau Mueller's sipping a cup of that stuff that passes for coffee or out looking for you."

"Mitch, I'm scared." She spoke in English, her voice hoarse. "What if we're separated forever?"

"That won't happen. It might take a little bit of time, but you will find her. You're too stubborn not to find her." He couldn't let her sink into despair.

She tipped her head to the side and brushed a strand of hair from her eyes. "Thank you for those encouraging words." The pins that held the rolls on the top of her head had come loose. Here, in the middle of a war zone, in the midst of all this death, he wanted to pull out all of those pins and run his fingers through the length of it.

He forced himself to turn away and keep to the topic at hand. He propelled her forward with a slight touch to the small of her back. "You need to rest."

Like a little child, she allowed him to lead her home. At each corner, he verified that they were headed in the right direction. She answered only with a nod or shake of her head.

The streetcar, limited as it was in its run, clanged a few streets over. Women hustled past, heading home with the meager food-stuffs they had bought for their families.

And then he peered at Gisela once more.

Mitch couldn't stand it. She looked defeated. Deflated. Done in. About a block from the apartment building, he stopped. She turned to look at him, her amber eyes full of questions.

He drew her close, could feel her heart beating furiously against his chest. She trembled much like the little bird he rescued from the ground when he was a child. Gone was the stubborn, infuriating woman. For a moment, she leaned against him, her arms snug around his middle.

He breathed in her amazingly fresh scent. "You aren't alone."

"I know."

"I'm going to stay with you. Through the rest of this crazy war, I'll stay with you."

She pushed away from him, her gaze directed over his shoulder.

Gisela blinked and blinked again, staring over Mitch's shoulder. A woman turned down the block. The woman's shape, posture, and gait were all familiar. The way she bustled about with an air of purpose and efficiency.

She pushed herself out of Mitch's embrace. "Mutti? Mutti?"

He spun around, following her line of vision. "Is that your mum?"

Gisela nodded. "Mutti!"

The woman never looked up. She didn't acknowledge her call. He held her arm, but Gisela slipped from his grasp and marched toward her mother. "Mutti."

The figure turned down a side street. Where was she going? Thankful this block had sustained little damage, Gisela sprinted in Mutti's direction. Hadn't she heard her daughter calling? "Mutti!"

Her lungs cried out from the exertion, but she ignored their protests. In the matter of half a block, she caught up to her mother. "Mutti."

The woman pivoted and looked around. "Are you talking to me?"

It couldn't be. The woman matched Mutti in size and stature, her plain brown coat just like her mother's. But the eyes were wrong and so was the tilt of her chin. Gisela's heart slammed against her ribs. "I'm so sorry. I thought you were someone else."

The woman nodded, turned, and walked away. Mitch came huffing beside her.

"It looked so much like her. She even walked like Mutti does, like she has a very important place she has to be. But it wasn't her. How could it not have been her?" Disappointment exploded in her stomach.

Mitch opened his mouth, sure to apologize again. His words would sound like teeth against a metal spoon.

"Don't say you're sorry. Please, don't say that anymore. I can't stand it. You didn't do anything. I did. I left my mother to do the laundry. And now she is—where? We don't know. We may never know. What do I do?"

"We can figure it out later. Right now, let's go home."

Home?

She didn't have a home.

Kurt wandered the desolate streets. The setting sun cast a red glow in the western sky, and Russian artillery fire colored the eastern sky crimson. The cool air refreshed him for a brief moment. Weak from months of hunger, he became winded far sooner than a man his age should.

All day, he had searched for Gisela's mutti. If he found her, Gisela would owe him a debt of thanks he intended for her to repay.

He had pondered turning in Josep numerous times. Only his concern that Gisela would mourn for the man caused him to hesitate. He could comfort her in her grief, but would she recover from another loss?

Nein, the situation demanded that he proceed with care.

And he had been unable to locate Frau Cramer. He balled his single fist in frustration. The woman had disappeared from the face of the earth. Not uncommon these days, but he had hoped to bring the best of news to Gisela tonight. Before Josep got the chance to play the hero.

Before Kurt lost the music forever.

He came to the bombed-out apartment building. The bodies he had helped lay in a row this morning reposed under their coats.

For a while, he paused in front of them, silent, his mind abuzz with ideas to impress Gisela. He tossed each away like the morning trash. Until one idea came and refused to leave.

He didn't relish the idea of ransacking the dead. To him, it resembled stealing far too much. But then he imagined Gisela's face when he brought home more ration coupons. Perhaps the dead woman had coupons for extra milk for the kinder. Gisela would run into his outstretched arm and kiss him on the cheek.

He rummaged through the pockets of the old couple that took in Bettina and Katya. A few cards, partially used.

He came to the bodies of the woman and three of her children. They hadn't found the others. As he reached into the pockets of the coats that covered them, he diverted his eyes from the children's bloated faces.

Just little kids, full of life, full of promise.

What are we doing here? Is this what I gave my arm for? What Hitler demanded of them? And all for what?

He sat back on his haunches and went to rub his right arm, the pain in it growing in intensity. Nothing but air met his hands.

Off in the distance, the air-raid sirens screamed their warning yet again. How many did this make today? He had lost count.

The cards he pulled from the children's pockets would be able to supplement the meager bit of milk the girls were allowed each day.

At least one small victory for him in Gisela's eyes.

Mitch sat on the hard kitchen chair, swirling water in his coffee cup. The walls of the small room closed in on him. In the living room, Gisela reclined on the couch, her head back, mouth open. At least she had given in to sleep. Light from the marble-based lamp spilled onto her hair, which shimmered gold.

He wanted to bang on the wobbly table. Why hadn't they been able to locate her mum? More than anything, he wanted to erase the worry and fear clouding her eyes. She stooped like an old woman. Was this what war did to them?

The sagging front door opened and Kurt stepped inside, peeling off his brown officer's coat and hanging it on the peg. He scanned the living room, a glint touching his cold eyes when he found Gisela.

He sat beside her and she stirred. "I'm sorry. I didn't mean to wake you."

Mitch detected very little sincerity in his words.

Gisela sat upright, searching Kurt's hard face. "Do you have news? Did you find Mutti?"

He shook his head.

She slumped.

"But I did come home with a good thing." He reached inside his shirt pocket.

Mitch wandered into the living room.

Kurt pulled out a handful of ration cards. "Extra milk for the girls."

A smile, small but there, lit Gisela's face. "Oh, Kurt, danke. This is so good. I've been worried about them since they were sick. They will have a few extra calories at least. When Ella comes for them, they will be more than just bones." She brushed her lips against Kurt's angular cheek.

Mitch's stomach boiled. His words slithered from between his teeth. "Where did you get them?"

A muscle jumped in Kurt's jaw.

Gisela waved him off. "I don't want to know. I don't care. This is the best gift I have ever received. Better than any Christmas present. Only Mutti coming home would have topped this."

Mitch turned and stomped back to the kitchen, choosing to sit in the chair with his back to the living room.

Gisela may not have cared to know where the ration cards came from, but Mitch had an idea. If she ever found out, she would be horrified to know that Annelies and Renate drank dead children's milk.

TWENTY-NINE

Gisela waited in the long bread queue with Audra, clutching her purse strap like it was cemented to her hand. The patent leather of the rectangular-shaped pocketbook was scuffed and scarred, but its cargo was precious. It held the extra ration coupons Kurt had procured.

A look of triumph had hardened his angular features. He had grabbed her around the waist and twirled her around the living room, whooping. Mitch had tried to sour the moment, but she wouldn't let him. At this time, she needed good news and relished in it.

The extra coupons came in very handy today. The twentieth of April. Hitler's birthday.

They had been told they were to be given an eight-day ration. And it appeared as if that was the case—a tin of vegetables, a few ounces of sugar, and a tiny bit of real coffee. What a treat that would be. And with the extra coupons, they would have even more.

Audra shifted her weight from one foot to the other. "You must be eager to return to America."

Gisela nodded. "Though I will miss Josep very much."

"But you won't go to England?" Audra sounded almost insistent.

"Why do you ask?"

"You're from America. That's where you want to go. And England is so cold and rainy. Maybe we could go to America together."

Gisela shrugged. "Perhaps." A movement across the street caught her eye. There stood a young boy, no more than thirteen years old, not yet grown, not yet matured, holding a rifle as large as himself. His drab brown uniform hung from his shoulders and his pants legs dragged on the ground. He had cinched a rope around his waist to hold up his trousers. A shock of yellow-blond hair stuck out from under a cap with a hatband that buckled at the bottom.

Today the artillery sounded closer than ever. She and Audra didn't want to be out, standing in line, waiting for food. But it couldn't be helped. They had to eat. They had taken to cooking on the old wood stove in the basement. They resided in the shelter these days, to save energy from running up and down the stairs during the almost-continuous air raids. No one minded the mice and the spiders as much as they once did.

Gisela had thought about taking the girls with her this morning, then decided to leave them at home with Mitch. The choice was easy. Out here, no one was safe. The Luftwaffe had been all but wiped out and the Allied planes met little resistance. The air-raid sirens didn't always sound.

She couldn't risk having Mitch go out. He drew too much unwelcome attention unless he pretended to have lost an arm. And then he wouldn't be able to carry as many provisions. With eight days of rations, perhaps they would have enough for the duration. The next time they had to venture out, maybe the skies would be quiet.

Though the wait was lengthy, the queue picked up speed more than other days. Today women hurried home, their precious bundles hidden beneath their coats.

Explosions rocked the ground and rang in Gisela's ears. She shivered and hugged herself. "That shelling is so close. Right in the middle of city by the way it sounds."

Audra nodded. "When will the Americans come?"

Since the death of President Roosevelt, Frau Mueller had been pulling out her battery-operated radio and listening to the BBC for a short time each night. They both knew the Americans wouldn't come. "Sixty miles away and they are letting the Red Army do all of the work. With the Russians, we trade one bad thing for another."

The women around them murmured in agreement. A tall, thin lady shook her head. "The Soviets are already at Seelow Heights and Baruth. It won't be long now."

Suburban Berlin. Mere kilometers away. No, it wouldn't be long now. Not long at all. And then what would happen to them?

Another loud explosion shook the ground. Oh, for it to be still for a moment. Often it felt like they were on a ship on the ocean, the land under their feet always swaying.

Every few minutes, she glanced at the very young man nearby standing guard. If only she could help him. The Nazis robbed him of his childhood—and likely, his life.

Audra shifted her weight from one foot to the other, the worn-through toe of her brown lace-up shoes stuffed with paper. "Josep gave me some of his rations yesterday. He said a beautiful woman like me shouldn't be so thin."

Gisela turned her attention from the boy-soldier. Why on earth would Audra tell her such a thing? "That was kind of him. He is a good man." A good man who made her heart flutter in a much different way than falling bombs made it pound.

"I notice the way he looks at me. He thinks I don't see him, but I do. He has invited me to meet his family in England when the war is over."

Gisela tapped the heel of her oxford on the pitted pavement. He had never spoken such words to her. Had he turned his sights on Audra? Did he stay to be near her?

Everything was crumbling around her. All of these days and no sign of Mutti. Gisela struggled to hold out hope for her. Now Mitch was interested in Audra.

Her heart shattered like the panes of glass during *Kristallnacht*. By the end of the war, she would have nothing left.

They spoke no more as they waited their turn. At last they reached the counter and presented their coupons and their money. As they exited, they clutched the precious packages to their chests, unwilling to lose even one crumb.

The boy with the rifle remained rooted to his spot. As anxious as she was to get back to the girls, the young man intrigued her. She broke off course and headed toward him.

A fat tear rolled down the child's sunken cheek.

Gisela handed him her handkerchief. "What are you doing here?"

"I was told to stand here. I have to shoot the Soviets when they come." His entire body, head to toe, trembled, his voice high and clear.

Her temperature rose a few degrees. How could those Nazis recruit children to fight a lost cause? It was one thing to draft old men like her father, but this . . . "Are you scared?"

He straightened his spine and clutched his weapon so his knuckles turned white. "I am not."

"Do you want to kill people?"

"Ja." But the tremor in his voice exposed him.

"Why don't you go home to your mutti?"

"Because the SS will hang me and shoot Mutti. I don't want anything bad to happen to her."

If the boy stayed and shot at the Soviets as they entered the city, he would die for sure. Gisela scratched her forehead. Either way, the kid was doomed.

"What is your name?"

"Jorgen."

"How old are you?"

"Thirteen."

"What are you going to do, Jorgen?"

"Stay here, build my trench, and fight the Russians."

At thirteen, this boy hadn't begun to live life yet.

"The Red Army will be here soon." His words were brave, even as his gun slipped from his grip and clattered to the ground. He hurried to retrieve it, and his hand shook when he reached for his weapon.

Another loud burst of artillery rang through the air. Gisela's head pounded and her ears buzzed. She grabbed Jorgen by the hand. "Let's get out of here."

"What on earth are you doing?" Audra shouted at Gisela, but she chose to ignore Audra. She couldn't close her eyes to the boy with the face of trust and innocence.

So much like the faces of her cousins.

The threesome ran through the streets of Berlin, around the wreckage, over heaps of rubble, Gisela clutching a package of food in one hand and with the other pulling Jorgen behind her. When she turned to him, he held to that menacing-looking weapon.

"Drop it. Drop the gun."

He shook his head.

She had to make him obey her. "Get rid of it or we'll get shot."

Again he shook his head.

Gisela's heart pounded in her chest, her lungs ready to explode. "Drop it."

At last he flung it away. They continued to run. She pulled

harder on Jorgen's arm to keep him going. "We are almost there."
Another round of artillery fire crackled not far from them.

Audra pulled ahead of them. "Keep going. Come on."

Nothing had ever looked as beautiful as the war-scarred building where seven frightened people huddled in the lower level.
Counting Audra and herself and now Jorgen, that brought their
total to ten.

Gisela pushed Jorgen up the steps. Once inside, they paused,
hands on their knees. Her breathing and heart rate refused to slow.

Mitch clattered up the stairs to greet them. "Who is he?"

"This boy, a mere thirteen-year-old child, stands guard on
the corner by the grocer, ready to shoot the Russians when they
arrive."

"Tell me you didn't."

"I did. I had to. He faced certain death there. At least here, he
has a chance."

Mitch touched her face and her cheek burned where his fingertips rested. She wanted to kiss his palm. Then she heard Audra
harrumph and remembered her earlier words.

"You are beautiful. Exasperating, but beautiful." Mitch touched
the small of her back. "We had better get downstairs."

The shriek of bombs falling drove them forward. The Russians
were shelling them while the Allies conducted an air raid. In
America, they would call this "double trouble."

She got Jorgen settled on the bench that ran along one wall.
He hadn't said a word to them since they took off. He wrung his
hands together, looking more like a playmate for Annelies than a
warrior.

"Any word about Mutti?"

Mitch shook his head. He needed a bath and a shave. "Nein.
No one has come."

"Is the message still there?"

He nodded. "I checked this morning. No one has posted any-thing else."

"Why can't we find her? Why has no one come to us with information? Where is she?"

Mitch rubbed her arm. She backed away. "I don't need comfort. I need Mutti."

A bomb burst nearby, so close that limestone from the ceiling rained on them. "I wish I knew what to say to you."

"Say you have found her."

"What about the boy?"

"He's staying here." She switched to English so Jorgen wouldn't know what she said. "If the SS comes, we will have to hide him. Maybe dress him like a little girl. Keep him safe. He was going to die out there. I can't leave a child to die."

"If they discover Jorgen here, the SS will kill every one of us."

"You pose as much of a threat. You could be hung or shot as a deserter. Every one of us in here stands in peril. We have to make sure neither the SS nor the Soviets find any of us."

That task would be harder than climbing the Alps.

Mitch flicked a glance at Jorgen. The boy sat on the hard wood bench, his shoulders slumped, his eyes closed. "I'm not unsympa-thetic to his plight, but I've a responsibility to you and the others in the house. I need to protect you. My job just got a lot tougher."

"I couldn't leave him there. I couldn't."

He understood. Gisela collected waifs like other people col-lected porcelain figurines.

"Are you angry with me?" Hurt and disappointment radiated from her eyes.

"No. I can't blame you. I'm not sure I'd have had your courage. It was risky."

"You won't send him away?"

That would sign the boy's death sentence. "No, I won't. But you had better get working on a disguise for him. And burn the uniform. His, Kurt's, anything that would link us to Hitler, the Nazis, the army." Good thing Herr Cramer's books had all been destroyed along with their flat. The Soviets would have no mercy on any Nazi sympathizers. "And bury anything of value. Get rid of it. The Russians will take whatever they can lay their hands on."

Bettina clucked. "What are we burying, dearies? Hidden treasure? Could we search for it? What a fun game that would be."

Katya bounced Renate on her knee. "Oh my, ja. Is there a treasure map? We have to have clues where to look."

Gisela ignored them. "What if they find us? Then what?"

He refused to think about the possibility. *Lord, protect them. I can't do it.*

Then the loudest whistle he ever heard headed straight for them.

Audra screamed and clutched his arm.

His breathing ceased, and he couldn't feel his heart beating. He locked his knees and braced for impact. For the explosion and searing heat.

For death.

THIRTY

Mitch closed his eyes. The whistle of the approaching bomb pierced his eardrums. The others in the shelter screamed.

The ground shook and the upstairs windows rattled.

God, save us!

Then silence.

He counted to ten and started to breathe, then dared to open his eyes. He wrenched his arm from Audra's embrace. She resisted. The pressure of her touch reassured him that he wasn't dreaming.

Or dead.

He wilted in relief, his arms and legs going weak.

The others lifted their heads. A little at a time, they began to speak. They laughed and patted each other on the back. "We're alive."

Audra leaned against his chest. "We almost died." Her green eyes filled with tears.

"Almost."

Annelies whimpered in the background.

Audra batted her just-about-white eyelashes. "You protected us."

He sat back from her, steadying her with his hand, which he released as soon as she straightened. "Nein. Only God did."

"Where did it land?" Gisela, sitting on the bed across from him with the girls, spoke in his direction but didn't look into his eyes.

"Very close. In the garden, perhaps. Stay here. I'm going to check it out."

Gisela leaned toward him. "Nein. Don't you go out there. If it was a bomb, it could explode at any time."

He switched to English, not knowing the German for what he needed to say. "If it made it from the plane to the ground without going off, it's not likely to do so anytime soon. Just as a precaution, let me see what landed next to us."

She shot nervous glances at the girls and at him. Hurt and uncertainty colored her face.

"Stay here. I will be fine, I promise."

Kurt commandeered the spot next to her. "Ja, stay here with me and you will be safe."

Mitch's shoulders tensed. He turned and took the stairs two at a time and was soon blinking in the sunlight. The day was warm and calm.

He climbed over piles of rubble. He crept around the corner of the building, staying low, ready to hit the ground at any instant if the bomb should explode. Not that he would have a chance to react. And there, in the garden, a giant crater gaped where potatoes and cabbages had grown. Stepping lightly, going a few paces closer, he saw the tail fins of the bomb. The body of it was as large as a man's torso.

The real deal.

Thank You, Lord.

If this shell had detonated as intended, there would be ten dead people in the building's shelter.

His knees wavered and he sank to the ground, trembling.

Images of the carnage this bomb could have delivered slashed through his mind like a picture show. The blood in his veins turned to ice.

He hadn't stopped it like Audra gave him credit for. Nothing he did prevented the tragedy. He sat helpless in the basement, awaiting the end.

But it hadn't come.

"Why?" The word echoed in the soft breeze.

No sooner had the thought escaped his lips than he knew the answer.

God.

Only God.

Only Him.

He spared their lives. He watched over them all the way from the POW camp in East Prussia, through Danzig, and their days in Berlin. In fact, God had allowed the Germans to capture Mitch so he would spend the bulk of the war far from harm.

The warmth of God's presence flooded him and he shrugged off his jacket, looking to the heavens. "You are here, Lord, aren't You?"

A breeze tickled the back of his neck and a ray of sun warmed his face.

On his own, he was as useless as a puff of air against a brick building. It didn't matter what he did or where he went. God had his life under His control.

Even if this bomb in front of him had discharged, God would have kept him safe and delivered Mitch to his heavenly home.

In the recesses of his mind, he heard his father's voice reading the Bible the night before he left home. *Hear my cry, O God; attend unto my prayer. From the end of the earth will I cry unto thee, when my heart is overwhelmed: lead me to the rock that is higher than I. For thou hast been a shelter for me, and a strong tower from the enemy.*

He could hear the pop of the fire on the hearth and smell his father's cigar. *I learned these verses from Psalm 61 when I fought in the*

Great War." His large hand caressed the Bible page. *"You would do well to remember them, no matter what happens in your life."*

These words from his father were wise. Whether or not they agreed about the course Mitch's life should take, his father had Mitch's best interest at heart. He didn't want his son to experience the hardships of war. He knew them well enough. All too well.

Mitch sat on the ground, head in his hands, for a long while, enjoying the feeling of peace and contentment. He had done the best he could under the worst of conditions in Belgium and France. No one knew where to go. No one saw the panzers coming.

And in the heat of battle, God had kept most of his chums alive. Captured, facing hardship, but breathing. If they had been able to return to England and then back to the battlefield, how many of them would be alive today? Perhaps not any of them.

An object blocked out the sun, cooling Mitch's back. He turned and Gisela stood behind him. He hadn't heard her coming.

"What are you doing?"

He stood, his legs cramped. He stretched his muscles. "That is a bomb, no doubt, but it never exploded."

"A dud."

"Yes, a dud. God sent us a dud."

Gisela stared at the rusty-looking metal bomb. "Wow." That was the only word her tumultuous brain could conjure.

"That's a good word for it."

"We came so close to dying." Dying. She should be dead now. A tremor passed through her body.

"Very close. But God took care of us. He is the one who delivered us."

"A poor bomb maker in the Soviet Union delivered us."

"No, God did. What could you and I have done to prevent this shell from detonating?"

She studied the small crater. Mitch had a point. "Nothing. We were helpless."

"Don't you see? God is the one who, as the hymn says, brought us safely thus far." In the midst of the battle, the heartbreak and sorrow, he lifted his beautiful tenor voice.

> *Amazing grace! How sweet the sound*
> *that saved a wretch like me!*
> *I once was lost, but now am found;*
> *was blind, but now I see.*

> *'Twas grace that taught my heart to fear,*
> *and grace my fears relieved;*
> *how precious did that grace appear*
> *the hour I first believed.*

She joined him, adding her alto harmony.

> *Through many dangers, toils, and snares,*
> *I have already come;*
> *'tis grace hath brought me safe thus far,*
> *and grace will lead me home.*

> *The Lord has promised good to me,*
> *his word my hope secures;*
> *he will my shield and portion be,*
> *as long as life endures.*

> *Yea, when this flesh and heart shall fail,*
> *and mortal life shall cease,*

I shall possess, within the veil,
a life of joy and peace.

They had come a long way. A very long way, through many trials and peril. "He has, hasn't He?"

"Do you know this in your head or in your heart?"

She didn't have an answer for that question. "We have no guarantee that we will live to see our liberation. No promise that you will ever see England again, or that I will see America. No assurance that you and Audra will get married."

He scrunched his dark eyebrows. "What? Married?"

She dismissed him with a wave of her hand. "It doesn't matter."

"It matters to me. I don't understand what you just said."

"You do."

"I really don't."

"Listen, we need to let the rest of the people in the cellar know about your discovery. We can finish talking about this later." Much, much later.

Although Mitch continued looking puzzled, they went inside together. He stopped her in the front hall. "Think about what I said. You and I have been so busy trying to make up for past wrongs, but we can't. God forgives. He protects. He gives life and takes it away."

It sounded so simple, to absolve herself of her guilt that way.

But she couldn't shake the truth that she had abandoned her cousins when they needed her most. And Opa and Ella and Herr Holtzmann. And Mutti. She had failed so many.

The next three days passed in a haze. The shelling in the nearby suburbs was constant.

The Soviets had the city surrounded.

The noose tightened.

The battle for Berlin raged.

The basement filled with people grew stuffy and confining. They had moved the couch, the kitchen table and chairs, and another bed downstairs. They lived here, ate here, slept here. Gisela was boxed in. The old women chatted about Paris and London and New York without ceasing. Where in the world they went on holiday changed on any given day. Any given moment.

Audra clung to Mitch. Kurt continued to sidle up to Gisela. With Mitch ensnared in Audra's clutches, perhaps she should turn her attention to the German soldier. He had never been unkind to her and had always been attentive.

Just the thought of Mitch made her heart thrum as if she had run a marathon.

It didn't kick up even a notch around Kurt. In time, could she love him, or would she always think of the British soldier with longing?

She studied Kurt's angular profile, handsome in a very Aryan way. Then she caught a glimpse of Mitch, his dimples creasing his face. Goose bumps broke out over her arms.

Renate crawled on her lap and stroked her cheek in the way children have. "Why sad, Tante Gisela?"

"Oh yes, dearie, you should not be sad when in Copenhagen. This is such a cosmopolitan city." Bettina waved her hands in front of her face. "And the food is the best in the world. Listen to the band striking up a tune. It makes me want to dance."

Mitch caught Bettina's wrist and kept her in her seat. "That's not music. For now, you had better stay here. We can dance later."

"We can dance here." Bettina pulled Annelies to her feet. "This dance hall is nice enough. Let me show you how to do the fox-trot."

The little girl giggled as she made a clumsy attempt to follow Bettina's zigzagging steps. Annelies stepped on her partner's toes more often than not.

Gisela pinched her nose to keep from crying. Mutti and Vater had waltzed like they were gliding across the floor. It was magical to watch them. Oh, that they might come home.

Renate bounced on Audra's lap. "Me too. I want to dance."

Katya rose to oblige the child. "I hope you are a better dancer than that other girl."

Renate nodded, solemn as could be. "I dance good."

"I am glad to hear that."

Gisela couldn't help but laugh as Renate did more hopping than dancing. Her laughter died when she noticed the way Audra stared at Mitch. Without words, she was inviting him to dance.

Katya paused in the middle of humming a tune. "You do dance very well, even though you could be a bit taller."

Across the room, Jorgen slumped in his seat, arms crossed over his chest. She thought that once she rescued him from standing sentry, he would open up and blossom. Instead, he hunkered on the hard bench, face downcast all of the time. He had said not more than two or three words since he arrived.

Gisela slapped her thighs and went to him, holding out her hand. "Will you dance with me?"

He shook his head.

She shifted her weight to her left foot and tapped her right. "Dance with me. A man shouldn't leave a woman sitting alone during a waltz."

Again Jorgen refused.

She lowered herself on the bench beside him and he scooted over. "Why won't you join in the fun?"

The artillery fire picked up in intensity, a brief spurt of machine guns.

"I don't want to."

"That's not a reason. My mutti never accepted that answer from me."

He pivoted to face her, his blue eyes blazing. "You aren't my mutti."

"I know that."

"She will be mad that you took me away. Mutti said I had to protect the Fatherland and Herr Hitler."

"You didn't want to sit out there with that gun."

"I don't want to be in trouble. I don't want to get you in trouble."

Gisela rubbed his back, afraid he would pull away. He didn't. "The Russians will be here in a day or two. Then it won't matter. It will be over and you can go home to your mutti. That is a gift I don't have."

His shoulders relaxed and the grimacing mask he wore melted away. The hard soldier persona left and he was a boy again.

"Now, come and dance and have a little bit of fun."

Gisela grabbed him by the hand and led him to the makeshift dance floor. He moved like a wooden toy soldier, but when Annelies and Renate fell to the floor in a puddle of giggles, a smile raced across his face.

Kurt came to her side and held out his hand. No smile crossed his hard features. "I am afraid I cannot hold you properly, but would you care to dance?"

And what could she say to that? Turn him down and hurt his feelings? He made the best of his disability and she didn't care to crush him. No matter how uncomfortable he made her. "I don't dance well."

"Neither do I, so it will matter not if I step on your toes."

She acquiesced and he pulled her a little too close to himself for a ballroom dance. They moved across the concrete floor, a cross between gliding and stumbling. Audra and Mitch sailed past them with pro-like grace.

Gisela shivered. She didn't glance into Mitch's chocolate eyes. To see his love for Audra written there would be worse than the pain from her blisters.

THIRTY-ONE

April 23

Frau Mueller bounded down the wood steps to the house's bunker, no doubt spilling much of the precious water she had risked her life for at the public pump. Her round face was red and she was breathless.

She set the bucket on the concrete floor and drew in several deep breaths. A tendril of gray hair had come loose from its pins and curled across her cheek. "You will never believe what I am to tell you."

Gisela sat forward, anticipation tickling her toes. The barest of hopes ran through her. "Tell us."

The rest of the cellar denizens, old and young, chimed in, each straining forward.

"She is going to tell us that she has arranged for a gondolier to row us around the canals of Venice." Katya's blue eyes gleamed in delight.

"Nein, not that." Frau Mueller's face returned to a more normal color. "Everyone at the pump was talking about it. The streets are abuzz because the government has been holding out on us. They have warehouses full of food—meat, vegetables, milk powder, flour, sugar—whatever you can imagine. People are running to get some before the Russians take it all."

Mitch scrubbed the dark stubble on his cheek. "By get some, you mean without coupons or paying? Looting?"

"Call it what you want. If we don't get it today, the Russians will dig in while we go hungry. Better we have it than them."

Before Gisela could utter a word, Kurt grabbed her wrist with a bit too much force and pulled her to her feet. "We volunteer. As a soldier, I will get preferential treatment. Gisela will help me carry the provisions." He had, so far, refused to burn his uniform.

She pulled herself from his grasp and stepped back. "Nein. The SS will kill whoever loots."

Kurt's face hardened and he straightened his shoulders. His icy stare gave Gisela a chill. "They won't shoot an officer who gave an arm to the cause. No one is safer on the streets than I am."

She couldn't verify that statement. And she didn't want to risk it. "We have enough for a few more days. By then, this will be over and the store shelves will burst."

"We don't know that." Frau Mueller sat on the bed with a thump. "The Red Army will take retribution on us and leave us with nothing."

Audra stood. "I will go." She gazed in Mitch's direction, almost as if she hoped he would stop her.

Which he did. "No women. Just men."

Gisela grasped the lapel of her gray sweater, her hands sweaty. "Nein, not you. They will hang you on the lamppost."

He steered her to the side, away from the eight pairs of ears. "I've not done a thing all war. Nothing. Nothing brave or heroic. Nothing for my country. The least I can do, the very least, is provide food for a group of women and children."

She wanted to shout at him that he was stealing. Yet she had taken the dead woman's coat and shoes. And he had taken the beer for her foot, and she had said nothing. The government stole from them this entire war.

"Hitler has been holding out, leaving his citizens to die."

"If they find out you're British, it'll be worse for you."

"Worse than hanging as a deserter?" He brushed a strand of hair from her face, his fingertips light as a breath. "I'll go with Kurt." With that, he turned away.

Gisela hated the thought of him out there. He may have given his heart to Audra, but hers continued to long for him.

With each passing minute, the report of machine-gun fire grew ever closer. The Soviets penetrated into the suburbs of Berlin. They were a few short kilometers from the heart of the city. Not much of it remained.

Mitch scanned the scene around him. Frau Mueller had been right. Hordes of people—the brave, the hungry, and the crazy— streamed from their cellars toward the shops and warehouses. They carried bags and baskets, like he and Kurt did. Others pushed prams, minus the infants, in hopes of returning with a stockpile of supplies.

They joined the almost-festive throng. The sky might have been black with smoke, but the people had something to look forward to for the first time in many days.

"Audra is a beautiful woman." Kurt clapped Mitch on the shoulder.

He didn't answer.

"She is very gentle and caring. You have seen her with the kinder?"

"Ja. She is nice."

"She would be a fantastic wife for you."

Mitch stopped in his tracks. "Wife?" The same as Gisela had said.

It wasn't Audra's green eyes that had chased away his nightmares. It was Gisela's amber ones.

"Ja. She is devoted to you."

"I heard you. You want Gisela for your own." He turned to face his foe. In that moment, he knew his heart. "So do I. She is the one I want to be my wife."

Kurt stopped short, balling his fist. "I will never let you take her from me."

If he wanted a fight, Mitch would give him one. He clenched his hands and stepped forward. "You never had her."

The German swung. Mitch ducked and he missed. With all his might, Mitch punched Kurt in the stomach. He doubled over and Mitch threw an uppercut.

The crowd halted and gathered around, cheering. Fists flew. Mitch didn't think. Just swung. Kurt connected with his eye, the pain blinding him for a moment.

Kurt's disability didn't hamper his fighting ability. Mitch had to give it everything he had. His arms grew tired. His face throbbed. Kurt got him in the gut. A second passed before he was able to catch his breath.

All for a woman.

His father would hate what he was doing.

A man stepped forward from the crowd. He pushed Mitch and Kurt apart, though both continued to lunge at each other.

"You should be fighting the enemy, not each other. What shame you bring on your country."

Kurt relaxed. Mitch only dared to let his guard down a bit. He stayed prepared for another round of fisticuffs.

With one push, the man separated them farther. Mitch stumbled backward, fighting to maintain his balance. "Gisela." His breath came in spurts and sweat dripped down his back.

"Ja." Kurt also huffed.

"We have to get the food."

Kurt nodded. Mitch picked up the bags he had discarded without thinking. He set a brisk pace in the direction the crowd streamed. If Kurt followed, he followed. If not, all the better.

Mitch pushed the fight aside, though his eye swelled and his vision blurred.

In his imagination, he couldn't have dreamed up a more surreal scene. Children sat crying in the rubble. Elderly men roamed the streets with aged guns. Women, old beyond their years, mourned over corpses in the streets.

As they approached the warehouse, the crowd picked up its pace. Ten-year-old boys, pregnant women, and teenaged girls sprinted ahead of them. In the opposite direction, in no less of a brisk pace, a similar group darted past, their carts and bags laden with butter and sugar. One woman, her face worn but radiant, dragged a rucksack behind her.

The throng pushed and shoved in a desperate bid to get their hands on the precious rations. The frenetic atmosphere that charged the air seeped into Mitch's veins. He must reach those food stores. He had to. Coming back empty-handed was unacceptable.

A ring of black-uniformed SS officers brandished their weapons. "Get back. All of you, get back."

Not a single person heeded the order.

A shrill voice uttered the crowd's plea. "Let us through! Give the food to us, not the Soviets!"

The chant rose. "Let us through! Let us through!"

A lucky few emerged with sacks of flour and tins of coffee.

"Drop it." The Nazi soldier fired into the air. "Drop it."

Those finished looting dashed away.

"Drop it!"

Shots rang out.

Two bodies fell to the ground.

"Let's get in there." Kurt shoved Mitch in the small of the back.

A few moments later, they popped through the doorway. In a burst of energy that was difficult to muster these days, they sprinted toward the pallets of food. The basics. Enough to keep them alive until peace arrived. They loaded sugar and a few tins of fruit into their bags.

Split sacks of flour coated the concrete floor. Mitch slipped and slid and grabbed a bag.

A group of soldiers—maybe half a dozen or so—entered the warehouse. "Out! Everyone out!"

Bullets ricocheted off the metal sides of the building. One zinged by Mitch's ear. He ignored it, intent on reaching the sticks of sausages a few meters in front of him.

In no time, his bags were full and his arms laden with more than he could carry. He headed toward the exit, having difficulty seeing through the one eye. If he got past the guards, he would be able to deliver this abundance to Gisela.

"Halten sie. You there."

Even before he reached the exits, Mitch's arms and shoulders burned with the load.

"Halten sie."

Mitch didn't think the Nazi spoke to him.

Not until the soldier jabbed his rifle into Mitch's side. He froze, shivering as the cold metal dug into him. Another scene from another day flashed in front of his eyes. He and his chums being marched off by the Germans. The enemy.

This soldier was not interested in taking prisoners.

Around him, starving people plundered the foodstuffs. No

one cared about him. They had a difficult enough job keeping themselves alive. A cold sweat broke out across his forehead.

"Drop what is in your hands."

He didn't want to. Didn't want that precious bag of flour to split open. He hesitated.

He winced as the soldier jabbed the barrel of the gun deeper into his flesh. "I said to drop it."

Mitch obeyed. The white powder flew into a cloud in the air.

"Deserter. Plunderer. Common criminal." The Nazi spit at his feet.

"Nein." His knees knocked. How could he defend himself? If he spoke, they would know he was British. If not, he'd swing from a lamppost on the Unter den Linden in less than an hour.

Death either way.

The heavy shelling continued, often rocking the little house and disturbing the peace of the eight people huddled in the cellar. Gisela attempted to interest Annelies and Renate in a game of pat-a-cake, but they didn't want to play.

Renate sucked her thumb with vigor. Annelies crawled onto Gisela's lap. "When will Mutti come?"

She looked at the child's precious face, gray eyes big against her sallow skin. "When the fighting is over, then she will come." *Father, may it be so.*

"When will that be?"

"You must give her a little time. She hasn't forgotten about you." Gisela stroked Annelies's tangled golden hair.

"And Opa too."

The chances of Ella making her way here were tiny. Almost nonexistent. And even less for Opa. But Gisela didn't want to tell the girl.

Bettina scooted over on the hard wood bench, closer to the child. "Is your mutti away on holiday, dearie? Rome, I imagine. The Trevi Fountain. Perhaps she will bring you a trinket. Would you like that?"

Annelies scrunched her little nose. "What is a trinket?"

"A small gift." Bettina smiled her gap-toothed grin.

"Ja, ja, I would like that."

Renate leaned forward. "I want one too."

"It's mine." Annelies pulled her sister's hair.

Gisela slapped her hand away. "No one will get any presents if they are mean and selfish. Or pull hair. Do you understand?"

Two heads bobbed in agreement.

Audra kneeled beside Annelies. "You didn't mean to be a bad girl, did you?"

"Nein. I want the present."

Audra presented Gisela with a triumphant look and a single nod. "Leave them be. They are tired and hungry and bored."

"It doesn't excuse Annelies's behavior."

"We are all short with each other now. That is what comes from spending endless days huddled in a shelter."

"There was no reason for Annelies to do what she did. Fighting will not solve problems. If we have learned any lesson from this war, that should be it."

Jorgen left his chair, grabbed a stick from the woodpile they had stacked in case they ran out of coal, and sat on the bench between Annelies and Renate. He pulled out a pocketknife. "Would you like to see what I am going to carve for both of you?"

The girls gave him their full attention and the gift was forgotten.

The boots of several German soldiers passed by the cellar window. Their feet shuffled up the steps and they pounded on the door. Demanding. Insistent. "Open up. *Schnell*. Schnell."

Frau Mueller went to answer their call and Gisela followed, curious as to what they might want. From her position behind the older woman, she saw three weary, dirty Wehrmacht soldiers, their gray-green uniforms tattered, hanging on their thin frames, their battered helmets askance on their heads.

"What is it you want?" Frau Mueller met them, hands on her hips. Her flowered dress contrasted with their drab clothing.

The apparent leader of the group, a towering young man whose pants legs ended above his ankles, answered. "Water. We have come from the front lines and have had nothing to drink all day. Give us a drink."

"Nein. We have no water."

They stepped over the threshold, and the tall one narrowed his eyes and glared at Frau Mueller. "You must have some. What else would you drink?"

Gisela stepped forward. "You'd be the one to tell us what we should drink, because we have nothing. We can't bathe or manage to keep sanitary conditions. There are two little girls here and two old women. How can we take care of them without water? It's dangerous to go to the pump to get any and no more flows from our faucets."

Annelies chose that moment to clamber up the steps, Audra right behind her. "I'm sorry. I told her to stay put, but she wanted to see where you had gone."

Gisela hugged the little one's shoulder, then peered at the ringleader. "We have no water. Even if we did, we wouldn't give it to you."

Frau Mueller shot her a warning look. Like she might have gone too far and provoked these men. Gisela didn't care. There was no way she would hand over their single bucket of that precious resource to them.

THIRTY-TWO

K urt watched from several paces behind Josep and the soldier. Josep dropped the bag of flour and it split open on the ground.

Even with his one hand, he had matched Josep punch for punch. His chin pained him and his midsection ached. But he would fight for Gisela. Never, ever would he let the music slip away from him.

And here lay his chance to win. To triumph. To take what belonged to him.

"Nein, nein." Josep pled for his life in that ridiculous, broken German. How the SS officer didn't notice the accent, he would never know.

He stood, watching the scene like a motion picture on the screen.

Gisela would be brokenhearted when he returned and gave her the news. But he would be there to comfort her. She would grow close to him as he stood by her side. Held her up. Ja, she would forget about Josep in time. They hadn't known each other that long. Their bond couldn't be that strong.

So he didn't move. He could go and defend Josep, tell the man with the rifle a story of how they fought together at Stalingrad. Earn the Brit's freedom.

Yet he didn't.

He narrowed his eyes and continued as a disinterested specta-tor. The soldier jammed his rifle deeper into Josep's ribs.

Kurt waited for the officer to pull the trigger. Why did he hesitate?

From the corner of his eye, Mitch spied Kurt. Standing with his arms crossed.

Mitch took a breath and held it. Waiting for the bullet. Waiting until his life ended.

He thought about Gisela. Kurt would win her. He hoped she would be happy.

He thought about his father. He'd never get the chance to tell him he loved him. Understood him now. How he only wanted the best for him. Wanted to spare him from the horror of war. Wanted him to live.

All of this took a split second.

Then the door came into focus. If he could get there, he might have a chance.

Why not try? Even if he failed, he'd be no worse off than if he didn't give it a go.

Still clutching the rations, he shot off like a fox in front of the hounds. A bullet whizzed past his neck. It dinged around him. The crowd screamed and scattered. A path opened in front of him.

Jackboots pounded behind him.

Already his legs and lungs burned from the effort. Each step, one closer to freedom. To life.

A searing pain ripped through his arm.

He blocked it out.

Steps from the door.

Lord, help me. Help me. Help me.

Daylight.

Shots.

"Get that man. He's a deserter."

Just keep running. Lord, help me. Help me.

Any second now, it would be over.

He pushed through the crowd. Surely the SS wouldn't shoot into the mob.

The crack of a rifle split the air.

Women shrieked.

Forward, ever forward.

Pain in his legs. Pain in his arm. Pain in his eye.

He couldn't see. He just ran.

With one surge, he came out on the other side. The street ahead was clear.

But he didn't stop sprinting. Eric Liddell would be proud.

He turned left at one street, right at the next, until the shouts faded and all he could hear was the blood whooshing in his ears.

At last he stopped, his legs unable to carry him any farther. He sucked in air like a baby would suck a bottle.

Once the world stopped spinning, he pivoted and looked around. No one followed him. The soldier was gone. Kurt hadn't struck out to find him.

The front of a building had been sheared away so Mitch could see inside. A couple sat at their kitchen table eating. They went about their business as if it were normal to have your flat exposed to the world.

Allied bombs had reduced several other buildings in the neighborhood into rubble. Nothing looked familiar. Where was he?

He walked to the intersection. Had he run in the opposite direction from home?

He wandered for a while. The sugar and sausages he carried grew heavy. Dusk fell. He walked until he had blisters on his heels. Until he despaired of ever finding home again. Across the city, an air-raid siren screeched. He ignored it.

When he felt like he couldn't walk any farther, he stumbled on the street they had come down a few days earlier: Unter den Linden.

Thank You, Lord.

He made his way home.

Kurt sat next to Audra at the kitchen table, now relocated to the center of the cramped, dirty shelter, and stirred his coffee. The aroma alone was enough of a treat. To have half a cup was more than he could have hoped for. He determined to savor every last drop.

Gisela sat across from him, her spoon clinking against the mug as she stirred her steaming brew, the note pure, rhythmic. Her gorgeous eyes, always tinged with sadness, shone like a child's on Christmas morning. She sipped a bit of the liquid from her spoon. "Whatever you did to get this, it was worth it."

"Ja, it was worth it." A Mozart piano concerto played in his head. "Punched in the stomach and the side of my head by others trying to stop me, but it was worth it." Never would he reveal the true reason for his injuries.

"Are you sure you aren't hurt? Should we have Dr. Liebenstraum look at you?"

Did he want tender concern from Gisela or admiration for his courage? "I'm fine."

She blew across the cup, then set it down. "Should we have waited for Josep?"

"Nein. Because we got separated, there is no telling how long it will be until he gets home."

"What if he got lost? Or stopped?" She rose from her chair and clasped her hands together. "Maybe we should go look for him."

"Nein, nein." She couldn't leave. He couldn't let her. "The sirens will sound again soon. It's too dangerous to be out there at this time of night. He's probably in a shelter somewhere. We would never find him."

She sat, a little of the sadness returning to her eyes. He rubbed her hand. "Don't worry, he'll be back soon."

How could the SS have let him get away? Kurt should be rid of him by now.

Audra sipped her coffee. "I agree with Gisela. He won't be able to find his way in the dark."

What was she saying? Josep couldn't return.

"Tomorrow. If he doesn't return by daylight, I'll go look for him then." He had no intention of ever finding him.

Gisela smiled, sunshine filling the room. "Danke. I hope he'll be safe tonight."

The music in his brain crescendoed.

For a while, they sat in silence. No sirens sounded, no bombs fell. The peace was broken by a knock on the door.

Gisela ran to answer it. Nein, nein. It couldn't be. *Don't let it be.* He followed.

She turned the knob. Josep fell across the threshold. She caught him, her arms tight around him. "Thank God, thank God, you're back." She kissed his forehead.

He held out the bag of sugar and the stick of sausage. She smiled and laughed and tears trickled down her cheek.

Like a needle scratching a record, the music stopped.

Gisela sat beside Mitch on the green couch, holding a cool cloth to his eye, careful not to cause him more pain. He was home. Safe.

Now, if only Mutti would come. And Vater, Opa, and Ella. "What happened?"

He looked up at Kurt with his one eye. Why? Kurt scowled. What were they hiding?

Mitch winced. She lightened her touch. "We had to fight for what we wanted."

"What were you doing out there? What took you so long to get home?"

"They shot at me." He held up his right arm. A red streak ran the length of it.

He'd been grazed by a bullet. "You never should have gone. I told you not to." She couldn't hide the tremor in her voice. She found an old roll of gauze in their first-aid kit, and after cleaning out his wound, she wrapped it around his arm.

She leaned over and whispered, "Now tell me what really happened. I haven't heard the truth."

He tipped his head, gave a wry smile, and exposed one dimple. "Why would you say that?"

She wasn't in the mood for his joking. "You didn't get separated from Kurt."

He sobered, his dark eyes clouding. "No, I didn't. But I don't want to get into the ghastly details now. Keep him away from me. If he gets close, I haven't a clue how I'll react. Or how he will."

"He gave you this black eye."

Mitch didn't answer. What had happened between the two of them?

A shiver ran down her spine.

April 25

The howling keen of the *Stalinorgel*—"Stalin's organ"—pierced Gisela's ears. The Holtzmann sisters covered theirs and whimpered. The multiple rockets from the launcher mounted on the backs of the Red Army's trucks found their targets not far from where ten frightened people cowered in the cellar.

Gisela's heart bounced around in her chest, no rhythm whatsoever to its beat.

The rising and falling wail from the powerful and deadly weapons continued around them. Like a baby crying but magnified ten-thousand-fold.

Annelies and Renate screamed at the sound. With shaking hands, Gisela sat beside them on the bed in the corner, gathered them close, and whispered to them. A loud whisper, to be heard over the screeching weapons. "This is the end, girls. Soon, one day very soon, it will be over. The air will be quiet again."

Another group of yowls rent the skies and shells landed in the garden. The hair on her arms bristled. "Oh God, bitte, bitte. Don't let them set off that bomb."

They didn't. A few bricks fell from the little house, splintering as they hit the pockmarked street within a meter or two from the cellar window. Glass rained down from the panes above, shattering upon impact. Light reflected off of their ragged edges, a prism shooting rainbows over the pavement.

Stone by stone, their shelter was being reduced to rubble.

Jorgen slid across the bench on the wall, closer to her. Gisela motioned him over with a flick of her hand. He came to the bed and nestled against her. If she had left him standing on that street corner with the rifle in his hand . . .

Another loud explosion rocked the building. Gisela shielded the children with her body as limestone dust showered them from the arched ceiling above.

As the ground stilled, she looked Mitch's way. He sat on the second bed beside the Holtzmann sisters, holding their hands, reassuring them that this was not the end of the world.

Or was it?

"Oh, dearie, dearie," Bettina chanted.

Katya gave her own plaintive wail. "Sister, my sister."

For a moment, the fighting subsided. Mitch slipped to Gisela's side. Kurt narrowed his eyes. He had been sullen and angry the past couple of days.

"How are you?"

"I'm fine." She nodded and smiled for the kinder's sake. They were frightened enough.

"You're as white as my mum's roses."

"That sound."

"The music of Stalin's army."

Exhausted after countless nights of little sleep, she rested her head on his shoulder. "What will happen to us when they arrive?"

"We won't worry about that now. God will take care of us."

"Shouldn't we be prepared? I heard some of the women in the bread queue talking the other day. If you are dirty and old, the Russians won't want you."

He gave a quiet little laugh. "You are neither dirty nor old."

"They said to put coal on your face and flour in your hair. Don't comb it or bathe."

"Not now. When the time comes."

His presence warmed her and the quiet lulled her to sleep.

She had just nodded off when the terrible screech of the Stalinorgel let loose once more.

Oh God, why not one quiet day? Why not one peaceful night?

Machine-gun fire punctuated the brief intermissions between the rounds of the rocket launchers.

She rose from among the kinder and peered through the narrow window above them. Wehrmacht boots and black SS boots dashed past. One shiny pair came to a sudden stop in front of the window, then lurched forward as a Soviet bullet met its mark.

Gisela turned away, unable to watch more. Kurt stood right behind her and she couldn't but help fall into his arms. "Come and sit. This is too much for you."

She trembled and allowed him to lead her to the cream-and-green davenport they had pushed against the far wall. He knelt in front of her. "There is nothing to worry about. I won't allow you to come to any harm."

"You can't say that. We're helpless against this assault."

"I won't leave your side."

She tried to take comfort in his words.

The gunfire ramped up once more, as did the howling squeal of the Stalinorgel, driving away the warmth in her limbs, chilling her all over.

Annelies covered her ears, missing most of the tale Mitch wove about princesses and castles, dragons and knights in shining armor. Even the beauty of his words could not overcome the ugliness on their doorstep.

Day turned into night. Neither the gunfire nor the Stalinorgel music stopped for a breath. Those dragons breathed fire and ravaged the decimated city.

At last, Renate and Annelies and the Holtzmann sisters gave in to their exhaustion and fell asleep on the bed. Gisela knew she would never rest while those monsters stood on the doorstep.

The thought of a good cry held some appeal.

She needed a break—a break from the boredom, the anticipation, the dread. She had to see something other than passing shoes—the tall, black boots of German officers, the midcalf brown boots of the field soldiers, the serviceable brown-and-white pumps of women scurrying to stock up on the necessities before the Russians arrived. She slipped from the shelter on the pretense of using the restroom and climbed the steps to the almost-empty second-floor bedroom that faced east.

Rocket fire colored the horizon blood red. A cacophony of shells and bombs and machine guns composed the strangest music. Explosions, like fireworks, lit up the heavens.

In a way, she believed this had to be a dream. Events like this didn't happen to average people. They lived happy lives with family around the table, plenty to eat, and the basics of existence. Not like clay pigeons, targets for whatever aircraft flew in the air. Not like sleepwalkers, passing the dead and bloated bodies of their school pals, neighbors, and family. Not like hungry baby birds, waiting with mouths open for the next morsel that might drop their way.

She pressed her nose to the glass, surprised that it bore no cracks or bullet holes. She closed her eyes, blocking out the nightmare.

A tap on her shoulder and she jumped as high as the Eiffel Tower. Clutching her chest, she turned to find Mitch behind her.

"I'm sorry. I tried to make noise"—he studied his stockinged feet—"but you were in a far-off place."

She touched his face, his beard coarse and bristly. "A place where this is nothing but a bad dream. A place where I will awake and find myself in my rose-papered bedroom in California, Margot asleep in the bed beside me."

"I have dreams too."

"Of flying?"

He nodded. He understood.

"Why did you come after me?" He should be with Audra, comforting her.

"You've been quiet."

"I don't want to talk."

"What did you mean when you spoke about Audra and me getting married?"

"Just what I said. It's a plan you two have, but one that may never be a reality."

"I haven't any desire to marry Audra."

She dared to look into his chocolate eyes. They were soft, kind. Perhaps loving. "Not now you don't want to marry her. When this tragedy finally ends."

"Never."

Could it be that the love she saw in his eyes was for her?

"I love another."

That, she couldn't bear. For half a second, she'd had hope. "Let's count to three and resolve to wake up." She closed her eyes. "One . . ."

"Wait."

"What?"

"In case this is a nightmare and we wake up an ocean and a continent apart from each other, I want you to know I love you. That has been the sweetest part of this dream. The part I don't want to wake from."

He loved her? "Do you mean that?"

"I do."

"I do too." Her heart dreamed along with his. "I'll be sorry to wake up and find you gone. Promise me you will try to locate me in California." Her heart pained her.

"I will. I promise. Will you slap me again if I kiss you?"

Part of her still didn't believe she had done such a thing. She shook her head. He leaned in for a kiss that she couldn't refuse. His lips came to rest on hers, the pressure gentle, soothing. Yet a fire raced through her and she pulled him closer. He held the back of her neck, his probing fingers pulling out her hairpins.

The passion intensified and he pressed his lips tighter to hers. The breath she drew wasn't sufficient. His heart beat over hers, their tempos in unison.

Mitch took her head in his hands and pulled away, his eyes intent on her. "You are the most incredible, beautiful woman I have ever met."

"Why did you stop?"

"Because if the kiss had gone on longer, I'd not have been able to control it. You fill me, complete me. I want you to be mine. I fought for you."

This had to be real. "You fought Kurt."

"He swung at me. I defended myself. Fought for you. He wants you as much as I do."

"No one has ever fought for me." That only happened at the cinema. It made her dizzy to think about. At the same time, anger surged in her toward Kurt. Didn't he understand she wasn't going to be his? Ever? "No wonder you don't want to be near him. I'd throw him out on the street if it wouldn't be his death sentence. But he won't get me. I love another."

His smile, his dimples, his love left her woozy.

He brushed his hand over her lids and she closed her eyes. "You have been the most beautiful dream. One, two . . ."

THIRTY-THREE

N o. Wait." Gisela broke off counting, pink rising in her pale, sunken cheeks.

He held her close in the freezing bedroom even as artillery fire screamed around them. The kiss had warmed him through and through. Almost too much. "Don't you want to wake up?"

"No, I don't." She slid from his embrace and held his hands, her touch light. "Even if I have to suffer through this nightmare of hunger and fright and death, it's worth it to be with you. I don't want to leave you."

A shell exploded nearby and the wood floors shook beneath them. Yet another shower of plaster rained on their heads. Mitch had enjoyed their game, but reality intruded. "We don't have to wake up. Because we aren't dreaming."

"I know."

"When the war is over . . ."

He wanted to commit to her, but she hushed him with a finger on his lips. "If I have learned nothing else from this horror, I have learned not to think about tomorrow. First, we have to survive today. So many don't have a future."

"But a pledge between us will keep us going until freedom comes."

"I don't want to break your heart. You don't want to break mine. Let's get through today, then the next and the next. Whatever that may hold for us."

He struggled to understand her resistance. Perhaps he had read her wrong. "Do you love me? Be truthful."

Her eyes sparkled. "If not for this war, things would be so very different."

"Why not take advantage of every moment we have, no matter how few or how many are left? Because of the uncertainty of war, we should grab each second and live as if every tick of the clock was our last."

She stepped to the other window on the wall and stared at the carnage on the streets. A large fissure ran the length of the pane. "It's dangerous to love me."

He went to her and massaged her shoulders, whispering into her ear, "Dangerous to my heart, yes. I've lost it to you."

She leaned into him. "I would fail you."

"Never."

"Why did I run from Heide and Lotta? Why did I value my life more than theirs?"

"You were frightened and acted on instinct. There's no shame in that."

"I knew better. All my life, my parents had trained me to put others ahead of myself, but I didn't do it that night. Even when I heard their screams, I kept running." She shivered.

For a few minutes, he allowed silence to invade them. Just a bit. Gisela relaxed as she rested on his chest, her back to him. Explosions burst in the air along with the constant firing of machine guns.

"What could you have done to save your cousins? You told me yourself that there was no escape for all of you."

"Then why did I go first? Why didn't I push them ahead of me?"

"Did they push and shove to get ahead of you? Did you knock them out of the way?"

Her breathing rate increased and he knew she had traveled to that ghastly night. "I can't remember. Maybe I did push them out of the way. Maybe, because I went first, they didn't have a chance. I don't know."

He wrapped his arms around her and grasped her hands. "What happened after you opened the window? Relax and think."

Gisela had heard the heavy Russian boots enter the parlor that night. They shouted, "*Uri,* uri," wanting the watches. Glass broke on the floor. Tante Sonje would have bent to clean up whatever had shattered.

Gisela huddled with Heide and Lotta in the corner of the bedroom, behind the bed. She prayed, her lips moving, no sound emanating from her. The Soviets shouted in Russian. What were they demanding now?

She heard a thud, then Tante Sonje screamed.

"My aunt screeched and screeched. 'Get out. Get out.'" Gisela shuddered.

Mitch's whisper came from behind her, the edges of his voice softened by her vision. "Keep going. To the part where you opened the window."

"We didn't move at that time. More screaming. Crying. Then shots." She couldn't block out the sound of her aunt's body hitting the floor.

Mitch rubbed her arm.

"They would come for us. We had to get out, so we opened the window and held it in place with a board my cousins kept in the room for that very purpose." She paused as the scene played in front of her eyes. She looked across the bedroom at the large featherbed she and her younger cousins occupied. Heide and Lotta's dolls lay scattered across the pink-and-green rag rug on the floor.

Her attention returned to the matter at hand. Boots clunked on the stairs. If the soldiers found them, they would kill them too, like Tante Sonje.

Her heart raced as she knew they had very little time to escape.

She jolted back to reality and spun to face Mitch. "I remember. Oh, I remember." Emotions almost cut off her breathing.

"What is it? What happened that night?"

"I tried to get my cousins to go out that window. I pulled them and tugged on them. Neither would cooperate." A sensation of frustration overcame her. "Why wouldn't they go out that window? Their mother was dead, their father out fighting. But they wouldn't budge."

"You did all you could. You offered them a means of escape, but they chose not to take it."

"They told me to get out, to leave. That they would be fine. As they closed the window behind me, the Russians burst into the room." Her knees went weak. In her head, she heard the Soviets shouting at her cousins. Even when she ran, the sound of those soldiers rang in her ears. "Maybe I should have stayed with them."

"So you could be a victim too?"

"Family doesn't leave family." She had left so much family.

Mitch scrubbed his face. "What else could you have done?"

She thought and thought. They were determined not to go. They told her to take the only way out. She hadn't decided for them. They had decided for themselves.

She left his side and paced the room. "I could have grabbed

them and pushed them out of the window like they pushed me. And I never bolted that bedroom door. If we had locked it and pushed the wardrobe against it, that would have bought us time. Time for me to convince my cousins to run."

"You could have moved a wardrobe?" One corner of his mouth turned up.

"Why not? The three of us would have been able to do it."

Mitch folded his arms and leaned against the wall. "And then what? Supposing you could have moved the wardrobe."

"There were a hundred other things I could have said to make them leave. I was an adult. They should have listened to me."

Mitch uncrossed his arms and tented his fingers even as she continued to pace. "Like you are listening to me."

She had never met such an exasperating man. "I left them. I left Ella. And Opa. And Mutti. How many more people I love will die when I leave them? And Margot left me." She covered her face and bit back the sting of tears.

"God saved you. And the girls and the Holtzmann sisters. All of us. It was nothing we did. On our own, we are unable. It is His hand that plucked us out of our situations and that has sustained us."

"This far."

"Yes, this far. Perhaps further. Perhaps not. But it's not up to us."

"I didn't fail them?"

Mitch gathered her to himself, his arms warm, his chest firm. "No, you didn't fail them. You can't save the world. That is God's job."

Gisela laid on the bed from upstairs. Audra snored softly beside her. Bettina's snore was a little more raucous. Kurt dozed on the davenport, Mitch wrapped in blankets on the hard floor. Everyone slept but her. The howl in the street had calmed a bit. German soldiers patrolled their neighborhood, not yet under Soviet occupation. But sleep remained as elusive as a butterfly.

She mulled over her memories and what Mitch had said. "I didn't fail them." The words snuck past her lips.

She had been trying to save the world in her own way. All along, she wanted to be the one to rescue these people. They would hail her for saving their lives. Like she couldn't save Heide or Lotta. Like she couldn't save her sister.

She thought of the scene playing in front of them. Today or tomorrow or the next day, the Russians would take their street and wouldn't relinquish control. This was what it was like to be in the midst of battle. If only Hitler would surrender.

And where was Mutti? If she still lived, had the Russians discovered her? What horrors was she surviving? Had she survived?

Lord, watch over her. Protect her. Bring her back to me.

She climbed out of bed, careful not to disturb the others. After tiptoeing to her rucksack, she rummaged through the few contents, discovering her Bible in the folds of her sweater.

She opened to the page with the daisy. Memories of Oma and Opa flooded her. Of good times. Of peaceful times. Times that ended, as surely as daisies faded.

She went to close the cover when the words of Isaiah 43 caught her eye.

> *But now thus saith the LORD that created thee, O Jacob, and he that formed thee, O Israel, Fear not: for I have redeemed thee, I have called thee by name; thou art mine. When thou passest through the waters, I will be with thee; and through the rivers, they shall not overflow thee: when thou walkest through the fire, thou shalt not be burned; neither shall the flame kindle upon thee. For I am the LORD thy God, the Holy One of Israel, thy Savior.*

She sat on the cold floor, her Bible in her lap. The screeching, the shooting, the anguished cries faded.

The words from her Lord seeped into her like the balmy California sun. Warmth spread through her and she could almost feel the soft grass between her toes. She fingered the flower tucked in the pages.

Opa had given it to Oma. And now to Gisela. And this was the passage he wanted her to remember. He quoted from it when she saw him last. *"'When thou passest through the waters, I will be with thee.'"*

That was why he had asked her to put it in this passage. She remembered his words, like he wanted.

"'Fear not: for I have redeemed thee, I have called thee by name; thou art mine.'"

She bit her lower lip to stem the tide of tears welling in her eyes. God had redeemed her from her wrongs. Getting the girls out of East Prussia hadn't accomplished that feat. Keeping the Holtzmann sisters together body and soul hadn't done it. Even if Gisela could locate Mutti, the redemption would not be complete.

Because it took Jesus to pay the ransom price on the cross.

April 27

From the cellar, Mitch and the other residents listened to the rounds of gunfire outside the window. Across the room, Frau Mueller's lips moved in silent petition. Gisela sat next to him on the bench. He squeezed her hand.

He hadn't been this frightened in Belgium or France. Perhaps wanting a future with this woman changed his outlook. Or being responsible for nine others, all of them helpless.

Yes, helpless. God would have to save them.

More Stalinorgels. Only God could save them.

They picked at their food, though they now had a few supplies. No one spoke much. Hour after hour, they sat in the dank semidarkness of the lower level, wondering if they would die in the next instant.

Renate had never sucked her thumb so vigorously.

The day wore on. Gisela dozed on his shoulder. He stared out of the window.

A wild screech, almost like the American Indian calls Mitch had seen in the motion pictures, pierced the air. The style of boots remained the same, though now the pants were greener. A few feet were wrapped in nothing but rags.

Gisela sat up straight at the yelling.

A tank rolled past the window, down the narrow street.

Mitch pushed to his feet and gazed out the small, dirty pane of glass. The faces of the men in the tank were not German. Their greasy hair was black and stuck straight out of their fur ushanka hats. Their dark, slanted eyes gave away their ethnic origin.

He had difficulty drawing a breath. He clenched his jaw.

Gisela stepped behind him. "Mongols," she whispered, shuddering.

They watched the foreign troops process down the road. For the people on this street, the war had ended. They were now in Russian-occupied territory.

When he could watch no longer, he turned to her, stroking her upper arm, trying to warm her. "Now might be a good time for that coal and powder."

"What about you and Kurt and Jorgen? They'll shoot you on the spot."

"Kurt and Jorgen, maybe, but not me. I'll explain to them that I'm British."

"And how will you do that when you don't speak Russian and I doubt any of them speak English? What are we going to do?"

Then he would fight them. Fight them for taking away Xavier. Fight them for what they did to women and children. Fight them to show he wouldn't surrender this time.

THIRTY-FOUR

April 28

K urt watched as Gisela grasped the lump of coal and rubbed it over Audra's face, then massaged precious flour into the other woman's hair. With its light color, it didn't take much to turn Audra gray. She did appear to be quite a bit older than her twenty or so years. And much uglier. Not good if she was out to impress Josep. He clenched and relaxed his sore fist.

Then again, Josep only had one good eye.

Not a word passed between the two of them since that day. They remained across the room from each other. His anger had cooled into determination. Josep and Gisela spent more time together than ever. But he would have her. She would be his. Even if he had to fight Josep again.

Audra kneaded the white powder into Gisela's hair. "When we get to America, we can dye our hair any color we want to." She worked in more. "Yours, being darker, isn't as easy as mine. We'll use up every bit of flour we have left."

The music faded. He hated witnessing Gisela's beauty being hidden.

"Don't do that." She held a mirror up to inspect herself, then turned to Audra. He didn't recognize her face. Nein, she couldn't disappear.

She tipped her head to the side. "Deepen the crease marks around my mouth and eyes and that will have to be sufficient."

The demanding foreign voices with their harsh-sounding language approached ever closer. His palms sweated and he managed a breath every ten seconds or so. Gisela huddled in the corner of the basement beside Mitch. Audra slid into the empty spot beside Kurt.

He leaned over to whisper in her ear. "You can't let them get this close. Not at a time like this. You should rely on him; she should be here with me."

"I'm watching. Trust me."

Kurt wiped his damp hands on his rather tight khaki pants, borrowed from Frau Mueller's much smaller husband. They had at last convinced him to burn his German officer's uniform. He shouldn't have to be ashamed of who he was.

"You'd better work fast. This war is almost over. And then what? They will run away to the west and leave us alone here. We can't let that happen." He didn't know if he was more afraid of the Red Army or of losing his muse.

Bettina sat at the edge of her seat. "Moscow, Sister, can you imagine? Remember being here years ago? Let's go see the colorful roofs of St. Basil's."

Frau Mueller grasped Bettina's arm. "Later, ja? Soon it will be supper time."

Jorgen sat dazed between the Holtzmann sisters and listened to them argue about what they would order in the Moscow restaurant tonight.

A higher-pitched scream broke out, cutting off the sisters' banter. Frost formed on the inside of Kurt's blood vessels. Gisela rose and snuck to the narrow window.

"Women. Large-boned Russian women high on the tanks, shooting their guns in the air and hollering like cornered rabbits. The Mongols weren't as bad as them."

"These are your allies, Josep. The people you have teamed up with to defeat Germany. What do you think of them now?"

Josep didn't answer, but fire smoldered behind his eyes.

While her back had been turned, Audra had snuck into Gisela's vacated seat next to Mitch. She clung to his elbow, her head on his shoulder. "I can't take much more of this. All of this yelling and shooting is frightful. How will any of us survive?"

No doubt about it, she batted her eyelashes at him. She practiced her English on him. "Please, tell me about England. I go to your house."

Mitch shot Gisela a glance, one dark eyebrow raised. She shrugged.

Kurt patted the empty spot next to him on the bench. "Come sit here, Gisela."

Mitch raised his other eyebrow. Good, raising doubts in his mind.

She moved like a wooden toy and took the seat beside him.

"There is nothing to worry about." He patted her knee.

"I wasn't worrying."

"Those communists won't harm me. If Josep can pretend to be German, I can pretend to be English. I will say I lost my papers and identification in the POW camp." Kurt reached for her hand, which she pulled away to scratch an itch on her nose. This wasn't what he wanted. Had Josep told her what happened at the warehouse?

"You sound rather confident."

"I am. When this is over, I will take you to my parents' home in Bavaria. You can rest and enjoy the quiet of the forest and the mountains. The air is fresh and clean, the countryside beautiful. Perhaps Oktoberfest will begin again in Munich. I want to show you the sights." If she saw his home, she would want to stay.

"That is a gracious offer, but I have to find Mutti. Ella will come for the girls, I will take the Holtzmann sisters to their niece, Vater will return, and then I will leave for home."

"This is your home."

"America."

Kurt shook his head. "Nein, you are German through and through. What little bit of American you had in you is gone."

A shadow passed over her heart-shaped face. The music in his head turned soft and slow. "I'm sorry. I didn't mean to hurt you."

"Please understand." She turned to him, her gaze holding his. "Germany hasn't been kind to me. I lost my sister here. We were closer than most. America is where my happy memories are. Where I want to be. Away from the war and death this place brought."

She couldn't leave him. He couldn't allow it. "You have awhile to decide. I will help you situate both sets of sisters and locate your parents. By then, Germany will have healed." If he could convince her to stay . . .

"You need to return to your home and your family, and I need to go to mine."

He grabbed her hand and pressed her fingers into his palm. "You must come with me, for the music."

Her forehead scrunched. "The music?"

"When I am near you, I hear the dancing of the notes. The music I thought I had lost along with my arm."

"I don't give you the music."

He sat straight. "But you do."

"Music comes from the heart." She touched his chest. His lungs expanded. "When you hear it, your heart is speaking to you. Not me. At home, the place you love, the music will come back. And I will be in the front row of your first concert."

"Don't you see? There will be no more concerts. A one-armed man will never play the piano. The melodies in my head are all I have left."

"God will give you the music. You could direct. Or teach."

"I could never do it. I was born to play."

"With God's help, you can do anything. Look at what we have survived."

She was slipping away from him, though he squeezed her hand. "I love you, Gisela."

She yanked her hand from his. Kurt's mouth went dry. "It's not me you love; it's the idea of me. You love the music you think is only with you when I'm nearby. But you don't love me. And I don't love you, Kurt."

He stared at the gray concrete floor, clenching his jaw. Without her, without the music, his life would be empty.

"God will give you the music. Trust Him. Love Him. It will come."

Kurt first fell in love with music in his hometown church. The swelling of the organ filled his soul. Once he had joined the Nazi party and entangled himself with them, that music failed to stir him. Could the Lord give back that gift?

She touched his shoulder. "When you go home to Munich, one day a woman will come along and you will love her. All of her. Not just the idea of her."

A requiem played in his head. Yet he heard the organ chords, and a spark lit deep inside. Perhaps, just perhaps, he needed to pray for the return of his beloved music.

Across the room, Audra touched Josep's stubbly cheek.

And the Mongol-Russians arrived at the door.

"Uri, uri, uri," the Soviet conquerors screamed as they clattered up the stairs. They wanted watches. And they would get them any way they could. These present-day yells mixed with the past ones in Gisela's memories. Goose bumps covered her arms. Each breath she drew was jerking and halting.

The women of the house crouched in the back corner of the cellar.

Kurt hid behind the oxygen pump with Jorgen.

Mitch stood tall in the middle of the room, waiting to face the Russians.

Would they take the time to find out he was British? Her stomach clenched. She went to him and tugged on his arm. "Please, go hide. In the time it will take you to explain to them who you are, they will shoot you. Go with the other men."

He rubbed her arm but didn't say a word. A study of his dark eyes told her what she needed to know. Nothing would dissuade him from confronting the Red Army head-on.

He guided her back to her spot with the other women. "Pray."

With a great crash, the soldiers broke open the heavy wood door. They thundered down the stairs, their boots stomping on the wooden steps. "Uri, uri," they continued to demand.

They turned the corner to the shelter. Within seconds, they raised their rifles and pointed them at Mitch's chest.

Oh God, spare him. Spare us, Father.

The answer to her prayer came to her as a soft whisper. *Fear not, for I have redeemed thee.*

Yet panic rose in her throat and threatened to choke her.

"English, English, English." Mitch shouted at the Soviets, his voice strong and clear. From his pocket, he withdrew a piece of paper. When he unfolded it, Gisela saw that he had colored a Union Jack. He waved this in front of his face. "English, English. Now get out. Leave here." He pointed to the stairs.

"Nein. *Germanski.*" A rather squat, Asian-looking soldier cocked his rifle, five watches glinting on his arm. He shook his head so hard, his ushanka hat tilted on his head. "Uri." With a jerk of his chin, he motioned for his cohorts to search the building for watches.

Mitch stared right back, his dark eyes focused on their guard.

Pressure built in Gisela's forehead and a wicked headache picked this moment to erupt. She sat and rubbed her temples. *Dear God, help us. Make these soldiers go away.*

She gripped the edge of her chair, digging her fingernails into the wood.

Mitch waved his homemade flag. The soldiers cared nothing for his nationality. "Leave this place." He took a step forward. A muscle jumped in his jaw.

The soldier cocked his gun. Mitch took another step forward. "Go. Go. Go." Another step.

The Mongol peered through the sight.

Mitch ran at him and kicked the rifle out of his hands. It clattered to the floor. Gisela sucked in her breath and shook all over. Mitch grabbed the gun and pointed it at the Mongol. "Out. Get out. Now." He spun the soldier around and marched him up the stairs.

Gisela clasped her hands together and hugged Annelies close. Russian voices floated from upstairs, harsh words she couldn't understand.

More clomping of boots on the stairs, Mitch's voice, the door slamming.

But who left?

Mitch leaned on the door, trembling like a nervous dog, his ears ringing.

He had sent the Russians a message.

How long before they returned the favor? With shaking fingers, he locked the door. He had to will his legs to carry him down the stairs to the bunker.

He sank to the floor.

Audra rushed to his side. Her hands were cool through his thin shirt. "Are you injured? Did they hurt you?"

"Nein, I'm fine."

She wrapped both hands around his upper arm. "You were so brave. I can't believe you stood up to those monsters. And they left here without hurting us. I owe you my life."

Gisela gathered a fussy Renate in her arms and came to stand beside him. "What were you doing?"

He managed a small grin. She didn't reciprocate and he sobered. "I couldn't let them come and have their way here. Not after what they did to Xavier, shooting at him from the sky. Not with what they might do to you. And the others."

Audra kissed him on the cheek. "Danke for saving my life. I will be forever grateful. I will do anything for you."

Mitch didn't doubt that she would. He pushed himself up and left her squatting on the floor. From the corner of his eye, he watched Kurt crawl from behind the oxygen pump and sit on the bench.

Mitch approached Gisela, who paced this small dungeon bouncing Renate on her hip. She wouldn't look him in the eye.

"What is it?"

She turned on him, fire in her amber eyes. "They could have shot you. They could have shot all of us. What kind of craziness was that?"

"For Xavier."

"Is that what he would have wanted?"

She had a point. A very good point. "No."

"They'll return. And they may not be so understanding next time."

Mitch bowed his head. "You're right. I'm sorry. It was foolish and, well, I didn't think. But I did take this from one of the soldiers as he left." He held out her gold watch.

She took it from him and stared at it. "You remembered this."

"The last link to your sister. I couldn't let them have it."

She touched his cheek. "Thank you. You were crazy and don't ever do that again, but thank you."

Kurt approached them, his gaze darting between them. "From now on, Gisela, you will go behind the oxygen tank with me. Josep is trying to get us all killed. You need to stay somewhere safe. With someone who will keep you safe." He gripped her elbow.

She wriggled away from him and a little closer to Mitch. Kurt clenched his fist.

Gisela hunched her shoulders. "It's only a matter of time until they take one of us. All of us. They will kill some of us and rape the others." Her voice broke as she studied Renate, now quiet in her arms. "God help us, our fate is sealed."

THIRTY-FIVE

May 1

For days, the screech of the Stalinorgels echoed in Audra's head. The cadence of machine guns lulled them to sleep and woke them in the morning. One day blurred into another. The Holtzmann sisters argued and bickered as did Annelies and Renate. Kurt was short with her, and Jorgen snapped at anyone within ten meters.

The only ones who got along were Gisela and Josep.

There had been a change in their relationship. They were closer, looked at each other with a tenderness that reminded Audra of her parents. They were in love.

And her dreams of a life of fame and fortune in the West were shattered.

The men left the shelter to work on securing the front door. From below, Audra heard them grunt as they picked up Frau Mueller's hutch and carried it to the entryway. The wardrobe would be harder as it had to come downstairs from the bedroom.

Gisela sat beside her on the bench and rocked a dozing Annelies.

Audra rested her back against the cool concrete wall. "Will the furniture keep the Soviets from getting in?" She had never been as frightened as when the soldiers had burst into the shelter. If they took her virtue, they would take everything she had left.

"Nein. It may delay them, but they will get in one way or another."

"And then?"

"You know."

Audra clamped her hands together.

"Put it here." Josep's voice carried down the stairs. The piece thunked on the floor.

Frau Mueller sat at the table on one side of the cellar, her red tongue stuck out in contrast to her pale face, as she concentrated on the strange markings she made on the paper.

She had written Тиф карантин—TYPHUS QUARANTINE— in big, bold letters. The Russian she had learned when she gave refuge to a woman fleeing the communist revolution years ago might be what would save their lives. They would post the paper on the front door and pray that whoever tried to force their way into the house could read.

And would be afraid enough of typhus to stay out.

The agonizing screams of women and girls echoed down the street, their purity and innocence snatched from them. Right on their block, the laughing, mocking voices of the soldiers continued day and night. When the women's cries died out, the wailing and mourning began.

They had traded one form of fascism for another.

Gisela turned to her. "You like Josep, nein?"

Audra smoothed back her movie star-colored hair. "You like him."

"I love him."

The swelling in her throat blocked anything Audra might have said. If Gisela would take her to America, then she could have everything she wanted. The fame, the fortune, the handsome man on her arm. "You will go to England?"

"Why do you want to be an actress so much?"

"In the West, I don't have to be poor anymore. No more awful handmade clothes. No more sharing the last piece of bread with your younger brother. No more sleeping four or five to a bed. If I could go to Hollywood and be famous, I would never have to worry again. Ever."

"I understand."

"You didn't answer my question about England. Will you go there?"

"I don't know what will happen tomorrow, much less after the war. I want to go to America, to California. When we lived there, I was happy. I want that again." Gisela clamped her hands together. A single tear escaped down her cheek. "I want you to come to America with me."

What did she say? Wiping her face, Audra turned back. "You would take me with you? You really would?"

"I would help you get a visa to come, help you get started."

"Why? All I've tried to do is keep Josep from you. For my sake. For Kurt's sake. He asked me to work with him."

"We know. Josep and I have known since one of the first nights we were here."

"Then I truly do not know why you would offer to help me. I don't deserve it."

Gisela's brow furrowed. "Everyone deserves a fresh start."

"What do you want in return?" The price might be too high. The last of her tears dried. Gisela must want something.

"Your friendship. Nothing more."

"You want more than that."

"Nein." Gisela rubbed her brow. "Everyone makes mistakes. If we could go back in time and make different choices, we would.

Each of us. But we can do nothing but move forward. I've made plenty of mistakes in my life. God has forgiven me for each and every one, washed me clean in His Son's blood. Given me redemption. That is what I'm offering to you."

"Redemption?"

"Something like that. Not from me. From the Lord."

From deep inside her welled a spring of tears. She couldn't stop them from running down her cheeks, even though they washed away the coal dust. And her sins.

The men returned to the bunker as the shelling continued, fiercer than ever. The noises of battle came from within the heart of the city. The Reichstag building must have fallen by now. Deep underground, below the Red Army's boots, was Hitler's bunker.

For Gisela, the hours passed with maddening slowness. Together they ate their meager meals. Jorgen carved little horses for Annelies and Renate, who played on the large blue-and-green rag rug in the middle of the concrete floor.

Drunken Russians soldiers, imbibing confiscated liquor for their May Day celebration, roamed the streets. The screams of the women being raped threatened to overwhelm her. How could she stand this any longer? Oh, that the cries outside would stop. That the cries in her memory would cease.

Darkness fell, deepening the shadows in the cellar. Outside, nothing stopped. The inebriated victors celebrated by molesting as many women as they could find. Annelies, Renate, and the old ladies fell asleep.

Tonight Frau Mueller pulled out the rectangular brown Bakelite radio set with its arched dial. Since the Russians had ordered all radios to be turned in a few days ago, she had hidden this battery-operated unit under the bottom stair. The victors wanted to take these magical boxes to Russia with them, not understanding that most needed electricity to make them work. Electricity they didn't have.

Mitch came to Gisela and pulled her close. She trembled against him. "I can't make the noises go away."

"Focus on God. He brings us through the raging waters."

"Isaiah 43:2. I've been reading that. My opa quoted it to me right before we left Heiligenbeil."

"Cling to it."

"I miss him terribly. I can't stand to think what happened to him."

"Then don't. Remember the good."

"And you too. Remember the good. The good of your time with Xavier. The good of the time with your father."

Frau Mueller turned the knob and the radio crackled to life. The adults sat on the davenport, huddled around it.

Surprise rippled through the group with the first words they heard.

"*Achtung*! Achtung! The German broadcasting system is going to give an important German government announcement for the German people."

But no statement came. The broadcast turned to classical music.

Gisela hugged herself. "What could that be about?"

"I didn't understand all of it." Mitch's voice held a trace of worry.

"A special announcement. Not from the Führer, but the German government."

Kurt moved beside her. He rubbed his hands together. "News of a great victory, no doubt."

But doubt it Gisela did. The sounds outside their cellar were not the sounds of triumph but of utter defeat.

They sat, hardly daring to breathe, not daring to move.

Just before ten o'clock, the achtung warning was given again and the broadcaster began to play the slow movement of Bruckner's Symphony no. 7, a well-recognized piece of music in Germany.

Gisela worried the cuff of her sleeve with her fingers. "How long are they going to make us wait? The batteries will die before we find out what they are going to say."

Mitch took her hand in his. "All in good time."

She jiggled her leg for a while, then paced the small room. Bettina and Katya snored so loudly Gisela was sure they would drown out the radio. The minutes ticked by. How long was this music?

It was close to ten thirty when the music came to an abrupt stop. Three drum rolls followed. Gisela couldn't swallow.

"It is reported from *Der Führer's* headquarters that our führer Adolf Hitler, fighting to the last breath against Bolshevism, fell for Germany this afternoon in his operational headquarters in the Reich Chancellery."

A collective gasp went up. Gisela bit back tears. Could it really be true? Might this be over? Mitch slipped his arm around her waist.

"On 30 April, Der Führer appointed Grand Admiral Dönitz his successor. The grand admiral and successor of Der Führer now speaks to the German people."

Admiral Dönitz took the microphone. "German men and women, soldiers of the armed forces: Our Führer, Adolf Hitler, has fallen. In the deepest sorrow and respect, the German people bow."

So it was true. *Dear God, You are our Savior.*

Her tears flowed freely, as did those of the other cellar residents. All except for Kurt. He hardened his face and clenched his hand. While the others rejoiced, he mourned. It must be hard to know your sacrifice had been in vain.

With her thoughts whirring, she missed some of the admiral's remarks. She concentrated on his words once more.

"It is my first task to save Germany from destruction by the advancing Bolshevist enemy. For this aim alone the military struggle continues. As far and for so long as achievement of this aim is impeded by the British and the Americans, we shall be forced to carry on our defensive fight against them as well. Under such conditions, however, the Anglo-Americans will continue the war not for their own peoples but solely for the spreading of Bolshevism in Europe.

"What the German people have achieved in battle and borne in the homeland during the struggle of this war is unique in history. In the coming time of need and crisis of our people, I shall endeavor to establish tolerable conditions of living for our women, men, and children so far as this lies in my power.

"For all this I need your help. Give me your confidence because your road is mine as well. Maintain order and discipline in town and country. Let everybody do his duty at his own post. Only thus shall we mitigate the sufferings that the coming time will bring to each of us; only thus shall we be able to prevent a collapse. If we do all that is in our power, God will not forsake us after so much suffering and sacrifice."

Gisela's knees buckled and Mitch led her back to the couch. "It's not over."

He shook his head. His trademark dimples had disappeared. "No, it's not."

Wracking sobs overtook her.

He drew her close and held her, whispering words into her hair she couldn't understand.

Kurt rubbed her back. "I know Der Führer's death is a great blow, but you heard Admiral Dönitz. The fight continues and we will be victorious."

"No one will win. This will never end." Her tears soaked Mitch's shirt.

"It will. It will."

But Gisela saw no end in sight. With or without the Führer.

May 2

Mitch sat on the long wood bench in the cellar, bouncing Renate on his knee. His attention, however, was focused on Gisela. She lay on the bed, eyes glazed, hair tangled.

He was at a loss as to what to do. She became despondent when Dönitz announced the war would continue. How could he help her?

Today was quieter. Perhaps he imagined it, but the fighting seemed to have subsided a bit. At least moved farther away.

Was it the calm before the storm? Or the harbinger of peace?

After the rest had finished their meager lunch, Mitch went to Gisela. She rolled over and opened her eyes. Red rimmed them and dark bags hung under them.

"Sit up, please. Eat a little bit."

She complied, nibbling at the crumbling piece of stale bread. It had to be comprised of at least half sawdust. But they ate it, hungry stomachs winning the battle.

He stroked her hair, longing to draw a brush through her soft brown tresses. Even broken as she was at this moment, she was beautiful.

No matter what it took, they would survive this ordeal. When they did, he intended to make her his own. Even if he had to fight Kurt again for her.

"Are you feeling better?"

She gave a slight nod but no smile. He missed the light in her eyes and the brightness in her face.

And suddenly, the guns and Stalinorgels fell quiet. For the first time in weeks, the air was still. Not a soul stirred.

It was not like the church-quiet from his childhood—holy and serene. It was a fragile quiet. At any moment, it might shatter and the bone-rattling noise would start once more.

For a while, the momentary peace held. No one in the cellar spoke. To do so would bring the war crashing around them.

A truck passed down the street, its engine the only sound in the neighborhood.

A blaring message pierced the air. "General Wilding has surrendered Berlin. Cease all fighting immediately. Berlin has fallen."

The message repeated several times before Mitch understood its full implication.

Berlin had come under complete Red Army control.

With Hitler dead and the German capital in enemy hands, it would be a matter of days before the most horrific war in European history would end.

Mitch couldn't help it. He whooped and his feet moved of their own volition and he danced a jig. Annelies and Renate laughed and joined in the festivities. They were the only celebrants.

Gisela frowned. "This isn't a time to rejoice. Look how many hundreds of thousands, even millions, have died. Life will never be the same. Under Stalin, nothing will change." She pinched her nose and swallowed hard.

His momentary joy evaporated.

Gisela crushed the bread crust in her hand. "The nightmare has only begun."

THIRTY-SIX

May 4

Wild Soviet troops patrolled the streets. They screeched, "Germanski kaput, Berlin kaput," and looted whatever they touched.

From her perch on the shelter's wood bench, Gisela listened as the Russians entered the houses around them. How many times had the women in them been raped? Frau Mueller's sign was a blessing.

And the only thing keeping her from the same fate.

But what about Mutti? Had God spared her?

That this carnage continued was insanity. The world had gone mad. Hitler had taken everything. Stalin demanded more.

She couldn't sit still. She walked a circuit around the cramped room several times. This must be what it was like in prison. Like it was for Mitch in the camp. She was a caged bird, beating her wings against the bars.

She couldn't breathe anymore. With ten people down here, the place was cramped. They ate together, slept together, fought together. The stench from the overflowing toilet upstairs permeated even to the cellar. The odor of all of those unwashed bodies was almost too much to bear.

Mitch teased her about going crackers, but she believed she might be on the verge of insanity if she stayed put one more minute.

After a while, the street in front of them quieted. The Soviets must have satiated themselves for the time being.

Good. She had to get outside.

Without a word to anyone, she slipped out of the room. While this usually meant a hurried trip to the bathroom, she went to the back door. The men had slid a desk in front of it. She moved the piece of furniture, unbolted the door, and slipped through.

Her hand froze on the door frame. The destruction of Vater's beloved city was complete. Not a single building remained unscathed. Berlin had become a burned-out ghost town. She half expected tumbleweeds to blow down the street.

She inhaled, hoping for a lungful of fresh air. But even out here, it was not meant to be. The smells of death and destruction were too strong. Instead, she covered her nose with her handkerchief so she wouldn't gag.

A quick look to the left and then to the right assured her no Soviet troops patrolled the area at the moment. With haste, she made her way to their bombed-out apartment building. The notice for Mutti had disappeared. Perhaps a vagabond had scoured the area for any useful item. Perhaps a Red Army soldier had removed it on purpose.

Mutti would never find them. Neither would Vater.

Gisela climbed over the rubble, searching for the brick with the message. She slid on the unstable pile and scraped her knee. She couldn't find it.

For as long as she could, she sifted through the debris, not knowing what she was searching for. Some clue about Mutti's whereabouts? Some sign that she was alive? Or dead?

Whatever her search, it proved fruitless. Once more, she climbed over the pile. Her left foot slid in between two bricks at a strange angle and pain ripped up her leg. She bit back a whimper and fell on top of the debris, the sharp edges of bricks digging into her backside.

Oh Lord, please take me home. End this misery for me.

Mitch played horsey with the girls until his bony knees ached from the hard concrete floor. He sat back on his haunches. "Everybody off. The horse is tired."

Annelies turned her sad gray eyes to him. "Bitte, Onkel Josep, just one more ride?"

Her expression almost did him in. He hated to disappoint her.

Renate clapped her hands. "Me too."

"Later. I promise. The horse has to rest. Play with Tante Gisela."

Annelies stomped her little foot. "She isn't here."

Mitch surveyed the room. She was right. Gisela had left to use the loo awhile ago and hadn't returned. He hopped to his feet, his knees protesting. Had she gotten sick?

"You stay with Tante Audra while I look for her." He nodded in her direction and she nodded back, some expression in her green eyes he couldn't read.

He took the steps two at a time, the upstairs cold and dark. The door to the loo stood ajar. "Gisela? Are you in there? Are you sick?"

No answer. He dared to take a peek. The room was empty.

He searched the other rooms. No sign of her. In her state, there was no telling where she might have gone. Doubting she had left the building, he conducted a thorough search, up and down and underneath and behind.

Fruitless. All of it fruitless.

With trembling legs, he climbed to the attic. Suicides were rampant in the city. Before they had been confined to the basement, they had heard reports of hundreds of women taking their own lives, either because they had been raped or so the Soviets wouldn't touch them.

The attic stairs creaked under his weight and he held his breath.

No Gisela. He released the air from his lungs and relaxed against the wall.

But if she wasn't here, where was she?

Gisela sat amid the rubble of what had been her home. Amid the rubble of her life, a light mist fell.

Her heart ached for Mutti and Vater. Where were they? Were they alive? And what about Ella and Opa? Gisela might never get the answers to those questions.

The war had torn so much apart that it could never be repaired.

She lifted her face to the heavens. *This is not fair, God. Not fair. I shouldn't be here.*

Tears streamed unchecked down her cheeks. Her bloodied hands ached. Her heart could hold no more.

Then, from the corner of her eye, she spied a splash of green against white concrete. Instead of limping on her sore ankle, she crawled to the spot.

Her daisy scarf had survived. She pushed aside the rubble to free it. It had unraveled in one spot, but nothing that couldn't be fixed. The day was cool and damp enough that she didn't feel funny about wrapping it around her neck.

She recalled Mutti draping it over her shoulders as she stood on the train platform two years ago, bound for the east. "I won't be there to comfort you, my darling, but this will keep you warm."

Three months ago, Ella had handed it to her on her way out the door, reminding her to keep bundled.

She fingered the edge of it. The daisies had remained intact. She swiped away her remaining tears.

"Remember, my Gisela, daisies are forever."

"O Israel, Fear not: for I have redeemed thee, I have called thee by name; thou art mine."

She had to cling to that hope—that one day, all would be restored. If not in this life, then in the next.

Her heartache eased a little. *Lord, please let my family survive. Reunite us.*

The Russian-imposed curfew would go into effect at four o'clock and she had no idea of the time. A shiver passed through her with the deepening chill.

And the raucous voices of the Russians.

Putting weight on her ankle proved to be painful. She winced as she stepped on her right foot, which then twisted slightly on the uneven ground. How would she ever get off of this rubble heap?

A block away, a group of four Russian soldiers turned the corner and began walking down the street.

In her direction.

Mitch resigned himself to the fact that Gisela wasn't in the house. Though he had a difficult time believing it, she must have gone out.

The question remained—where? Seeing the desk pulled away from the back door confirmed his fears.

He stepped from the house, half afraid of another encounter with a Red Army soldier. Gisela wasn't by his side this time.

He had to find her. Fast.

His first thought was to go to the apartment building ruins. She could well have gone there, hoping for a message from her mum. Before he could turn in that direction, though, the neighbor across the street appeared on her front stoop.

She greeted him with enthusiasm. "The baker has bread. A pound for everyone with the new stamp on the old coupon book." She bounced down the step and set off in the opposite direction.

Gisela must have heard the news and struck out for the bakery. He followed the neighbor several blocks through the destruction. He couldn't compare it to anything he had ever seen or heard. He closed his mind to the sights of the bloated bodies lining the street. Many of them were women, blood covering their lower torsos.

He fisted his hands and tried not to gag.

A group of nervous women queued in front of the small shop. They never stopped scanning the area for their brutal occupiers, despite being dressed in rags, hair unkempt, faces smeared with coal.

An officer appeared from the back of the bakery, followed by a thin woman with large blue eyes, her arms loaded with bread. To a person, they knew how this girl had come away with such riches.

Though he felt like a coward, he scooted behind a woman with a long black coat and crouched to avoid the Russian's roving eye. Easier than being shot on the spot, mistaken for a German soldier.

"Frau, *kommen*." The Soviet motioned to Gisela's neighbor. She hesitated.

Mitch didn't.

Gisela sat as still as a rabbit in the crosshairs. Every instinct screamed at her to run. But doing so would draw unwanted attention to herself. She kept her breath as shallow as possible so her chest wouldn't rise and fall.

Sweat broke out over her entire body despite the coolness of the day. Her heart galloped faster than a wild mustang.

The troops moved ever closer, each step nearer to where she cowered. Time ceased. The world narrowed to a tunnel, her fate awaiting at the far end.

Their heavy footfalls echoed down the street, their feet now encased in SS boots stripped from dead Germans.

Dear God, don't let them see me.

Perhaps she would pass out from fright. They would think she was dead.

Play dead. Of course.

She sat upright, though, and that complicated matters. Moving might cause them to notice her.

Her mind rushed between her two options—sit here perfectly still or slump over and fake her own passing.

Each second brought them another step closer.

They spoke, loud and drunk with their own successes and exploits.

Her stomach twisted. Thoughts of their hands on her tightened the vise on her lungs.

From the corner of her eye, she watched them stumble down the road, weaving around the rubble. Three were about the same height and build, much larger than she, the other slighter. The Mongol was dark, the Russians fairer.

One of the tall, fair ones pointed in her direction.

They had spotted her.

THIRTY-SEVEN

The look in the Russian soldier's dark eyes as he raked his gaze over the woman in the bread line didn't escape Mitch. Instinct took over.

He rushed forward and planted himself between the woman and the Soviet, legs spread, hands on his hips. "You will not touch this woman."

The infantryman raised his sidearm.

Mitch stepped back. "British, British," he shouted, pointing at himself.

The soldier shook his head. "Germanski."

"No. British." With trembling hands, Mitch withdrew his dog tags, tugged them over his head, and handed them to the man for verification.

The soldier didn't give them much more than a glance before he tossed them to the side. He shouted something Mitch didn't understand. Probably along the lines of, "This is a trick." At no point did he lower his sidearm.

Mitch yelled right back. "British, British. Not Germanski." He spit on the ground as if the people of Berlin left a bad taste in his mouth.

His adversary's shoulders relaxed.

"Stalag." Mitch bet the man understood that German word for *prison*.

If he comprehended, it didn't make a difference. What kind of people were these? Britain should never have aligned with them. With his weapon aimed at Mitch's chest, he reached around Mitch and grabbed the woman's hand. "Frau, kommen."

The woman let out a strangled cry.

Mitch chopped away the soldier's hand. *"Nyet.* Leave her alone."

The barrel of the firearm dug into his stomach.

"I said to let her go. Don't touch her."

Another soldier appeared. With his mouth drawn into a tight line, he assessed the situation. He spoke a few words to his comrade who flashed Mitch a warning look. But he backed down. His superior nodded away from the bread line and the lower-ranking officer marched in that direction.

As Mitch watched them leave, he spied a familiar form approaching them.

Gisela had seen the gruesome sights, women stripped, abused, and left to die. Those were the lucky ones. The most unfortunate lived.

Lord, don't let it happen. But if it does, may the end come quickly.

He would have to be the one to save her. She couldn't do it herself.

She had a difficult time sitting still because every inch of her body quaked. Every tick of the second hand passed like an eternity. Yet the soldiers approached all too fast. They must be taking meter-long steps.

She braced herself for the inevitable. Through her mind flashed memories of Mutti and Vater, their time in California, Margot and Gisela playing on the tire swing or in the sand at the beach. She thought of the kisses she had shared with Mitch, the most beautiful moments of her life. She would never experience the joy of the marriage bed, the joy of loving a man—Mitch—with all she had.

She bit back the metallic taste as blood seeped from the teeth marks in her lip.

The soldiers laughed and jabbed each other with their elbows, one of them almost falling to the ground in his drunken stupor.

She determined not to cry, not to make a noise. They would not have that satisfaction. She wouldn't plead with them for her innocence or beg for her life.

They reached her. Two of them climbed over the remains of the apartment building. Each took one of her arms. The warmth of their hands seeped through her cotton blouse.

With little regard for her arm sockets, they lifted her to her feet. A sharp pain raced through her shoulders. She locked her teeth shut so she wouldn't wince as they forced her to stand.

But she couldn't control the retch that wracked her stomach.

Mitch rubbed his eyes to make sure he wasn't seeing an oasis in the desert. No, the figure he spied down the block bore the same shape as Gisela, had the same soft sway to the hips. It had to be her.

With the neighbor behind him shouting her thanks, he sprinted away. The scattered debris slowed his progress and frustrated him.

"Gisela! Gisela!" The woman didn't turn at the sound of her name.

"Halten sie! Halten sie!" He raced as fast as he could in her direction, his lungs protesting at having to do two jobs at the same time.

This time the woman stopped, spun, and leaned forward, like she was attempting to decipher who was calling her. "Who is that?"

"Gisela, it's me."

She didn't move but waited for him to draw closer. He was impressed with the job the powder did on her hair, making her appear much older.

When he was about ten or fifteen meters from her, he realized that the gray in the woman's hair wasn't from powder. Though the woman bore a striking resemblance to Gisela, it wasn't her.

"Kommen, kommen." The rough man who reeked of alcohol didn't care that Gisela had vomited on his shoes. His lack of concern over the incident only stirred Gisela's stomach further.

She thought she might be sick again.

The two dragged her over the rubble and to the street where the others stood waiting. Waiting their turns to have their way with her.

Her heart had stopped beating and she couldn't take a breath. She limped beside them. Why had she thought she would be different from the rest of the women in the neighborhood? None of them had escaped this dreadful destiny. Neither would she.

Oh God, save me. Don't let the waters or the fire consume me. Deliver me. Please, deliver me.

With her legs as wobbly as a toddler's, they dragged her down the street. Few buildings stood in this area. Would they have their fun with her in the open?

She tamped down the bile rising in her throat.

Down another block, the facade of a shop sat tall among

the destruction. The inside had burned completely, but the shell remained.

The soldiers pulled her by the hair from the road to the back of the empty building. The one with the dark hair grunted and pushed her against the rough brick wall. If he hadn't pinned her there, she would have sunk to the ground.

In one swift motion, he tore open her blouse.

"Frau Cramer?"

"Josep? Is that you?" The woman buried her head in her hands and cried.

Mitch had not been imagining things and didn't think she was a vision. He wanted to shout. After all of this time, all of this searching, all of this heartache, he had found Gisela's mum.

He closed the space between them in a few strides. "Frau Cramer, it is you. Where have you been? We've been so worried."

"Where is my Gisela? Is she alive? Bitte, tell me."

He hugged the woman. "She is fine." That was true. He didn't have any information to the contrary. Not yet, anyway. "She misses you terribly. Didn't you see the message we left for you?"

She lifted her head and touched his face. "You are real."

He nodded.

"When you hadn't returned by the time I finished the laundry, I set out, thinking I might catch up to you. The next thing I remember was waking up in a strange house with a strange woman taking care of me. Days, maybe weeks, had passed."

"Why don't you wait with the story until we are together to hear it?" He didn't want to tell Gisela's mum that she was out here, somewhere, alone.

"Ja, that I will. I want to see my daughter."

Father, may she be at home, safe and sound. Even as he prayed the prayer, his gut clenched.

He squeezed Frau Cramer's hand and led her through the streets toward the place they called home. The neighborhood they traversed had been razed. Here and there the shell of a building remained, stark against the fiery sky.

Women's screams echoed in the late afternoon air. Much as Mitch tried to shut them out, they penetrated his brain. Sounds he would never forget, no matter how long he lived.

One screech in particular caught his attention. It had a familiar tone, a familiar timbre to it.

But it couldn't be.

Oh, dear God, don't let it be.

THIRTY-EIGHT

Mitch heard nothing but the blood pounding in his ears, saw nothing but the brick facade of the empty building, thought of nothing but her. And what those brutal Russians might be doing to her. "Gisela! Gisela!"

"Mit—!" The answer to his call was cut off, as if someone covered her mouth.

He ran faster than he had ever run in his life, yet it took forever to reach her.

A Soviet with a machine gun met him.

Over the man's shoulder, he saw Gisela, her blouse ripped, her eye black and blue, blood running from her nose. Her white chest rose and fell at a rapid rate.

"No Germanski. British." He slapped his chest, then pointed to Gisela. "No Germanski. American."

Tears streamed down her face, washing away a bit of the blood. Her eyes were wild, like those of a rabbit cornered by a wolf. They pleaded with him.

What had these beasts done to her?

He didn't have a plan. If he attacked them, they would shoot him. If he was sure it would save her dignity and her life, he would do it.

But he had no such guarantee.

Without thinking further, he pushed his way past the startled Russian and sprinted to Gisela, positioning himself between her and her attackers. She clung to the back of his shirt.

He didn't turn to look at her. "Are you hurt?"

"Not that way, no." She trembled.

His throat constricted. "American. American. Leave her alone. Don't touch her."

With one eye on the four Soviets, he squatted and picked up two bricks. The roughness of the blocks scratched his palms. Their weight gave him confidence. He hoisted one, prepared to pitch it. "Go away. Get out of here and leave her alone."

The dark one of the quartet spit on the ground and dug the heel of his boot into the soft dirt. He flailed the hand that held the rifle and spoke.

Mitch narrowed his eyes, cocked his right arm, and took one step forward. He made his intention clear, no matter what the language barrier.

The Mongol trained the barrel of his weapon at Mitch's heart.

Mitch grasped the bricks. "Run, Gisela, run."

She didn't hesitate for a moment but sprint-limped away.

Now the soldiers could do whatever they wanted with him.

Gisela dashed out of reach of the Soviet monsters—as much as she could hop on one foot. She leaned against the building, panting, the lone branchless tree spinning. Her hands quivered so much, she had a difficult time doing up her buttons. The ones they hadn't torn off.

She would never be able to wash away the feel of their hands on her. She bit back another bout with bile.

What was happening to Mitch? Would they kill him?

The thought slammed her harder than the Soviet's fists.

She didn't want to—couldn't—live without him. Her life would be empty. She loved him so much it hurt, yet it was wonderful and bright.

Someone tapped her on the shoulder, her heart rate jumping to an unhealthy level again. She spun around, hands fisted.

Then she saw the most beautiful sight of her life. "Mutti. Oh, Mutti, is it really you?"

Her mother fell weeping into her arms. Gisela couldn't believe she was here. Alive and well. Her tears mingled with her mutti's. At last Mutti loosened her grip on her only child. "What have they done to you?"

Gisela touched her sore cheek. "Nothing that won't heal."

"My daughter, my daughter."

"Mitch saved me."

"He found me."

"What if they hurt him?" Gisela stumbled from her mutti's grasp.

"Where are you going?"

"Stay here." She took a few steps away, then turned to reassure herself it truly was Mutti.

"Gisela, you can't."

"I love him. I have to."

She left Mutti on the street and hobbled along the side of the building, then stopped a moment to pick up a chunk of concrete, then peeked around the corner.

Mitch had dropped one of the bricks but continued to clutch the other.

The glare in the soldier's eyes left no doubt as to their intentions. They didn't believe Mitch was an ally.

Or else they didn't care.

One of the fairer men stood closest to her, his back to her. He wasn't much taller than she was.

Gisela licked her lips and focused.

She steadied herself on her right foot. Like Samson and his final fit of strength, she prayed for power, pushed off with her throbbing foot and, with everything in her, hefted the concrete.

Mitch leaned against the building's rough brick wall, wondering when the Russians would finish their job. The methods he used before to prove he was an ally had failed. Of course they would. This had nothing to do with nationality. He had spoiled their fun.

A loud thud came from Mitch's right. One of the smaller soldiers fell.

Mitch raised his arm and chucked the remaining brick as far and as hard as possible. Then he took off like a rabbit before a hawk. He rounded the corner to the street side of the building. Frau Cramer spun, panic in her eyes. Gisela limped in front of him.

Mitch grabbed them and dragged them down the street, away from the Russians as fast as possible. Between Frau Cramer's age and Gisela's limp, they didn't gain the speed he would have liked. He was grateful they didn't stop to ask questions but trusted enough to follow where he led.

He didn't think, just moved his legs forward.

He prepared himself for a bullet in the back.

He didn't even twist around until they were about to turn the corner onto Frau Mueller's street.

No soldiers pursued them. No Russians bit at their heels.

Only a crazy man would slow down, though.

In no time they climbed the back steps of Frau Mueller's home, slid through the doorway, secured the bolt, and pushed the desk back into place.

His precious Gisela was bruised, her hands bloodied, her shirt torn. "Are you hurt? Did they . . . ?" He couldn't speak the words.

"Nein. Nein. You came just in time."

With God's help, he had saved her.

Gisela sat on the edge of the desk against the door and pulled her blouse tighter around her with her blood-caked fingers. That Mitch had seen her with her shirt open began to sink in. She stared at the floor.

He stepped in front of her and lifted her chin. "Let me look at you. Are you sure they didn't hurt you?"

She dared to peer into his warm eyes. Instead of the disgust and revilement she expected to find, she only saw compassion and tenderness. And love.

"I'm fine. Are you hurt?"

"Not a scratch."

"Mutti?"

Her mutti sat beside her on the worn desk. "I went out to look for you. I don't remember what happened, but I ended up with a bump on my head. An older woman took good care of me and my injury is healed. So many times I wanted to find you, but there were things I had a hard time remembering. But I could never forget you, my darling."

Gisela couldn't stop her tears. Mutti had been restored to her. God had brought her back. She clung to her.

"Oh, Gisela, I wondered if I would ever find you. Now I know we will be fine. Vater will come home and life will be sweet once more."

"I thought you were dead." In a way, God had brought Mutti back to life.

"The Lord spared me. He spared us. We owe so much to this man." She gestured toward Mitch.

He held Gisela's hand and squeezed it. His mere presence brought her comfort. "You owe me nothing. I love your daughter and would do anything for her."

Mutti glared at Mitch. "And what do you plan to do about this?"

"I plan to make your daughter my wife. For real."

Her stomach tripped, though the words had little chance to settle in before footfalls flew up the steps and Frau Mueller appeared, red-faced and panting.

"Frieda, is that you?" Frau Mueller embraced Mutti and the two friends laughed and cried. "I have a little broth on the stove in the cellar. Let me fix you a bite to eat. Then we want to hear about your adventures. You will stay with me until your husband comes back."

Two little girls clattered up the stairs. "Oma, Oma!" They attached themselves to Mutti, one on each leg. "Come see the horses Jorgen has carved for us."

"And who is this Jorgen?"

Annelies tugged on Mutti's arm. "He's my friend."

Mutti turned to Gisela. "Her friend?"

"A boy soldier I rescued. When this is over, we will reunite him with his family. Right now it's too dangerous for him on the streets."

"And those crazy sisters? Are they here?"

"Ja, until I can contact their niece in Düsseldorf. Go on down with the girls. Mitch and I will be there in a bit. Don't start the story until then."

The welcoming party left Mitch and Gisela alone in the back hall. A sudden shyness overtook her, and she limped down the hall to sit on the bottom stair.

Mitch took a seat beside her. "Did you hurt your foot?"

"I'm fine. Thanks to you, I'm fine." She swallowed hard. The ending would have been much different if he hadn't appeared when he had. "You saved me."

She dared to hold his hand. "Do you think less of me? Because of what they tried to do? Do you hate me?"

"Never." He clutched her in a sideways hug. "You weren't at fault. Nothing could make me think less of you."

Warm relief flooded her. "God brought you to me at just the right time."

"Yes, He did."

Mitch touched her bruised cheek, his fingertips just brushing her skin. She shivered even as heat raced through her body. Catching his hand, she kissed the inside of his palm.

A small sigh escaped his lips. "You ought to be a cricket bowler, the way you threw that brick."

"I wonder if the New York Yankees would draft a girl."

"I would want you on my team. When I told your mum that I wanted to marry you, I meant it. And I am willing to raise the girls if Ella doesn't return." He leaned in as if to kiss her, then pulled back. "With my whole heart, I want to kiss you."

"You may."

"Are you sure? After your ordeal . . . ?"

She nodded. His peck on her lips was short and sweet.

He wanted to marry her. And care for Annelies and Renate. Every bit of the horror and suffering faded away. Her timidity fled and she returned his affection with ardor, pulling him close, wanting him always. To be one with him.

He pulled away, breathless. "I love you, Gisela, with everything I am. Please tell me we have a future. I will follow you to the ends of the earth."

Could you sink to the depths and soar to the heights in one day? She studied his face, his dimpled cheeks, his crinkled eyes. Even the bright California sun paled in comparison to her passion for this incredible man. He filled a void in her, made her feel clean and whole. If she had to go through this ordeal again just to get to this ending, she would. "I love you too, Mitch. You don't need to follow me. I'll stay with you forever."

She knew their love would last far longer than the faded daisy pressed in her Bible.

EPILOGUE

LOS ANGELES, CALIFORNIA

October 1946

Gisela pulled her lightweight jacket around her as the sea breeze whipped across the tarmac, tangling her green silk skirt around her legs. She craned her neck to look into the blue sky. The buzz of the plane's engines grew ever louder as it approached its landing.

She stood on her tiptoes, as if she might be able to reach up and pluck it from the sky. It took eons to circle the airport, tipping its wings in one direction, then the other, finally straightening.

"Is the plane here yet?" Annelies mimicked Gisela and stretched. Renate copied them both. "I want to see too."

"It's coming, it's coming." If only the plane would contain Ella. It had taken some doing, but several weeks ago they received word of Ella's and Opa's deaths. She wiped away her stray tears.

She returned her attention to the aircraft mere feet from the runway.

When its wheels touched the ground, they sent up a puff of dust. Gisela had all she could do to keep from dancing in circles. She silently urged the ground crew to hurry and wheel the stairs to the doorway.

Mutti held her shoulder to restrain her from climbing over the fence to the runway. "He will come soon enough. All of your jumping around will only tire you out and make you warm."

Gisela aged another ten years before the cabin door opened and the passengers began to disembark.

Her breath caught in her throat when he appeared at the head of the stairs. He was more handsome than she had remembered.

She waved. Even from this distance, his smile shone, his dimples deep. He took the steps two by two and raced across the airfield.

"Oh, Mitch." She fell into his arms.

He picked her up and swung her in circles. "Yee haw!"

She laughed. "What was that for?"

"Isn't that what you Americans say?"

"No, we say this." She kissed him on the lips, hard, not caring if Mutti saw them.

"I'm so glad you got out of Berlin."

"It's good to be home. You finally came." The past year of separation while both of them had waited for permission to come to the States had been excruciating.

Mitch leaned in to whisper in her ear. His breath tickled her neck and started a funny fluttering in her stomach. "I have three surprises for you."

"Isn't you being here enough excitement for now?"

"Look." He stepped out of the way and pointed to the airplane.

At the top of the stairs came a wonderfully familiar silhouette.

"Vater! Mitch, you brought Vater home to me." She hugged Mitch's neck.

"Thank you, thank you, thank you."

Hand in hand they raced across the tarmac.

She fell into Vater's arms, but only for a minute. He released his hold as Mutti joined them, tears racing down her cheeks. The three of them clung to each other.

"We thought you were still waiting for approval from the embassy."

Vater stepped back, wiping the dampness from his wrinkled cheeks. "That is cleared up. But I didn't tell you because I wanted to surprise you. Mitch worked to get me on the same flight as him from New York. You have a very fine man, Gisela. I'm proud."

Then, from the corner of her eye, she noticed a woman with platinum-blond hair. "Audra." She turned to Mitch. "You brought Audra too?"

Audra laughed. "I'm in California. Where Hollywood is. Are there actors and actresses here?"

Now Gisela giggled. "Not right here." Then she embraced her former foe. "I'm glad you are here. May all of your dreams come true."

Gisela turned to Mitch. "That's only two surprises. What's the third?"

Right in front of the whole world, he got down on one knee. Her hands shook. Could he really be . . . ?

"Gisela Cramer, will you do me the honor of being my wife? For real this time?"

She squealed like a little girl. "Oh, yes yes yes."

He pulled a box from his pocket, opened it, and slipped a ring on her finger. The engagement ring had a large center diamond with small diamonds surrounding it. It looked like a daisy.

"It's gorgeous." She helped him stand.

"No more beautiful than the woman with whom I'm going to spend the rest of my life."

No more beautiful than the life they would have.

THE STORY BEHIND THE STORY

The author with her aunt, Lillian Tolsma, the inspiration
for this book and a truly courageous woman.

Ruth Sabine Hildegard Lippert, seventeen years old in February 1945, is the inspiration for the first half of this story. In her own words: "Soon thereafter, on February 8, the Russians marched into our city; we escaped by night, in temperatures of minus 20 degrees, launched into a four-week *Flucht* [escape]. Through the Lord's grace and shielding, I was able, as a fearless leader, to save a group of about ten people from certain death or captivity."

They crossed the frozen Frische Haff, were shot at by Russian planes, and rode in trucks and on trains. She endured many trials and hardships and finally arrived at home in Bad Homburg four weeks later, only to be bombed out of her home the same night she arrived.

The second half of the book is based on the stories told by my aunt, Lillian Tolsma, born in the United States to parents of German descent. In the late 1930s, her family decided to return to Germany. She spent the last part of the war in Berlin, surviving almost constant bombing raids and having her apartment building bombed out while she was away from home. Once the Soviets entered the city, she had to hide from the Russians soldiers, escaping their clutches more than once.

These women's stories demonstrate that the war affected ordinary citizens on both sides of the conflict. The courage it took to survive one of the darkest periods in history was amazing.

READING GROUP GUIDE

1. Did Gisela make the right decision to leave Ella and Opa in East Prussia? What might you have done in that situation?
2. Was it Mitch's fault that he and the men with him were taken prisoners by the Germans at the beginning of the war?
3. Is the lying and stealing that take place throughout the book commendable or condemnable?
4. What effect did her sister's death have on Gisela?
5. Kurt and Audra used Mitch and Gisela for their own ends. What other ways could they have gone about reaching their goals?
6. What kind of emotional toll did the near-constant bombing of Berlin take on the characters?
7. Mitch says of Gisela, "She collected waifs like people collected porcelain figurines." What does that tell you about her character?
8. How is levity added to the story? Why is it added?
9. Mitch and Gisela were both searching for redemption. Did they find it? If so, where did it come from?
10. How has the story changed your view of the everyday German citizen during the war?

ACKNOWLEDGMENTS

My deepest appreciation to Lillian Tolsma and the family of Ruth Lippert for sharing your stories with the world, so we may know what true courage looks like.

Thank you to the fabulous staff at Thomas Nelson Publishers. I have enjoyed working with my editors Becky Philpott and Julee Swarzburg. You have made me a better writer. Many thanks to Ruthie Dean, my former publicist. Your help was so appreciated. Thanks also to Becky Monds, Jodi Hughes, Daisy Hutton, and all of the many, many wonderful people there. I cannot begin to thank you enough for your care and concern for me during the illness I battled while editing this book. What a joy to work with people who understand what is important in life.

Thank you to my agent, Tamela Hancock Murray. Your support and availability throughout this process have been a true encouragement to me.

Without my terrific critic partner, Diana, this book wouldn't be what it is. It's fun "thinking with my fingers" with you. Thank you for spurring me on to be better and for telling me like it is.

Thank you to my eighth-grade locker partner, Ruth Lyons,

for your translation of Ruth Lippert's biography. You helped me to truly understand her story.

My family's love and support allowed me to follow my dream and write this book. Thank you to my children, Brian, Alyssa, and Jonalyn, for being flexible and understanding when dinner was late or nonexistent because of a deadline. And to Doug, thank you for holding down the fort, for cleaning and cooking and carting kids around so I can follow my passion. You make me a better person.

And while so many people had a hand in making this book a reality, the truth is that without God's blessing, not a single word would have been written. He planted the desire and the ability in me and surrounded me with just the right people at just the right time. All praise to Him.

A STRANGER'S LIFE HANGS IN THE BALANCE.
BUT TO SAVE HIM IS TO RISK EVERYTHING.

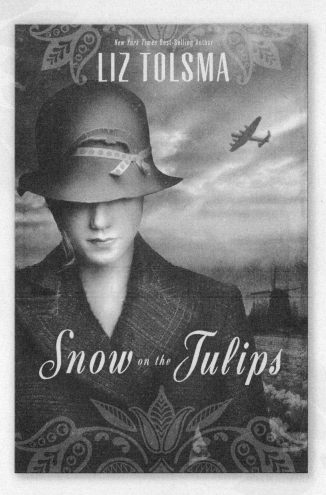

Since 1798

thomasnelson.com

Available in Print and E-Book

ABOUT THE AUTHOR

Photo by Bentfield Photography

Liz Tolsma has lived in Wisconsin most of her life. She and her husband have a son and two daughters, all adopted internationally. When not busy putting words to paper, Liz enjoys reading, walking, working in her large perennial garden, kayaking, and camping with her family.

Visit www.LizTolsma.com